Broken
Blessings

Broken Blessings

Christine Elder

Spirit Water Publications
Salem, Oregon

BROKEN BLESSINGS

SPIRIT WATER PUBLICATIONS
P.O. Box 7522
Salem, Oregon 97303

Library of Congress Control Number: 2010938001

ISBN-13: 978-0-9729460-3-2
ISBN-10: 0-9729460-3-9

Printed and bound by:
Gorham Printing
3718 Mahoney Drive
Centralia, WA 98531

Cover Art by Jeff Tiner
Cover Design by Janelle Wheeler Olivarez
Artwork by Jeff Tiner
Photographs by Rob Elder
Edited by Rob Elder

All biblical references cited from the NRSV

Manufactured in the United States of America

Dedication

This book is dedicated to all who battle the demon of addiction whether the struggle is their own or among those they love. I hope and pray that you will know joy in the midst of life's hardships, and that you'll find the serenity that comes not from an absence of conflict but rather from knowing deep peace no matter the circumstances. This peace is there to be found. It never leaves us, and it never fails. May we all have the hearts to see it and believe.

Contents

Acknowledgements

Throughout the writing of this book, I have been blessed by a rich and loving community of support. I would like to thank my dear friend Barbara who served as my first stop for advice and my constant companion through every phase. Not only was she one of the primary prompters for beginning the project, she also pushed me when I dragged and believed enough in the sharing of this story to selflessly invest much of her personal time and effort to see it come to fruition. Her candid help and support has been invaluable to me.

I'd like to thank my good friend Marva for being a steady rudder during the days and weeks at the hospital and afterward, for being one of the first to suggest I write a book, for giving me a copy of Brenda Ueland's *If You Want to Write*, and for being the cherished friend and colleague that she is. My thanks to all of the music faculty and administration at Willamette whose generosity, understanding, and help carried us through.

My gratitude also goes to the countless saints who prayed and watched over us with love, who wrote words of encouragement and support, many of whom also suggested this story become a book. *Broken Blessings* is here because of your gentle words of encouragement. Thank you.

I'd also like to thank my parents for nurturing a faith that withstands strong winds and moving earth. The countless theological and spiritual conversations we have shared through the years have laid the strong foundation on which I stand today. I am so grateful for your love given through these discussions and mutual seeking.

My gratitude goes to Janelle who assembled the cover design, and I am indebted to my friend and publisher, Sarah, who has been there for me in so many ways through the years. She is one of those friends I know I can call at any time, day or night to ask for help (and I have!). What a joy to now share a passion for penning spiritual encouragement and hope.

I thank Jeff, my friend and spiritual brother, for designing the cover art, for his permission to include other artwork and writings, for his ceaseless prayers, and for the gift of our friendship.

This book wouldn't be here without the generous permission of my son Michael to share his story with the world. He is a brave young man.

And finally I thank my husband Rob. Not only is he the primary editor of this book, he is my anchor, my partner, and my best friend. Over the years he has "re-taught me my loveliness," to paraphrase Galway Kinnell. I am a better person in the world because of him, and I am grateful for all that he has taught me about love.

Introduction

A friend of mine once said that God always makes us face our fears. I cannot say if this is true, but I do know that I came face to face with many of my deepest fears one night in October of 2009. My 17-year-old son Michael, who has struggled with drug and alcohol addiction for the entirety of his adolescence, hung himself. This book is our story: Michael's, mine and those who have borne witness, and it isn't an easy one. But while a nightmare may have come true that October evening, I have been reminded of a greater truth, that often it is within the folds of the deepest shadows of life that we are pierced most lovingly by the light. There is heartbreak in our pain, yes, but more than that there is hope. And when we trust that hope, we find the compass that guides us safely through chaos and loss. If we follow its lead, we can discover deep comfort, even peace, in moments wracked with immeasurable suffering.

My name is Christine, and there is much I want to tell you. I want to tell you about the death row inmate who began praying for Michael on his first day in the hospital and who continues praying for him to this day. He has become a good friend of mine, an unlikely spiritual brother. I want to share how I have mined precious jewels from the pit of my son's struggle with alcohol and drug abuse, a struggle that carried him to the point of death. I want to share how we have been broken and put back together by love.

This crisis brought us to our knees, and because we were so utterly dependent on the love around us to help us through, our perspective was surprisingly clear. I know God works this way, thinning the veil when we are laid bare by life, clearing out much of what stands between us and Heaven. It may hurt like hell, but it isn't all bad. In fact, when we are down so far that the only way we can look is up, the beauty we see can be nearly overwhelming.

Sometimes when I think about brokenness, I see a beautiful possibility. I envision our spirits like malleable glass, the substance through which the light and love of God moves. As the Spirit moves through, love is magnified and we are transformed, refracted, and arrayed into a beautiful spectrum of color. At times life stretches the glass too thin, and while God moves through easily then, sometimes we break. The break isn't necessarily wrong or bad, it is just what happens, though at times it can feel like too much. But now, as glass that has shattered into a million little pieces, we have infinitely more surface area for the love and light of God to touch. It may hurt, this much light in the brokenness, but it is also healing if we can stay with it. The light touches us on all sides, through and through, and eventually we are forged back together into new strength and purpose. There is much more love in us than there was before.

This story is about that love.

The narrative unfolds in real time using communications that began as a way to provide regular updates on Michael's medical condition to family and friends. Some interpolated reflections and background information stand outside of the chronological order. Over time, the story becomes as much about the inward journey as the outward one. My hope is that you might find encouragement in these words for your own walk, which doubtless includes significant challenge and hardship at times. This story, like all of our stories, is ultimately one of blessing no matter the outcome, because, as Betsie Ten Boom said, "There is no pit so deep that God's love is not deeper still." [1]

Chapter 1
The Bend in the Road

It had been a good weekend. My collegiate choir performed their first concert of the semester on Saturday night and sang beautifully, exceptionally so. They were a strong group, sensitive and mature, and the year held promise. Now it was Sunday evening and the work week was around the corner of one more sleep. I looked forward to seeing my class the next day and celebrating their musical accomplishments. As an added bonus, Monday was trash day. A friend of mine says trash day is her favorite day of the week because she gets a clean start every time the garbage vanishes. I too, like trash day. And since it was almost bedtime, I was feeling a familiar, happy anticipation. Since I'm not much of a night owl, I get excited each evening when 9:00 rolls around because, as I often tell my husband Rob, I really like bed. "Do you now?" he'll tease in a faux Scotts accent. Yes, I do. I frequently experience childlike delight as I snuggle down in the covers and prepare for the blessed suspension between waking and sleeping where my mental stream of words gives way to soft, morphing images. This fluid weaving in and out of consciousness is one of my favorite moments in the day, and I was almost there. Already in my jammies, I was about to settle in when the phone rang.

It was Kelley, my son Michael's girlfriend. I'm fairly sure she had never called me before. "Hi Christine. I'm sorry to bother you so late, but I'm really worried about Michael.

He is scaring me. He's talking about killing himself, saying he's going to hang himself from the neighbor's deck or something." Apparently Kelley and Michael had been fighting for several days, working toward a breakup. I spoke with her a bit more, hung up, and got dressed. It is difficult to remember the exact sequence of events that followed as the memories have rearranged themselves in my head over time. This is the order I remember now, the scene that plays itself like a movie that has made it beyond the editing room and become fixed in circulation.

I called 911 to report a suicide threat. I described what Kelley had shared. I described Michael. As I spoke to the operator I thought, "They won't do anything about this. What can they possibly do about this? They must get calls like this all the time and most of them amount to nothing."

After a bit of time spent wondering what we should do next, Rob and I decided we would drive around and look for him. We got the keys and headed out to the garage, just in time to see Michael duck down behind one of the cars. He remained motionless for a minute, like an animal in the wild who freezes in hope that the predator in his midst won't see him. He was crouched along the wall near the side door that goes out toward the yard. I tentatively said his name. "Michael?" He sprang up, looked at me, and then bolted out the door. He had something in his hands.

I will never forget the look of his eyes. They were crazed and wild, not his own, and unlike anything I had ever seen. My first thought was, "Oh God, this is bad. He's done some really serious drugs and is on a very bad trip." I knew right then it would be a long night. We went out after him and saw him running full speed down the middle of the street. We quickly got in the car and followed. This wasn't the first time I'd pursued him in a car at night. Near our house, just past the one on our immediate left, is a huge, downward sloping hillside that I call the ski bowl. A developer in town has divided its lots for sale, though we often comment someone would have to be crazy to build on such a severe incline as most of the house would be on air. Michael disappeared down the far end of the ski bowl, and we lost him in the darkness. After a bit he suddenly reappeared and was running toward our house, which was the strangest thing. When Michael is drunk or on drugs, and particularly when we're on to him, he doesn't come home. He disappears, and we wait. He usually drags himself home in the wee hours of the morning, somewhat sobered up or at least worn out enough to favor confrontation over remaining a fugitive. He goes to bed and I wait until morning before delivering the Speech of Reprimand and Consequences. I've learned the futility of either confronting or punishing him when he is in such a state. Through the years of Michael's drug and alcohol use I've learned a lot about waiting and staying calm. I believe I've learned much more than I ever wanted to know.

So when he headed back toward our house, we were puzzled. He ran just past it and down the hill on the side with the door and into the back. Our house is also on a slope, though not one as severe as the ski bowl. Behind us is a vacant lot with an immense maple tree in a field full of tall grass, blackberries and other untamed growth. Michael vanished into the thick, and we lost him again.

Unsure what to do next, we went inside to wait, thinking the drugs would have to run their course. But this waiting was different. The reported suicide threat nagged at me, as did the image of his crazed eyes. It left me with a bad feeling because this deranged look was a new and foreign element we'd never encountered. Time passed, I'm not sure how much. More than a few minutes, less than a long while. These particular minutes (were there 10? 20? 30?) are blank in my memory. They were dead moments, filler, time and space when we were removed from the action, suspended in the waiting. Rob was talking with Kat, a college student living with us, who suggested maybe Michael was just sitting out back in the field. Rob and I knew that would not fit

3

Michael's pattern, that he wouldn't hang around close by where he could be found. He always ran. But her words and Rob's mounting feeling that doing nothing was not a good option prompted him to go out back with a flashlight and look again. As I sat in the living room I received a quiet, inner nudge: "Call Kelley again." I did. I asked her if she had heard any more from Michael. She said yes, that he had called a bit ago. "Did he say anything?" "He said, 'I just wanted to hear your voice one last time.'"

Oh God. No...

"How long ago did you talk to him?"

"I don't know, about five minutes? Maybe more."

Panic bore down on me with a single, suffocating thought: We have to find him and we have to find him *now*. I ran out back to look again, and then I heard Rob. He had found Michael hanging and had been yelling for help but we hadn't heard him because the windows were closed. Rob had been walking through the tall grass in the field behind our house when he turned around and looked up toward the neighbor's house, and there he spotted Michael. At first, in the near blackness, he thought Michael was simply standing very still, looking at him. He even wondered if he might be violent or try to hurt him if he came near. Then he realized his feet were a couple of feet off the deck, that he was suspended, and he ran to him.

Never in a million years would I have thought as we chased Michael in the car that he would run back to our house to kill himself right behind us, or that he had already tried once and was about to try again. Days later we discovered a broken piece of thin rope hanging from our own deck, evidence of his first, failed attempt that evening, an attempt he had described to Kelley on the phone. Apparently he had gone back to the garage for a stronger cord, which was when we unwittingly stumbled upon him. The cord must have been what I had seen in his hand.

I now understand that the coordination of Rob's choice

to go out back and look and the prompt I received to call Kelley were two essential events in the sequence that led us to find Michael. This finely tuned orchestration brought both of us to him when there was no time left. It didn't feel like it then, but we had perfect help.

Michael was hanging so high that Rob had been unable to relieve much of the pressure on his neck by himself. I called 911 again, the second of three calls I'd make that night, and then we both struggled to release him. Rob, who is six feet tall, could just barely lift him by wrapping his arms around his lower legs and ankles, and neither of us could get anywhere near the knot in what turned out to be a thick, orange electrical cord. We were beyond distraught, desperate to help but without a way. His body was completely limp so every time Rob raised him to relieve the pressure on his neck, his head would flop to the side. Eventually I realized I could climb some steps to the side of where he hung and lean out crosswise to reach the cord. Since it was an electrical cord, the knot hadn't been able to pull tight from Michael's weight, so I could untangle it. We got him down and Rob began CPR.

Michael was completely motionless, lifeless. His skin was pale, but not a pale I've ever seen before. It was the color of death. He wasn't breathing and we didn't stop to check his pulse. I left then, though I can't remember why. I think one reason was to check on the arrival of the EMTs and another was to prevent anyone from stumbling onto the scene. I had an irrational fear of anyone discovering what we'd found. I felt protective of both Michael and others. For his sake (or was it mine?), I didn't want anyone to see him in this horrific state. I also worried about the trauma of such a morbid sight. My daughter Natalie came outside at one point and squeaked a small, "Mom?" I screamed at her to get back in the house, not to come down, to go inside. I told her we'd found him but that she couldn't come down. I'm sure I was hysterical.

While I was away from Michael's body Rob ferociously

compressed his chest, uttering a steady stream of orders and profanities. "You will not die. You will not do this to your mother, you little s***. Come on! Don't die on us. Don't you die on us!" I remember being in front of the house at one point looking for the ambulance when a dear neighbor came out to see if she could help. She is one of the sweetest, most genuine people I know, and I turned on her in rage, yelling, "NO! Go back inside! We don't need anything. GO INSIDE!"

I made several trips back and forth between the street above and the deck below where Rob continued CPR on Michael. At one point I spotted two emergency vehicles on the street behind our house, at the bottom of the ski bowl. Men were searching the grass with flashlights. I screamed, "Up here! We're up here!" but they didn't see or hear me. My desperation grew. I called 911 again and frantically told the operator that they were in the wrong place. I was shouting, sobbing, pleading. "Please. *Please*. They can't see us. Oh God, he hung himself. Please just get here. They're in the wrong place. Tell them they're in the wrong place! They can't find us. Oh God, please…"

On my last trip out front I saw a fire truck at the far, dead end of our street, three or four blocks away. I ran into the road, jumping in the air like a spastic spider, spreading my arms and legs as wide as I could with each leap to make myself as big as possible, yelling over and over, "Here! Here! We're down here! HERE!" The truck slowly turned and when its lights finally found my springing, hysterical form, it began moving our way. It had been eight minutes since my second call to 911, eight minutes since we'd found him hanging, still and lifeless in the dark.

I know that emergency responders are trained not to rush once they reach the scene. I know they are taught not to hurry and thus create mistakes or waste. But I can tell you that they all looked like they were moving through waist-deep molasses to me. In my mind's eye I can still see their

6

matching, emergency-responder boots slowly plodding in the dark, one after another, deliberate, and interminably slow. They moved down the slope leading from the street to the back of the house, carefully navigating the pitch black. Not only was there no light, the wooden steps under Michael were slippery with an algae-like substance that had covered the deck through the months of steady, generous Oregon rain. Their measured, slow steps did eventually lead them to Michael, and Rob, exhausted from the grueling stretch of CPR, gratefully stood down. Help was here now. They would save my son. They would know what to do. I was unaware that in their quiet they were already assessing his grave condition, a condition they would later note on his chart with a "Glasgow coma score of 3." The scale for this score is 3-15, with 3 being the worst and 15 being the best. There is no 1 or 2, and 3 is what you are given when you are not technically dead but may as well be. Perhaps Michael wasn't considered dead right then because his heart was beating, but that was only because Rob had been pounding on it for eight long minutes.

The EMTs did what EMTs do: they intubated him (with difficulty due to his neck injury), put him on a stretcher and loaded him into the ambulance. Each step seemed to take several long minutes. I noticed some others moving carefully in the dark on the slippery deck. There were policemen and men in emergency clothes. They asked us a few questions: our names, our relation to the patient, etc. One of them found Michael's cell phone below where his body had been hanging. They asked if they could take it to the police station. This was my first realization that they needed to rule out homicide and that we might be potential suspects. We said yes. We later heard about the painful trail of text messages he left with his girlfriend Kelley, right up to his last which must have preceded his eventual, unconscious dropping of the phone. As we made our way up toward the street behind Michael, one of the EMTs turned to Rob and said, "You saved his life." I remember feeling grateful beyond measure that they told us they would take care of the cord which still hung from the banister railing above us.

We went to our car to follow the ambulance to the ER. As we were pulling out of the driveway, another well-meaning neighbor rushed up to our car window and stopped us, frantically asking, "Are you guys okay? I just had to make sure you are okay!" Once again I responded like an angry animal, yelling, "We are fine but our son is not and we have to go!" I thought I would drive over him right then and there if he didn't get out of the way. Many times I have thought on that man's genuine concern for us and the way I bit his head off. It took me seven months to finally approach him one day as he worked in his yard and apologize for my outburst, and to thank him for his gentle approach that I met with blinding, desperate fear.

We made our way to the ER where Michael was now in a room on a gurney. His room had doors. I had only ever been in rooms in the ER with dividing curtains, not doors. Lots of folks were working on him and around him. At one point someone handed us a bag with the clothes that had been cut off of his body, asking us if we wanted them. No, you may throw them out. I realized I was calm. The hysterical screaming had passed and all of my words were even and unemotional. I navigated the busy freeway-like traffic of doctors, nurses and technicians in the ER with steady patience. They might be racing around like ambulances with their sirens blaring but I was simply slowing down and pulling over to the side of the road. It was here in my mental slow lane that I remember encountering the eyes of a certain policeman. I first saw him through the tiny, square window in the emergency room door. The view of his face was specific, like an intentional but unexpected framing of a subject in a picture. The top half of his head filled the little square. His partner came in and out of the room, asking us questions, but this other man didn't approach or speak. He simply observed, me in particular.

He had small, wire-rimmed glasses and steady, piercing eyes that bore into me every time I met his gaze through the tiny window. I felt I knew why he was watching me. In my mind he was watching to see how I was responding. I felt I wasn't passing the test because surely my calmness garnered suspicion. I understood that he was feeling out my potential as a murder suspect. This is what I believed as he silently hovered in the hall, and I thought, "I know why you're here. You'll figure out the truth about me over time."

About then we were told they needed to do some procedures on Michael and that we would need to vacate the ER. I don't recall asking what they were going to do. Maybe they told us, I don't remember. I didn't want to leave, but I followed instructions. We obediently went to a small conference room where people wait to hear news of their loved ones. This is the place where someone eventually approaches and says either "We're so sorry," or "You may come this way now." There were already people in the room— my daughter Natalie, Kat, Kelley, some friends of Natalie's and even one friend's mother. It was crowded. At some point Natalie's pastor showed up, maybe around midnight. And then a police chaplain appeared. Apparently someone had asked Rob (who is also a pastor) if we would like a visit from someone from Crisis Chaplaincy Services and he had said yes. So this uniformed man came to be with us, to talk and minister to us while we waited in the little room.

He asked Kelley questions about her relationship with Michael and she shared that he had been verbally abusive to her in horrible and demeaning ways that night. "Has this sort of thing happened before?" "No, never, he's always been completely sweet. He's never said anything like that to me before, ever." I thought how these are the words a mother longs to hear about her son, that he's good to his girlfriend and that he treats her well. But then he had treated her so badly this night. I began to realize that perhaps his suicide attempt could have been a way to punish her by hurting himself.

Then the chaplain turned his attention to us. "Now listen to me. Your minds are going to begin going down the 'what if' and 'if only' road, and I am telling you right now, don't go there. Don't even start down that path because it is the way of the devil, and no good will come of it. You can't help your son or yourselves one bit by thinking that way." My fragile, needy mind gratefully soaked up his words. I took them to heart and trusted them as truth because I recognized the saving wisdom in what he spoke. He was right, we had already begun to think that way, and to be tortured by it. I was already recalling in hindsight that Kelley mentioned on the phone that Michael had said he was going to hang himself on the neighbor's deck. But I hadn't paid attention to those words at the time. They didn't take hold in my mind because they were so preposterous and absurd, too random and too specific at the same time. Kelley had never once believed that Michael was serious in his suicide threat or the description of his attempts because everything he was saying was so completely out of character. She had even called me reluctantly, as though she felt maybe she shouldn't bother us or say anything at all. And of course that call was one of the things that saved his life. If he were to live.

At some point in the conversation with the chaplain in the little room I began to crater emotionally. My calm, even demeanor was sporadically interrupted with shaking sobs. The chaplain looked at me and said, "Let me explain what is happening to you right now. You've been riding on adrenaline for several hours and it's beginning to spend itself out of your system. As it goes, you're going to feel the crash: mentally, emotionally and physically. You'll probably fall hard, so don't be alarmed. It is just what is happening in your body, and you'll regain your balance eventually." I remember thinking, "What a good thing to know. That must be why I was able to be so calm in the ER, and it explains why I was okay just a minute ago and now I'm not okay at all. Maybe this nice man will go and give this report to the other policeman, the one with the watchful eyes behind the little wire glasses, and then that one will know I care about my son. He'll know I'm falling apart and thus won't think I tried to kill him." I never did see that other officer again.

These two bits of advice the chaplain offered, avoiding the "if only" road and not freaking out as I lost control of my mental and emotional world, were just what I needed to hear. Rob and I reflected many times in the days and weeks to come how crucial those particular life preservers of counsel were in our ocean of emotion that first night. And then the officer prayed with us. Natalie, her friends, Kelley, Kat, Rob and I and this wise man joined together in raw pleas for Michael's life as we huddled in the small, bad-news room. Then another call came in from a situation worse than ours, and the chaplain moved on.

I didn't know at the time, didn't find out until months later when I reviewed the hospital records, that Michael's body temperature was 91 degrees when he was admitted to the ER. I didn't know the only thing working in him was his heart, that his pupils were fixed and dilated. Maybe they told us this, but I don't remember it. We didn't know his Glasgow coma score, didn't know there was such a thing, and we didn't know a score of 3 means brain death. We didn't know that brain death is defined as "Irreversible unconsciousness with complete loss of brain function, including the brain stem, although the heartbeat may continue. Demonstration of brain death is the accepted criterion for establishing the fact and time of death. Factors in diagnosing brain death include irreversible cessation of brain function as demonstrated by fixed and dilated pupils, lack of eye movement, absence of respiratory reflexes (apnea), and unresponsiveness to painful stimuli. In addition, there should be evidence that the patient has experienced a disease or injury that could cause brain death."[1] I didn't know until I read the hospital notes that a reasonable course of treatment might have been to do nothing and let him go, but that "given the patient's young age, aggressive treatment is warranted and well justified."

When the doctor asked us how long his brain had been without oxygen, we estimated as many as ten minutes, not knowing that anything beyond five was in the morbid range. There was much we didn't know that night. We were given only a brief word from the ER doctor: "Well, you know the outlook is bleak." He emphasized the word *know*, as if we were fully aware of the gravity of the situation, as if we already understood that hoping would be a costly error in judgment. I simply figured he was saying this to prepare us for the possibility of Michael's death. I remember thinking that was fine, that he had to say those things to cover his tracks, but he didn't know the outcome and neither did we. That's all I knew.

Chapter 2
Bleak

Hospital

Hi. We're writing to update friends and family on Michael's progress in his recovery at the hospital and afterward.

Michael was hospitalized on the evening of Sunday, October 11th. He had been found not breathing, and after administration of CPR was taken to the ER and then to the ICU at Salem Hospital, where on Sunday evening and Monday he was cooled and sedated to protect his brain from any further potential injury. This process put him into a hypothermic coma of 90 degrees. After 24 hours they'll begin letting him warm, at which point we will see if he regains consciousness.

Thank you for caring. Thank you for praying for Michael and for us.

Further Information

Hi again. This morning they began allowing Michael's temperature to return to normal and reduced the paralytic drugs. When the drug dosage went down, he did wake up and open his eyes, but soon after began to struggle a little with the NG tube. He has been further sedated to keep him from fighting with the intubation. The family takes all of these movements as good signs, as he had no responsiveness when admitted.

He is currently fighting an infection and has a high fever,

most likely from pneumonia, which is not atypical after his kind of injury. So he has begun antibiotics. Tomorrow he will have an MRI to determine the state of his brain and neck. We'll know more about the state of his brain injuries at that point.

We really appreciate your interest and concern. We feel your prayers and know their power is real. We believe all of your prayers have carried him thus far. Please continue praying—for healing in his brain and from infection. We know your love for him sustains him and us.

In God's Hands

Good news! Michael responded to his name! He made purposeful, direct eye contact when his name was spoken and squeezed his right hand when asked. He turned his head (as much as is possible with the neck collar on) to look toward my or the nurse's voice, and then his eyes made contact. Thank you God, for your continuing healing in him, for all of the prayers of your people, for the gift of life, and the gift of each other.

The doctor thinks that they will try letting him breathe on his own today while leaving the tubing and ventilator in place to measure the extent of his ability. I know Michael would really love to have that apparatus removed.

I'd like also to share a story with you. Yesterday one of the hospital chaplains stopped by. He told us a bit about his prison ministry, and about a man who is on death row whose name I'll have to learn again. This man has been through a conversion along the lines of Saul to Paul[1] and now prays three hours every day. He gets up at 4:30 AM so he can pray before his block gets noisy. Each time he visits with the chaplain, he asks, "Who can I pray for this week?" Allen, the chaplain, gave him Michael's name, and told him a bit about his situation. Allen gave us a print of one of the prisoner's drawings. It is beautiful, this hand of God holding Michael.

Post - MRI

Michael's MRI showed some damage to the "deep, gray matter" of the brain. The ICU doctor said it was inconclusive what that might mean, perhaps issues with coordination, but he didn't know. He will be conferring with a neurologist tomorrow, and then we'll know more about the possible indications of that finding.

As for the breathing tube, Michael did breathe on his own for five minutes this morning, so his breathing capabilities are good. We still don't know whether he can fully support and coordinate his airway—swallow, etc.—and until that can be proven he will still need the intubation. They plan to revisit the possibility of extubation in the next day or two.

Here is another interesting bit of the story. Michael had some rather large bruises on the knuckles on his right hand when he arrived here. Apparently they came from an incident on Saturday. They worsened through Monday and Tuesday, as bruises tend to do. Today, Wednesday, they are completely gone. The skin is pink and healthy and shows no discoloration of blue, yellow or otherwise. It's as though they were just erased. I'm thinking all of these healing prayers are having effects we don't even intend.

Our daughter Natalie organized a vigil on Michael's first full night in the hospital. People gathered outside the hospital in an open courtyard near the entrance to the ER while Michael lay in a coma, four floors above them. More than fifty people assembled for nearly two hours. They prayed, sang, and wept, asking God for healing and strength. I was too fragile to join them, but on my way home for dinner around 8:30, I brushed by the edge of the circle and hugged a few friends. I couldn't believe how many people had come, how many of them I didn't know. Many who I did know I hadn't seen in a long while. It was powerful, this circle of love.

We truly had no idea of the miracle that occurred when Michael woke up. We were so unaware of the full scope of his prognosis that we didn't understand the significance of his immediate emergence from the coma. We were thrilled to see him regain consciousness, but we didn't share the depth of amazement that the doctors and nurses experienced. Since we still didn't know where he'd been, we didn't understand how far he had returned. Our faith was blind, but due to ignorance rather than trust.

And on the Third Day...

We have had a miraculous night. Michael went from slight cognition and response this morning to full out present personality and interaction this evening. I hardly know where to begin sharing the pieces of grace we saw. He was alert and emotionally connected, particularly to his sister Natalie who kept making him cry with wonderful things she'd tell him about how many people are praying for him, or about his mom sleeping here every night. Natalie and Kelley even got him laughing so hard that he broke into a ventilator coughing fit.

Earlier I showed him a small, fluffy, cream-colored bear I've had for years. It is a little angel with a heart-shaped bib with his name embroidered on it, and when I waved it at him and said, "This is you, Michael," his entire face broke into a smile, even with the feeding and breathing tubes stuck into him.

So, our dear friends, it has been a truly miraculous day. The hospital staff is also sharing our joy, as they have been tending and rooting for him ceaselessly. One of the nurses here said, "I've seen a lot of these come in as he did, and all I can say is that boy must have had an angel holding him up."

We love each of you, and we love God, the giver of all life, of every good gift and breath and joy. We praise God for the miracles working in Michael's life, through the great vast presence that is all of you and the angels and saints above.

All Glory be to God, the One in whom "we live and move and have our being,"[2] in whom and through whom all things have life.

Getting Some Air

Michael was taken off the ventilator and feeding tube this morning. We are so thankful for this progress. He has a fair amount of injury to the pathways in his neck, both from the event and from the intubation, so he is not yet able to speak (though he tries a lot). He also has limited coordination, as his motor movements are slow and labored. He is responsive and purposeful, but every gesture is in slow motion.

He has a lot of secretions in his airway and lungs, both from the irritation and also from the infection. He is working to clear those through coughing, which is fairly labored at present, and with suction. This is an important and difficult task for him.

We are grateful for the progress, and still we have such a long way to go. A neurologist will see him today, and if he gains enough awareness and is medically cleared, eventually a psychiatrist. He remains in ICU.

Wait on God, and God will give you the desires of your heart.[3]

So we wait. And we pray. And we trust. And we love all of you very much.

When the darkness closes in Lord, still I will say, "Blessed be the name of the Lord. Blessed be God's glorious name."[4]

Saying Michael was "working at clearing secretions" doesn't begin to describe the volcano of phlegm spewing out of him. It was an incessant, violent process of prolific mucous removal. He required constant assistance with a suction tube as once he coughed up the crud he had no ability to either spit it out or swallow it down. The forcefulness of the cough repeatedly splattered the TV screen on the opposite wall with fluid, a good 12 feet away. His caregivers (nurses and family) stayed near the suction at all times to keep him from choking, and Michael hacked constantly throughout the days and nights. Just like when my children were infants, I took to wearing only clothes that were easily cleaned and not highly valued since they always ended up covered with gunk. We all took direct hits in the face from time to time. The nurses and doctors were quick learners and soon wore splatter shields whenever they entered his room. Every now and then we'd get a new person on the rotation and after a quick eye splat, they, too knew the routine.

❧

Seeing More

Lots of tears today. The obvious becomes clearer. We are likely in for a pretty long rehabilitative haul for speech and motor coordination.

But just now he smiled at me and said, "Mom." So the tears are accompanied by laughter and small happiness.

This afternoon we had visits with the ICU trauma surgeon and the speech therapist. Michael seems to understand spoken words pretty well, though he is still very groggy a good deal of the time. The grogginess should subside as the meds are cut back. His body is more active each day, though there is no getting out of bed since he will eventually need to re-learn how to walk. When he reaches for a hand or the suction tube, his hand coordination is only approximate, like that of an infant discovering his limbs.

After the Visit with the Neurologist

Wow, is our world a roller coaster, so prepare for the fun part with the breeze at the top of the hill. We just met with the neurologist to go over the results of Michael's MRI. He said he expects Michael to make a complete physical recovery within a matter of weeks rather than months or years. He pointed out the two small dead areas in the basal ganglia that look like little strokes, each about a centimeter and a half in size, where his brain tissue died from lack of oxygen. He said Michael will be able to regain all functioning, that he may have some issues with memory loss, but that physically he should be fully normal. We were stunned and thrilled, asking, "Really?" and he said, "Oh yes!" The larger issue of psychological health remains and will take time to address, but we are surely buoyed by the miraculous news.

We'll be waiting to hear if Michael will be moved out of ICU in the next day or so, likely to the Neurological Trauma Care Unit, and eventually from there to an in-patient rehabilitation facility for two to three weeks. After that he'll be looking at therapy (physical or PT, occupational or OT and speech or ST) for at least three hours every day, possibly twice a day.

Thank you, thank you, thank you for all of your prayers, love and support. I'll conclude by sharing with you some words from a song cycle I'm performing soon, text by Brenda Ueland and music by Libby Larsen: "What do I believe? That love is the creative thing. That life is love. That is my belief. That perfection is in all, and we should love it in all; that is my belief. That I must love people, that I must love myself, that is my belief. That God is a person, that I must love people, that I must love myself, my reckless, arrogant, joyful self. *Memento Vivere.*" This last in Latin was Goethe's motto: *Remember to Live.* She finishes the movement with the words "To keep my face toward what is great, and lovelier, and move toward it." Yes.

Not There Yet

After the doctor's visit today it appears Michael will remain in ICU for a while yet. Our two biggest concerns are his inability to swallow and the secretions that he continues to cough up due to infection. If he continues to be unable to swallow properly, two things will result: a feeding tube and a tracheostomy. The tracheostomy (surgically creating an airway to breathe below his vocal chords) is reversible down the road if his condition improves.

His neck is still quite weak, which keeps him from holding his head upright, so he received a soft collar to support it and to help him move around in the bed without danger of injury.

Michael's afternoon was busy with visits from therapists. The occupational therapist thought his eye-hand coordination was improving (he was able to touch his nose with his left hand but not with his right), and a team of two physical therapists worked to help him to stand up for the first time, which he apparently liked very much given his broad smile. His girlfriend Kelley has been a tremendous help as she both motivates and cheers him up. He will do for her what he seems less interested in doing for anyone else.

Each day brings new challenges and also outpourings of grace. We are humbled by the way God is leading us deeper into love: its power, healing and compassion, both around and within us. We realize that we of our own selves can do nothing, but that we can do all things through Christ who strengthens us.[5] Christ is love.

Follow Up

This post is a follow up on the neurological report of the other day. We are receiving a more varied forecast, particularly from the members of the teams that work directly with his rehab (ST, OT and PT).

While everyone agrees Michael has an excellent outlook for recovery, the timelines we are given are anywhere from weeks to months to a couple of years. And while his prognosis is very good (his youth and strength work in his favor), there is no guarantee of the totality of his recovery.

So the news is still good, but we are learning how slow the process will be for the next weeks and months, and how many things are unknown. Also in the mix is his mental health, as the condition that led to this event is often exacerbated or intensified by the long, hard road he will face to return to functioning.

I have set a couple of self-care goals for myself in the coming days and weeks: regular exercise and an hour of singing per day. The rest of the days will be spent caring for and supporting Michael and attending to the daily tasks of life. I have not been back to work since he was hospitalized and will be off teaching at the university for the remainder of the semester unless his rehab progresses at a rate that facilitates an earlier return.

Through the years I've gone over and over in my head what I could have done differently as I parented Michael. During his and Natalie's grade-school and early adolescent years I was a single mom working a demanding, full time job as a music director at a church while teaching part time at a university in town. At home I was often tired or busy with domestic obligations. Many times I longed for my own time and space where no one needed me and nothing was required. Often when the kids did need me, I felt I wasn't as present as I should have been. I was well familiar with the "if only" road which the police chaplain warned us against that first night in the hospital. It led to thoughts like this: A good mother would have been able to prevent this. A good mother would have made a thousand different choices along the way, would have been stricter or more lenient, would have listened and loved better, would have tried harder, would have noticed warning signs sooner and would have responded more appropriately. A good mother would have been able to make her marriage work and spare her children the pain of a divorce. And a good mother most certainly would have thought to look on the neighbor's deck right away. If only I had gone straight to the deck. *If only.* The police chaplain was right. This sort of thinking is the way of the devil.

Sabbath

Three angels came last evening and relieved me from night duty—Natalie, Kat, and Kelley. They played with Michael, who apparently arm-wrestled Kat twice, pulling her arm to his chest and laughing. Kelley and Kat stayed the night while Natalie eventually went home to get more sleep. Natalie is hanging in there but is weary, and she is having some trouble concentrating. Rob has come down with a cold.

The speech therapy assessment yesterday showed that it is almost certain Michael will need a feeding tube tomorrow, as he isn't able to complete the motion of swallowing yet. We will also find out tomorrow if he will need a tracheostomy.

The best progress came in PT where he was able to stand and support his own weight. He wasn't able to coordinate balance or walking, but the strength of standing was progress from the day before. He spent most of the afternoon in a recliner chair rather than the bed, which, by the admission of one of the nurses really isn't very comfortable. He seemed to like it there. When asked if he wanted to watch baseball or football, he was able to articulate a vague "football," also a big stride. This morning he asked for his mom.

And now for the best news. Michael is graduating out of ICU this evening and on to the Neurological Trauma Care Unit, so we're moving from the 4th to the 7th floor. We have so much to be thankful for. He was playful and even ornery at times today—grabbing at his Tigger (his favorite gift from Kelley) and arm wrestling again. He made many other neurological strides, was able to connect thumb to various fingers, scratch his nose, and give a high five, to name a few.

We are also thankful for the abiding love and help of friends—elves who came and cleaned the house, those who make and share meals, and the countless saints who pray and love from a distance. We know that you are all part of this process, and we are indebted and grateful.

One of the opportunities this situation affords is a great deal of time for spiritual reflection and contemplation.

We've considered the possibility of the new life that is offered Michael through this transformative sequence of events. We pray for openness on all of our parts for the power and love of God to work through and in us in miraculous and life-giving ways. We know that God's strength is made perfect in our weakness,[6] which to me is a way of affirming that when "I" am out of the way, grace and love can flow through. We know that this love is available for all of us all of the time, endlessly, abundantly, and that our job is to recognize it and let it move and work. We trust this, and pray for the humility to both stay out of the way and to actively do our part. Blessed be the One in whom we all are one, who never leaves us comfortless. I'll close with this word from the Apocrypha: *For a good angel will go with him, his journey will be successful, and he will come home safe and sound.*[7]

Chapter 3
Graduation

New Digs

Michael had a good morning. With OT he put on socks, a shirt and pants, brushed his teeth, took steps with a walker and sat himself in a chair, threw and caught a small ball, and repeatedly wiped his face himself (there is still a lot of mucus coming up). He was able to successfully swallow some ice chips and a bit of apple sauce, so this afternoon he goes for a barium X-ray to make sure no matter is going down the airway or remaining in the back of his throat during swallowing. If he passes this assessment we will look toward the next step, which will be either a nursing care or in-patient physical rehab facility. The decision depends on his ability to respond to commands and to participate in three hours of therapy a day.

His speech is still very slow and nearly non-existent, so psychiatric/psychological therapy isn't on the table yet, though he is on a 24-hour one-on-one watch here in the NTCU. This is helpful as he is nearly constantly pulling things off—soft collar, IV tape, clothes, anything he can reach and manipulate. They've given up on keeping the stat lock on his catheter after too many removals. This boy is a busy handful, much like an active toddler in a 17-year old body. But busy is good, much better than the alternative.

Day is Done

More good news: Michael passed the barium x-ray swallowing test. Apparently his pharyngeal motion is good but his tongue and mouth activity lag behind. So we will be trying feeding for a few days. The speech therapist is skeptical about his chances because of the mouth coordination and also because his motivation for eating appears to be very low. If after a couple of days he still isn't getting enough nutrition, we will review other options.

Other good strides: He walked about ten feet with PT today.

The hard news: he has eruptions of anger and agitation that are a bit frightening. Apparently this can be a side effect of hypoxia (lack of oxygen to the brain), and we are hoping it subsides soon. It seems to flash through in very dynamic but brief episodes. I sense it is as frightening to him as it is to us.

This evening at 8:30 Natalie has organized another prayer meeting outside the hospital. We will be praising God for Michael's progress and asking for continued healing, both for his body and particularly for his spirit.

We know that darkness is real, and also that God is stronger than the darkness. Just as I was feeling spiritually overwhelmed by the struggle I see in Michael, I received a call from a friend who spent several years in deep depression, including several hospitalizations. She told me that it was indeed very dark there and so frightening, but that God shone in that darkness. She told me that it was because of those years and God's presence with her that she is now a minister of word and sacrament. We never know how God might use our struggles and painful encounters in transformative ways. I'm so grateful that God does, that even the most hopeless or painful things can transmute into joy if we are willing to let God take us there. So today we pray for Michael's spiritual transformation even as we pray for the restoration of his body. And we pray for that transformation in each of us, as we move "from light into light," as the hymn says.[1]

Over the mountains and the seas your river runs with
love for me, and I will open up my heart and let the healer set
me free. I'm happy to be in the truth and I will daily lift my
hands, for I will always sing of when your love came down.
I could sing of your love forever...
— Martin Smith

One Good Day Deserves....

I seem to see a pattern developing over the last few days: a good day followed by a not so good day. Today isn't the good day. While Michael passed his swallowing assessment yesterday, he has not yet been able to eat. The physical function is there, but the "will or desire to feed," as the trauma PA said, isn't. They said his MRI showed that the part of his brain that controls this urge may have taken a hit. We are approaching the marker where starvation becomes an issue, and are in a bit of a catch 22. The dietician and speech pathologist are not optimistic that he is able to meet his nutritional needs orally, and yet none of our options for internal feeding are too appetizing, as Michael is pulling at everything on his body. So yet again we are on a decision watch, as he should not go longer than one more day without nourishment.

I am learning that there are many ups and downs on this long, slow road. The positives feel very good, but the negatives are deeply discouraging and the altitude changes can be harsh and disorienting. So I will be seeking the place of equilibrium, or "detachment with love," as we call it in Al-Anon. No easy task for a mother.

I am reminded that the measure of our faith is not really discovered in the good times. Just as it is easy to be compassionate to those we love, the call that matters is to love our enemies. Likewise, it is easy to praise God when things go well, but I see that the choice of gratitude is all the more important when we are in the valley of despair. I

27

know at times God has said to me, "Okay, Christine, are you ready? Are you with me? This isn't going to be easy." And I remember that I answered, "Yes." I still do.

Have courage for the great sorrows of life and patience for the small ones; and when you have laboriously accomplished your daily task, go to sleep in peace. God is awake.
— *Victor Hugo*

Deciding Not to Decide

Hello friends. Onward into another day, and I'm happy to say it's true to our pattern, which means today is much better than yesterday (let's not talk about tomorrow just yet). Michael is still eating in very small amounts, but I was just told we can put off the decision about a feeding tube for a few more days. This is due to the good news, which is that his neurological and motor advancements of the last 24 hours are very strong. Last night he typed his name on a laptop. He got up several times and used the john, he said a version of "hello" to his dad on the phone, and something resembling "thank you" to one of his aids. He walked with minimal balance support from his physical therapist. He tied the cords on his scrub pants into a bow. It is amazing how exquisitely beautiful such a simple task can be.

This morning in OT he wrote several things on paper. Michael's normal penmanship (by his own, frustrated admission) is horrendous, and nearly illegible. And frankly it looks about the same now. But he wrote several sentences: "I'm Michael. I don't like it here. I want to leave. I want to go home and sleep. I threw up on Tigger last night." A bit later he wrote, "Mom, I love you. I'm so sorry." After his writing time we had a vigorous game of catch with Tigger, during which he repeatedly inched his sanitary underwear lower on his hips. His nurse said with amusement, "I have never had a patient who wanted to sag their Attends." Michael may be brain-injured, but he's still a teenage boy of the 2000's, so

28

even in the hospital he likes to wear his pants low.

We also have pinpointed the struggle with eating, which is the motion of his tongue. He was able to type answers to the speech therapist's questions, so we learned he feels like he's choking when he eats due to the lack of tongue coordination. She worked with him on sounds and motions to strengthen and retrain those muscles. This will improve each day with practice. He wrote, "How long?" to which she replied, "Probably you'll say a few simple words in one to two weeks." Speech is certainly one of the most intricate and complicated things we do.

I was reminded of two things in prayer time this morning. One is that darkness is really not so different from places of illumination. The light simply hasn't touched it yet. In essence, darkness and light are the same in that God is fully present in both and this truth of sameness is more important than any distinction. The other is that the everyday ups and downs, the emotions, the good news, the bad, the triumphs, failures, frustrations and even boredom, while these things are the essence of daily living, i.e. "life," they are not Life. Life exists below the surface of activity. So no matter if there is a raging storm or placid calm, the true substance of Life is always deep below where it is quiet, and its essence is peace. I was grateful to be reminded of this and was reminded also that even these moments of illumination are grace, gifts not earned by our own efforts. Thank you, God.

Michael conjured plenty of storms during his years of drug and alcohol abuse. I had repeatedly taken him to the ER for suspected overdoses, the first time when he drank two full bottles of cough syrup. I think he was in the 8th grade. I later learned that cough syrup taken in high volumes functions as an opiate. There were other hospital visits, and eventually Michael spent two stints in drug and alcohol rehabilitation, the first was when he was 14, the second at 16. Interestingly, the very competent staff of this particular dual-diagnosis, in-patient facility (they treat both addictions and behavioral/psychological problems in youth) told me that they could not give Michael a diagnosis of clinical depression in good conscience, because he did not fit that profile. He had situational depression due to drug and alcohol use, but not clinical. This distinction meant his insurance company would not cover the treatment.

By the time he had reached 17, we'd already traveled a long and challenging road, one that led me to reenter the program of Al-Anon in earnest (Al-Anon is the sister organization of Alcoholics Anonymous for families and loved ones of alcoholics). I had already grown in ways I had no interest in growing. I had completely restructured my parenting style (which had worked beautifully with Michael's older sister) since nothing I had tried up to that point had remotely tamed this beast of addiction. We were told by drug counselors that Michael ran the highest possible risk for continuing addiction problems due to a combination of early onset with genetic predisposition on both sides of his family. I was vigilant. I owned an alcohol breath-testing device and had a battery of home urinalysis kits. I had been through counseling with him, had attended countless family meetings in drug treatment, both in and out-patient. On more than one occasion I had opened the door for the police in the middle of the night. Through all of this we had found a way to manage his using, albeit not a very satisfactory one. He was biding his time and so were we. We all knew the routine, and the routine was what we planned to do until he was 18 and on his own. We imposed rules and

30

consequences but we knew they were only stop-gap measures. We fully expected that once independent of our reins, he would find his way to bottom. And we knew we wouldn't stop him. I clearly recall one conversation in particular: "Michael, when you are out on your own, if you get arrested, don't even think about calling me to help you out." "I know, Mom. Don't worry. I wouldn't." Once Michael turned 18 we would make the conscious choice not to be his safety net any longer. But since we were still his legal guardians and thus liable for his choices, and because we never stopped wanting and hoping for the richest possible life for him, we insisted on sobriety, holding him accountable as best we could.

Step-Dad's Corner

This is Rob writing at the moment.

I developed my second upper respiratory infection of the season at the end of last week, so I have been sidelined from the direct medical scene. Even so, being disqualified from hospital duty doesn't mean there is nothing to be done. I have found some ways to make myself useful. Today I decided to take on Michael's room at the house. If you read the cartoon strip *Zits* in the newspaper, you will have some idea what teenage Michael's room looks like; Although Jeremy, the teenager in *Zits*, might be a bit of a slacker in the clutter department when compared to Michael.

Seriously, Michael's room had taken on the appearance of a depressed person's quarters. The large closet (larger than his sister's!) has a string of empty hangers and a few boxes on the floor, some odd items on the shelf above the clothes rod, and virtually nothing on hangers in there. Nothing even tossed on the closet floor. No, every single item of Michael's teenage boy wardrobe lay on the floor of the room on one giant heap. As far as I could tell, nothing much in the pile had been washed since the end of George W. Bush's first term. There were empty soda and vitamin water containers scattered about. So I decided to clear the room out, wash everything on the floor (which meant, well, everything), and get the room in clean shape for when Michael returns. It was a good plan. It is now 7:30 PM, I am on my 5th or 6th load of wash with no end in sight. I think I have counted at least 10 pairs of jeans so far. I never knew anyone could possibly need so many pairs of jeans! When Michael gets to come home, he won't be able to find anything, I'm sure, because I am putting folded things on the shelves in his closet and in his dresser. I'm wondering if he'll ever think to look in his dresser...

A bright spot for me in the late afternoon today was when, since my cold is about finished, Christine called and asked me to bring the dogs to the NTCU to see Michael. If you ever want to be sure everyone in a hospital lobby looks at you, just stroll in with a couple of dogs sometime. To my surprise, no one stopped us, no one asked for I.D. or a note from our teacher. Christine met me downstairs and up the elevator we went with Sasha, our sweet little "cattle dog" mutt and Michael's first pooch, and Max, our Golden Retriever who loves everyone on earth without exception and wants to show them it is so. This did not even cause a slight stir in the NTCU. They encourage such visits to help the patients see some things from their normal lives while they are there. The CNA who was with Michael said it was okay for the dogs to get on the bed with him, and they didn't have to be asked twice. I am sure Michael is still covered with fur now, a few hours later.

At dinnertime, four lovely co-eds from Willamette University showed up at our door at home with all the makings for a very nice soft taco dinner. What we ever did to deserve such grace and generosity I'll never know, but then we know grace is never about deserving, and always about caring for one another in the spirit of Christ.

32

We continue to be pleased with Michael's progress toward health and wholeness. We continue to pray for his spirit and for those who are caring for him, and we continue to petition you for your prayers for Michael and for us. We are so grateful for you, our friends and family, who sustain us with prayer. We literally don't know if we could possibly get through all this without you. Thank you, thank you, thank you.

Still Not There Yet

Michael is still unable to eat, so likely a decision about a feeding tube will be made today. Our best option is a peg surgically inserted into his stomach. Given his record with removing things (IVs, arm bands, clothing, stat lock), we can't see that a tube through the nose would stay in for any length of time, and the peg can be wrapped and hidden (not that he's had any trouble removing wraps, though). Thankfully he can go under conscious sedation rather than going under general anesthesia for the procedure. At least we'll avoid further throat irritation from intubation as he continues to cough up secretions throughout the day and night.

His PT/OT progress is still very good: he rounded the unit supporting himself on a walker today, and can get himself to and from the john. We've complicated the Tigger catch game—high and outside, low and slow, etc. He's able to maintain his seated balance while playing, something he couldn't do yesterday. He also played his guitar today for ten minutes or so, and remembered at least three, maybe four chords.

Many of you have asked about the rest of the family. I know Rob gave you an update on his mountainous task of yesterday. WHOA what a room! Rob continues pastoring in Cottage Grove, and I have taken a leave of absence from the university. Our expectation is that I will be out for the remainder of the semester with the option of returning sooner.

I have been greatly blessed by the generosity, understanding, and compassion of my colleagues and administrators, not to mention my students whom I miss dearly.

Natalie is back in school full time, also at Willamette, going to classes and catching up on homework. She is also back to work, and is holding steady. Kat (our live-in, adopted daughter at present) has returned to classes at OSU, and she too is working and hanging in there with the family. You heard about the dogs yesterday. That's about it for the Elder clan. More as more comes, fellow travelers.

Gratitude

We're having a bit of déja-vu from last week, as yet again we are going to "wait until Monday" to make a decision on a feeding tube. Yesterday and today Michael ate enough for the doctors to feel comfortable postponing the decision. Once again we are hopeful he's turned the swallowing corner. He's eaten full bowls of pudding and just drank 240 ml of Sunny D. He's been downing the chocolate instant breakfast drink, too. YES!!!

As soon as he's eating regularly he will likely be cleared for discharge for the next phase: in-patient physical rehabilitation. If he keeps up on the meals this could happen as soon as Monday. His physical and occupational therapists told me today that he already meets the entrance requirement of tolerating three hours of therapy per day. So the only hold up at this point is nutrition, and I really do think we're very close on that. He's down over 20 pounds since he arrived, and he wasn't a chunky boy to begin with, but as the dietician said, he can make that up once he's back on track.

This morning Michael removed his IV for the third time. He's very quick at it, so even with three people in the room he slipped it by us. Thankfully the doctors have agreed not to insert another. Since he's been getting fluids, occasional pain meds and antibiotics through the IV, we'll be working to administer each of these things orally.

The IV removal is a symptom of a larger issue we're dealing with, which is his impulsivity. This issue is aggravated by his lack of comprehension. Just as his motor coordination improves in leaps and bounds every day, his cognitive awareness is coming along but is far from complete. The neurologist asked him yesterday, "Do you feel pretty with it mentally, Michael? Are you tracking pretty well?" He slowly shook his head no. He still doesn't know why he's here or how he got here, and the doctor affirms that he doesn't have the cognitive awareness to talk about that yet. Obviously that will be a major component down the road, but our focus for now is physical viability, strength, mobility, coordination, and independence. One of the doctors guessed that in four to six weeks he might be ready to address some psychological issues.

In-patient rehab will last ten days to three weeks. After that he will continue with out-patient therapies as needed anywhere from three to six hours per day.

I titled this post "gratitude" because I am filled with it today for so many things. I am grateful for Salem Hospital. The staff is wonderful, the new facilities lovely and aesthetically soothing. There is original artwork in every room and an obvious move away from cold, institutional ambience with appointments such as curved flooring pieces and soothing paint colors. I am grateful for the show of fall weather as I drove in this morning: blowing wet leaves and raindrops in a cascade of autumn colors on a backdrop of lovely gray (yes, I am an Oregonian). We are grateful for friends and family, for prayers, for meals, for understanding and compassion from those we love dearly and those we've never met. I'm grateful for Michael's life, for another chance, for the sweetness in his spirit and for the amazing strength and resiliency of his body. Human life is so astounding and miraculous, and clearly it is the body's nature to heal and restore itself. I am grateful for Dr. Vanderheyden, his trauma doc, who trusts this process and believes we should do as little as possible to interfere with the body's natural wisdom, but who is ready to make difficult decisions and to execute them competently when the need arises. I am thankful for the patience of his one-on-one CNA's who spend literally every minute by his side, speeding and tending his recovery with care.

Yesterday I wrote a friend that my worst fears in the last few years for Michael regarding his substance abuse were either death or severe disability. Now that we've crossed through and into both of those things (and by grace it appears most of it could be temporary), they are no longer huge, anxious monsters. They have become just things, decisions and processes we make and do one at a time. It's a strange reality shift, and certainly not a preferred alternative to the previous anxieties. I guess I'm saying it simply *is*, as my mother is fond of pointing out. So we are learning the "unforced rhythms of grace" (Eugene Petersen). I came to the hospital this morning thinking, "Life is good, so very, very good."

I've been working on this post for about two hours, in between all of the activity with Michael, and he just fell asleep holding my hand. Yes, life is good.

Michael once held my hand for a very long while when he was a tiny baby. He was on my lap in a huge, old, easy-rocking chair. His little body rested in the crook created by one of my legs as it crossed over my other knee. His hands were wandering as newborns' hands do when one of them latched onto my index finger. He gripped it reflexively. And then, as if he had just noticed that a whole person was attached to that finger, he looked me in the eye for a long, long while. We sat motionless, holding each other's gaze for a good 15 minutes. His focus was mesmerizing. I had no idea a small infant could fix his attention for such an extended period of time.

What is this communion like to this tiny, new being, I wondered. Some time later I wrote a poem about the experience, which I eventually set to music:

> *A hand, with eyes to match*
> *Finds its way into mine. I catch it,*
> *Soft and tiny, holding tight.*
> *It holds me like a dream*
> *Holds a mind. Firmly, but flowing,*
> *Knowing, but unknown.*
> *And through the eyes a*
> *Heart climbs into mine.*
> *Rests, and sleeps, and dreams.*

Birth Day

Today is Natalie's birthday and she's left her teen years behind. It is a good day in our family, which stretches beyond this group of people living on Fillmore, beyond the family in Portland, Seattle, Mississippi, New Jersey, Kansas, South Carolina, Colorado, Florida, Connecticut and California. So, big family, here is our news, and I'll begin with the physical: Michael exceeded his caloric intake goal yesterday. It's still a labor to eat, and it's messy, but it's happening, and he is motivated. He won't need surgery, won't need a feeding tube, and likely will be discharged to rehab soon. Every day he makes amazing strides in OT and PT. I learned that the primary window for recovery with brain injuries is the first year, and within that time frame, any early, significant progress bodes very well for the months to come. His medical team agrees that his progress is fantastic.

Michael is most frustrated with not being able to speak articulately. Today (and some yesterday) we have been able to make out a few of his words, but most of the time he still needs to write things to communicate clearly. Other skills are coming along beautifully: walking, bathing, eating and playing.

His mental clarity, however, is widely inconsistent. For instance, he repeatedly puts his bottle of Sunny D into a little clothes closet that his nurse affectionately calls "the fridge," while other aspects of his daily routine appear completely normal. So I've been unsure about when to talk with him about what. I spoke with a psychiatrist yesterday who told me that with this kind of injury he may or may not ever really process his choices. He might want to talk about it, might not, and her ten years of experience with teens and children have taught her that dredging up painful subjects when the youth isn't ready tends to produce a great deal of emotional disruption and very little help. She mentioned that often the primary need to process belongs to family members and friends rather than the patient, and their insistence on verbally working through painful subjects or events on their timetable rather than the patient's is often harmful. So the word was let him initiate. If he asks, talk about it and go from there. If not, let it be.

And yet again, God is so good. We had just talked through that advice as a family, and then this morning when Michael was alone with Natalie, almost on cue he wrote, "So what exactly happened?" Boom, he opened the door, so she told him. She followed her instincts and God's lead and walked Michael through the events of that night. He was shocked to the point of disbelief, but thankfully the Spirit gave her the words to meet his discouragement and disillusionment. And then he pulled her close and put his head on hers. His next words were, "I want to go to The Way." The Way is Natalie's Portland church and has been a powerful light in her own faith journey. I thought of how many times we have prayed for God to open Michael's heart, to open him to love, and here he is broken wide open, taking in the love of family and friends like cool water after a long walk in the desert. His spiritual openness is astounding.

Yesterday these words came to me: "I tell you the truth,

unless you change and become like little children, you will never enter the kingdom of heaven."[2] I see such childlike innocence in Michael right now, in his sweet, open spirit, and I see that he has the chance to let the light in, to know God's love and abundance. I thought about how his actions initiated a sort of huge spiritual intervention, and with that thought I considered how our connections in the family of faith have expanded over the last two to three years. After a decade of being nurtured in a single congregation (for me, Natalie and Michael, and much longer for Rob), we have now disseminated our church experience in so many directions: Rob to Las Vegas and Cottage Grove, me to the First United Methodist church here in Salem, Natalie to Outward and The Way. And still Michael's prayer circle reaches far beyond these six "home churches" into other congregations and communities, and the breadth of it amazes me. It's a big body, indeed.

Still, a long road stretches before us with no guaranteed course and many unknowns. I realize every person's journey is between them and God and is not for another to orchestrate or control. I feel a mother's pain in my heart that I'm not able to direct Michael's life more pointedly (oh, such an al-anonic I am!), the pain in the futile desire to shield him from loss, or control outcomes. Yesterday as I walked through the hospital parking garage I sensed God's presence saying to me, "Do you remember I told you I've got him, that he's mine?" I recall receiving this word years ago in prayer. I laughed out loud and said, "Yes, I remember." Just then Kat texted me and said, "Natalie and I are praying for Michael at The Way tonight. He is God's."

I thought again of how our culture equates worrying with care, as if worrying means we love someone more. It strikes me that worry is so far from love. Concern and care may be from the heart, but worry, no. Worry is akin to fear, the exact opposite of love, and it seems to suck the life out of situations and people. Worry is a brain activity and thus is more closely aligned with ego, while concern is from the heart. I learned this week that about ten years ago medical science discovered a nerve running directly from the heart to the brain, and the heart initiates the impulses. The heart directs the brain, in a sense. This is something we've known spiritually for eons, that seeing with the eyes of the heart is truer than any kind of ocular vision. I've also learned that worrying about people is a way we leave ourselves and go out toward them on a current of fear. Often we pray this way, while praying for them in love is more like steeping in the Presence and then drawing them in. This seems much preferable to me.

I'm so happy to share our good news with you today. There is more to come, no doubt. Michael is God's, as we all are. I'm so happy we're related.

Over time I have realized I have a rather illogical denial of Michael's mental illness, or at least of his depression. Granted, there is no denying that he took his life, and I say "took" rather than "attempted to take" because he underwent 20 minutes of resuscitation somewhere during the couple of hours we were in the little waiting room. I didn't know this until weeks later when I received the hospital bill and noted the $420 charge for those minutes. But I confess I eventually agreed with the doctors at his addiction treatment facility when they insisted that he was not clinically depressed, and I didn't think he had been so the night of his suicide attempt. You might think I am crazy to make such an assertion in the face of his actions, that I am the one lacking a healthy grip on reality. That is possible. But what I saw in Michael's eyes in the garage that night and in his subsequent choice was something altogether different than despair. It was either a psychotic break or an old-fashioned demonic possession. Maybe both. His mental condition was clearly aggravated by the combination of extreme distress over his relational difficulties and his alcohol and marijuana use earlier in the day, but there was something else. His blood alcohol level was below the legal limit when they ran the lab tests that night, and while he tested positive for THC (marijuana), there was nothing unusual or extreme about the result. Clearly the combination of the pot and alcohol had unbalanced him, and this imbalance was then exploited by a third force. I was coming to believe it was this other demon, whether it was the unique composite of previously named factors or a new entity altogether, that fired his dogged determination to take his life.

Identifying this third element helped me later to understand why he ran back to the house that night instead of away from us. This bizarre, unnamable aspect is the only piece that completes the picture for me. Otherwise I cannot understand the unrelenting momentum driving him toward his intended goal, cannot understand why I missed his brazen and illogical action right under my nose. Perhaps a psychologist better versed in these matters could explain more to me. Perhaps all of these details simply indicate he didn't want to die and that he wanted very much to be found. Surely he wanted his girlfriend to stop him. He had given her a play by play of each of his actions by text message: his first attempt on our own deck where the rope broke and then his intention to make a second try next door. But of course she didn't believe him because he was out of his mind and nothing he said made sense. He wanted her to save him, but God had a different savior in mind.

All Shall Be Well

It's a quiet day at the hospital. It turns out Michael has a thrush infection in his throat, likely either from the antibiotics or the intubation. I'm always amazed how one medically saving process often leads to the next problem.

He is busy with his computer today, both MySpace and iTunes. Unfortunately for those working and residing in the hospital, he has a lot of rap on his play lists. He wrote, "That cranky lady over there doesn't like my music," referring to his CNA. No doubt. When I walked in today his computer was shouting profanities while the TV answered by blaring back a 700 Club program on the Christian Broadcasting Network. His CNA was doing her best to cope. I explained to him that not everyone in the hospital shared his musical tastes so he'd need to keep the volume down.

Michael hasn't regained much self-consciousness yet, so he lacks both the amenities that come with it like modesty and consideration of others as well as the restrictions it imposes, thus his openness. I remember watching the light bulb of self-awareness pop on in both of my children when they were small. Once that corner was rounded they never returned to that former world again. They suffered a loss of innocence but also gained a beautiful measure of awareness. They had begun that fantastic life journey into consciousness that we all travel. It is strange to see Michael poised to pass through such a juncture again, especially with playlists full of rap on his computer.

Today I consider addictions and the darkness they bring. I have learned that the genesis of addiction is physical, that particular conditions predispose a person to the problem. It is not due to moral degeneration or weakness. I was amazed to learn that the brain's firing of the pleasure response in an addict's brain is 12 times that of a non-addict's, whether that response is to caffeine, nicotine, alcohol, or drugs. Those who struggle with addiction face a physical and mental battle hard for non-addicts to imagine.

And then there is something that happens between the original predisposition to addiction and the use of substances over time. Repeatedly succumbing to the pull opens the door for all kinds of darkness to enter where it then manifests in states of mind like discouragement, depression, alienation, or poor choices in the area of friends, surroundings, finances, and life pathways.

Last night Michael stared at the clock for a while and then began packing up. He got his retainer, shaver, computer and two pairs of socks and was headed out the door. I said, "What's up?" He said something I couldn't understand and then wrote, "25 minutes past room change!!!" He was correct in a sense, it was 25 minutes past shift change, but in his head he thought he moved to a new room every time they changed personnel. So I explained that he's always been in this room, that his nurses vary, but he never changes location. He looked at me, thought about it, and then unpacked his stuff and lay down. When I couple that kind of confusion with addictive urges, well, you get the picture.

Addiction strikes me as fully physical, mental and spiritual. And there is only one power that I know that can heal such a malady, and that is the power of God. Today God reminded me how ultimately time is not linear, how it is possible for Christ to return to traumatic or painful times in our lives and heal us in the now, even if those events are far past. We can invite Him there, even if we don't know where "there" is. While we may be limited by kronos (chronological time), God works in kairos (the fullness of time) and it is a beautiful, unbounded space. I love thinking about Christ meeting Michael in that dark space he visited and binding him up, body, mind and soul.

So today I pray for healing of the chemistry in his brain, for his heart, which holds so little self-affirmation, and for his spiritual substance, the essence of him. I affirm that the unseen reality is greater and stronger than the seen, that we are first spiritual beings and secondarily physical persons, and that God works through Spirit to affect us on every level. As Julian of Norwich said, "All shall be well, and all shall be well and all manner of thing shall be well."

Take Two

Will there ever be a morning? Is there such a thing as day?
Could I see it from the mountains if I were as tall as they?
— Emily Dickinson

Oh yes, there is morning. I love mornings. Emily may have been a night owl, but I am a morning bird. Light comes to me in the morning just as it comes into the world, and I've been drinking it in, even on this very rainy, gray Oregon fall day.

Michael's two main tasks today are to follow commands and pass a psychological evaluation. In order to be discharged he needs to control his impulsivity and get by without a one-on-one CNA in the room, and he needs to prove he has no desire to hurt himself. To test and tame his impulsivity, they've given him a written set of instructions entitled "How to Call for Help." He's to call and ask every time before getting out of his bed, and so far so good. He seems to understand that this is the way to rehab, and he wants to go, because he knows rehab is the way to home. He's graduated to some solid food for lunch, and can almost handle thin liquids (he's been on an all nectar-thick diet). I am able to understand some of his speech now. No one is talking about a feeding tube. Apparently that has slipped permanently off the radar (he did eat two trays of breakfast this morning). Thank you God. The expectation is that in the next day or two or three (nothing is ever a given, I'm learning), he'll move to phase two. The duration of this phase will depend on his needs as well as the amount allowed by insurance coverage.

Last night I felt rather broken and tired. I recognized it as grief, and as so many know, there is nowhere to go, internally or externally, to escape grief. You can't sleep it away or swallow it down with a good meal. It is just there, with you, in you. I have thought so much about how this story is everyone's story, only the details are different. These details may be particularly horrific, but there isn't a person out there who doesn't know brokenness and sorrow, who at some point faces that which is overwhelming or too difficult or wrong. My mother mentioned that all of life is about two things at the core: love and forgiveness. Each of our stories leads us ever deeper into knowing and sharing these parts of the Divine. God is leading me so deeply into love it hurts.

Chapter 4
Onward

Night Travel

After 17 days in the hospital Michael has been released to in-patient rehabilitation. This means he passed his psych evaluation and is following commands. We moved him this morning at 10:00. He'll be busy during the days continuing the various kinds of therapies he began at the hospital: speech, OT and PT, with a greater focus on cognitive processing and speech. His evenings are free. Some things are the same and some are different. He started with a hospital bed here but is now in a Posey bed, a tent that zips around the mattress at night so that he can't wander. He likes it. They will provide him with some one-on-one supervision after all. He'll continue to work on basic functions such as hygiene, ambulation, and cognitive skills, but he'll get to eat in a common dining hall now and will have more time in the various therapies. His daily schedule will be posted on a board so we can keep track of him when we visit. I will be participating in his training, learning as much as I can.

I am feeling the familiar settling of gratitude alongside persistent questions about the unknown. I have already encountered deep compassion here: in the eyes of women who ask me how I am and then genuinely watch and wait for the answer, in the receptionist who is the mother of a friend of Michael's, who looked at me with knowing and love, in the care of medical personnel. Gratitude comes like a cloud of knowing and is both internal and external, around me but fully within. It has a familiar, comfortable weight these days, and I recognize it as a friend.

Sitting with gratitude are many questions about the future. I'm told that when Michael finishes the recommended 8-12 days he will be released to home where he will require 24-hour supervision. Safety concerns are primary. For instance, he has a burn on his hand from a night stroll around the neuro-trauma unit at the hospital. A nurse was with him but with impulsive speed he made it to an instant hot water lever on a coffee machine and pulled it before he could be diverted. He still wavers and loses balance. So we'll be watching him in the same ways parents watch small children, making sure he doesn't turn on the gas stove or fall down the stairs or wander out into harm. We'll be learning more about what his home care will look like as that time approaches.

One of the staff told me, "Time is your friend right now. Be willing to let it take its course." This is the word I hear over and over with brain injuries. I think of how many things in life can't be hurried: babies in utero, the blossoming of a flower, our unfolding into consciousness and grace. We have no idea what time will bring for Michael, what kind of a friend it will be. We don't know if he'll regain his memory or cognitive functioning or if his personality will be the same. He no longer remembers how he got here though we've explained it all to him several times. He does remember my phone number and his dog's name and that it's 2009. He still has a sense of humor, though it's different and more primitive than before. I played Tic Tac Toe with him for 30 minutes this morning and watched him struggle to remember strategies. Interestingly, one thing he couldn't spot was the possibility of three in a row when each of the outside pieces was in place. That hole in the middle was a blind spot for him. After we finished he looked at the games on the paper for a long while and even played more against himself, trying to remember what he once knew. Thankfully thus far he isn't impatient or angry about his deficits. Just now his laptop died while he was watching *Behind Enemy Lines* and he simply rolled over without protest and tucked under his blanket for a rest.

Our progression is like driving at night. The headlights illumine enough for us to proceed but do not reveal much beyond an immediate view. Isn't this always the case? I think our journey will be long with numerous twists and turns, and I recognize my desire to see what lies beyond the curve as a need for control and omniscience, powers that do not belong to me. I once asked Rob why, when my daily prayer meditation time is the richest, most nourishing thing I know, why do I still resist going into it? He answered, "Because in prayer we have to admit we are not God." I can honestly say I have not resisted much lately. I am learning so much about surrender, and thankfully I find ego more easily abandoned through this crisis, a crisis that is now birthing into a new way of life. I see some of the unnecessary self of ego being crushed out of me, and this is a good thing. I'm also reminded that here in Earth School, Heaven isn't much concerned with our comfort. Over and over I see how God has such intimate, ultimate concern for us, but this concern doesn't extend to our comfort. So as I watch the amazing journey of Michael's recovery, his effort to relearn and remember, I try to remember what I know: God is good, all the time. God's grace is sufficient for my needs. And as Brenda Ueland said, "Perfection is in all, and we should love it in all."

Signs of the Times

Michael is settling into his new routine. He has seven different therapy sessions today, has completed six, and is growing tired. The speech therapist taught him about the hard vs. soft swallow. A hard swallow is done with your teeth clenched and activates the tongue more specifically. This helps eliminate some of the choking/coughing while eating. She'll be focusing mainly on his eating skills as triage puts safety first, with speech taking a back burner for now. His voice is nasal most of the time so they think his soft palate may have suffered damage from the throat injury. He's also working on slowing down, whether while eating, walking, or getting out of bed. His impulsivity persists, though it isn't as dramatic as it was a week ago. While he isn't fully steady on his feet yet, he thinks he is, so he tends to take off like a skateboarder headed downhill. He worked on concentration, focus and memory in OT and said he really likes practicing these skills. He worked on balance and strength in PT, even did six push-ups at the urging of his friend Chris who was visiting. Then he rolled onto the pillows on his back on the therapy mat and heaved a sigh. His body is still weak, but his will is making an impressive showing.

I can see that God prepared me in so many ways for this juncture. While there was no knowing, no way to ever imagine exactly what this is or would be, I can look back now and see markers along the way. The markers act as a compass, as points that say, "You are here and it is right." No, that isn't quite it. Truer would be, "You are here and I am with you. I was with you before and I'll be with you in the future." And of course it is only with hindsight that I understand the significance of the reference points. The following story is one of those markers.

Rob's first interim ministry appointment was at Mountain View Presbyterian Church in Las Vegas. This began less than a year after we were married and continued for 15 months or so. Through the generosity of the church he was granted a travel allowance that covered a commute home about every other weekend. Most of those weekends he came to Salem, but occasionally I went to Vegas. We always flew on Southwest Airlines and were well-versed in their seating system where passengers line up numerically according to the number they were given when they obtained a boarding pass and then choose any available seat when they board. The numbers are assigned in three groups, A, B and C, with about 50 numbers per letter.

One time and one time only I prayed as I got on the plane, "God, please place me where I am supposed to be today." I had a good number, somewhere early in the "A" group, which meant I would easily be able to choose an aisle or window seat. But after that prayer I was led directly to a middle seat near the front of the plane. A man was in the window seat and the aisle seat was empty. I thought, "Are you kidding? Who would choose the middle seat?" but the internal prompt was persistent and bossy so I quit arguing. My first clue that something was odd was when the man frantically fumbled to help me with my seat belt, straightening it and handing it to me, messily inserting himself into my personal space before I'd even sat down. I thanked him and settled in, and within 30 seconds he said to me, "Are you married?" I answered, "Yes," and he said, "Too bad." As we taxied for take-off I unwrapped a piece of chewing gum and he asked, "Do you have any more gum? It will be good for when we talk." I gave him a piece and our conversation began. His name was Craig.

As an aside, the only other person I remember from my Vegas flights was a man who approached me during the boarding call, asking the usual "What's your number?" question, the one we all ask and answer as we line up. I told him 11. He said, "I should have known it. You have 11 written all over you." I mentally rolled my eyes and thought, "Did you really just say that?" He was tall, handsome and confident, and clearly had pursued this course of conversation before. He went on to ask if I lived in Vegas or Portland (he was from Vegas, where we were headed), and then whether I was traveling for business or pleasure. When I told him I was visiting my husband who worked there, he asked the question I had been waiting for: "What does he do?" "He's a pastor."

Normally when people first learn that Rob is a pastor (which happens to him a lot on planes), they immediately become self-conscious and a bit uncomfortable, thinking they are being judged or evaluated by a standard they hadn't previously considered. Usually this unintended effect is a bit frustrating and Rob finds himself wishing people didn't immediately judge him the way they assume he is judging them. But I confess I was hoping for exactly this result by sharing my husband's vocation with Mr. 11. I thought it might discourage him, but I was wrong. There was a quiet, awkward moment as he digested the information and then he resumed his persistent, oblivious banter. As we boarded the plane he indicated two open seats near the front. I moved past them without comment, thinking, "There is no way I'm sitting next to you on this flight." I passed another eight or ten vacant rows before I found a seat at what I considered to be a safe distance. Mr. 11 got the message and turned his attention to the next available number.

But back to the Portland flight with Craig. It was clear he had some sort of mental disability but I couldn't place it in any familiar category. His speech was blurred most of the time, but occasionally it would clear. He was talkative, though, and told me many things, including how he held the course record for golf at his club. Hmm. He didn't move or act much like he could golf now, and eventually he explained that was a while ago, before his accident. He told me it happened on New Year's Eve when he was 18, though he didn't remember any of it because he ended up in a coma. I imagined the scene: a young man, attractive, well off and talented, out with friends on the holiday. Maybe it was a car accident, probably there was drinking. I wondered if he was driving, wondered what happened to others, and I thought, "You are what I fear for my son."

Craig and I talked much of the trip from Vegas to Portland. We were almost exactly the same age, and he was on his way to a family reunion in Neskowin, a little town on the Oregon coast where I had spent many weekends through the years on church staff retreats. He lived in Texas, apparently somewhat independently because he was meeting other members of his family in Oregon. He told me he had short-term memory issues and would give me an unintentional demonstration of this deficit by asking, "What's your name?" about every eight or nine minutes. In a bemusing way it was like riding next to Dory from *Finding Nemo*. Each time I'd tell him, "Christine," he'd say, "Oh yeah! Like the haunted car!" Apparently there is a movie with a haunted car named Christine. Who knew? He was sweet and genuine, if obviously different from who or what he had been before.

As we approached our destination he said, "I want you to meet my mom." I told him that might work out, but why didn't we just see. After exiting the plane I stopped at the restroom and lost sight of him. Then as I was leaving the security area I realized he was just a few feet in front of me. His gait was awkward and effortful. And then I saw his mother. Her entire being lit up when she spotted him. With difficulty he sped his struggling steps toward her wide-open arms. The joy and love on her face brought tears to my eyes. She reminded me of my mother, looked like her, even dressed like her. She was classy and down to earth at the same time.

I am not sure what I learned from my flight with Craig that day, but I know that it mattered. I knew it then and I know it more today. That encounter was a thread woven into the fabric of my life, and it's color has changed over time. Maybe I saw that for Craig, while many things were obviously lost, the most important things appeared to remain. His mother's love was beautiful, full and strong. And Craig was a joyful man. Whatever he lost in his accident, it wasn't joy. Perhaps he gained it there, I don't know.

Prayer

I asked Michael today if he ever prays. He thought about it and shook his head and said simply, "Nope." "Would you like to?" "Sure." He turned off his music and closed his laptop. I found it wasn't easy for me to explain. Prayer is mostly a state of being for me, but that isn't the most obvious place to begin with a brain-injured teenager. So I described it as conversation, the opening of a door. We can talk, ask, complain, listen, thank, or simply be, but the important thing is to open the door to the Other. We talked about how over time prayer can fill and build us up on the inside. He thought about it and said, "Are you talking to a friend or a parent?" I said, "Well, could be either, or both." He said, "But they're very different." Good point. I suggested beginning with friend. We talked about what that might be like, and after some consideration he asked, "Do I have to say it out loud or can I just think it in my head?" The quiet was sweet.

The Night of October 11

This one has been working its way through me for nearly three weeks now. I haven't written about the night of Michael's incident, or named it, though many friends and family know details. But there is an important witness to be borne in this part of the telling, and I pray now that I might be faithful to that witness.

This is our part of the story. It isn't about Michael's choice or what led him to it or what he experienced. It is about what we found and saw and how we have seen God's saving presence in the midst of engulfing, terrifying darkness.

We found Michael hanging from the deck of a vacant house next door. I should say Rob found him, and I was shortly behind. We had been looking for him after his girlfriend called and told us he had threatened to kill himself. He was unconscious, not breathing, and completely limp. His face was eerily pale. I have since learned that this look can be indicative of death by carotid artery obstruction.

Rob was with him some moments before I arrived, and had been trying to figure a way to get him down or at least relieve the pressure on his neck as Michael was hanging very high. After I called 911 we realized I could climb some steps and reach the cord to untie it. We got him down and Rob began CPR and continued this for eight minutes until the EMTs arrived. He has told me that he knew with an assurance beyond reason what he was supposed to do and that he'd be able to do it. He credits part of this confidence to his training as an eagle scout as a youngster and part of it to God giving him the knowing. His last CPR class was in the mid-1980's and many things have changed since then. But, as grace would have it, both Natalie and Kat had just taken a mandatory CPR course as part of their training as group ride instructors at an athletic club here in town, and dinner conversation just two nights earlier had been about that training and the updated techniques.

Those eight minutes were some of the longest of our

lives. I was in a helpless and nearly insane panic as I watched the ambulance and fire truck go the wrong way on the wrong roads of our poorly marked neighborhood streets. Some vehicles were on the street below us where we could see and hear them clearly but where they were fully out of earshot of my frantic screaming. They surely couldn't see us in the pitch black up the hill. Eventually one of them made it to our street but yet again went the wrong way. As I desperately leapt and shouted and screamed and cried in the street they finally turned around and saw me and headed to our door.

Rob has told me that when he found Michael, the darkness was so pervasive that his first thought was one of hopelessness. The ugly weight was powerful and palpable and all he could think was, "It's too late, he's already dead." His next thought, which pierced that first idea and then required some conscious strength to maintain, was, "NO!" As Rob administered CPR he talked to Michael, not particularly gently, telling him not to do this to his mother, that no, he couldn't die, wouldn't die. As the CPR went on and on and on he became light headed and weak. He thought he couldn't go on. Just then a swift, new strength flooded him and he knew he had the endurance to last as long as needed.

Once to Michael, the EMTs intubated him and then transported him to the hospital. When he presented in the ER Michael showed no reflexive responsiveness. The police questioned us and requested permission to confiscate his cell phone, obviously needing to rule out a murder charge. We gave them our full if bewildered cooperation.

I suffered some PTSD symptoms from that night. For the first 36-48 hours after we found Michael, any time I would start to fall asleep the image of him hanging would flash before me and I'd be jolted into a state of emergency again. The trauma surgeon at the hospital told me that treating this response very early on helps prevent long-term symptoms and suggested I talk to my doctor about something to help circumvent the mental loop. The idea is to prevent the brain from wearing the groove too deeply too quickly. I took her advice to heart and with very minimal and intermittent medication have remained free from the flashing images. My dreams have begun to work on me, but I was alerted to that possibility and given some coping strategies. I see this medical advice as another manifestation of the presence of God.

The scene we found haunts both of us. Most disturbing was the pervasive sense of evil. The darkness was so thick, and it wasn't just the absence of daylight. In one particularly haunting mental flash I saw Michael hanging and all around him a huge, black, beastlike face bellowed and howled. Sometimes in those early days in the hospital I saw the same terrifying, crazed look in his eyes that we saw that night. It reminded me of the beast, and was so frightening. One such time I took his face into my hands and, bringing it within inches of mine and boring steadily into his wild eyes I said, "I command you in the name of Jesus Christ to be gone, not to return, and to do no harm in your leaving." Michael's eyes changed, and suddenly he appeared confused and uncomprehending, looking as scared as I felt. I saw the crazed look in his eyes only once again, and I said, "I am not talking to you. I am only talking to Michael." Darkness is real, and we are fools if we think it's only the stuff of Halloween fare. The evil we encountered that night was strong and insistent, but it wasn't the final word.

I couldn't see it at the time because I was consumed with fear, hysteria and pain, but I have since been able to look back and see Christ there in the midst of the horror, right there, unwavering, unfaltering, unassailable. Rob and I have talked about it, and he sees the image of Him standing, present and calm. I see and feel Him as light, and I know it was and is a saving light. That light was present in the phone call of Michael's girlfriend, in Rob's efforts that saved Michael's life, in the girls' CPR training the week before and the seemingly random conversation about it, and in the love of those around him.

That first night at the hospital I had a clear sense of Michael's spirit being out of his body. We had been asked to wait in a room while they did some procedures. At one point I felt him hovering in the upper corner of the small space where many of us gathered. He was light and buoyant and joyful, saying, "It's good here, Mom. There is no more struggle and I'm so happy." I looked toward him in my mind's eye and said, "I understand that, but you need to come back. You have more to do. You can't leave yet." I told him I understood that ultimately this was a decision between him and God, but if God agreed, I felt very clearly his earthly life hadn't yet reached completion.

Rob has often said that it is impossible to be neutral in the world, that if you don't choose something, something will choose you. I want people to know that we have seen both realities side by side and we proclaim with the hosts of heaven and earth that nothing can defeat Love, including death. The light of Christ truly does pierce every darkness, and God has the final word, saving us from ourselves.

The Presence that was with us that night continues in so many ways. I often reflect on how I am managing to cope right now, and I know it isn't through strength of my own. I am well aware of the wave of love and support that you all are creating and sustaining for us and for Michael. It is powerful and keeps us on track. Many of you have shared that you are blessed by our sharing. I know it helps me to write, and the fact that it may be a good word for others confirms that God is at work. As Rob once noted, grace doesn't move only in a linear fashion, from person to person or back again, but rather it spreads like a flood and touches areas we never imagine.

I'll close with a song and a prayer:

What if my joys and comforts die? I know that truth is living. What if the darkness 'round me close? Still truth its

light is giving. No storm can shake my inmost calm while to that rock I'm clinging. Since Love is lord of heaven and earth, how can I keep from singing?
— Robert Lowry

For this reason I bow my knees before the Father, from whom every family in heaven and on earth takes its name. I pray that, according to the riches of his glory, he may grant that you be strengthened in your inner being with power through His Spirit, and that Christ may dwell in your hearts through faith, as you are being rooted and grounded in love.
I pray that you may have the power to comprehend, along with the saints, what is the breadth and length and height and depth, and to know the love of Christ that surpasses knowledge, so that you may be filled with all the fullness of God.
Now to him who by the power at work within us is able to accomplish abundantly far more than all we can ask or imagine, to him be glory in the church and in Christ Jesus to all generations forever and ever. Amen.
— Ephesians 3: 14-21

Puzzling

Michael is sleeping. He returned from his first counseling session with a psychologist and fell fast asleep.

He's been busy again today with swallowing therapy, OT and PT. I enjoyed sharing some tips for eliminating nasality (who knew being a voice teacher would be helpful in a situation like this?) and he was able to implement some of them with practice. This was hopeful to me. He got to take a walk around the block and it is a beautiful day: overcast but almost balmy, with lots of colorful, wet leaves everywhere. He was so happy to be out and walking, and talked about how good it smelled. Afterward his legs were fatigued.

Today I'll share the technical report from OT. Michael was given a cognitive assessment test and on a scale of 1-6 his current score is a 5.2. The good news is he is a smart boy, and his intelligence is evident. Particular areas of concern are memory and abstract reasoning. The challenges here affect many things. For instance, he does best with instructions that are physical, visual or tactile rather than verbal. He is often unable to recognize secondary effects or consequences of choices. Accordingly, his decision-making is impulsive, unorganized and erratic. This applies to social decision making as well. Not surprisingly, his thinking tends to be black and white. For instance, Kat was here and said, "I'm glad to see your progress, Michael!" He corrected her, saying she wasn't seeing the progress but was hearing about it from me and that I, Mom, had actually seen it.

At this level, structure and coaching is needed for successful completion of tasks or appropriate interaction. The good news is that the prognosis is positive for eventual independent living, with some continuing need for cognitive assistance.

I haven't been able to ask yet what the possibilities might be for advancing or improving in these cognitive areas. I know they are working on many of them in OT. I've also been informed a secondary goal is to develop compensatory strategies for permanent deficits.

Michael was always a subtle and sensitive thinker. One of his elementary teachers saw this clearly and tested him for the TAG program (Talented and Gifted). While he ultimately didn't fit that academic profile, his ability to perceive and draw subtle and complex connections was ahead of his time. He could read people well and his insights were often surprisingly mature. This sensitivity was also often a vulnerability.

So many things have changed in him. It's as though God took the puzzle pieces that made the picture of Michael and tossed them heavenward. They are reassembling now on their way down but the image they are creating is different. The DNA may be the same, but the way it's going to land on the page is not. I'm guessing some pieces may float off into space and never return, and others will fall back into place very slowly, as if subject to their own personal version of the law of gravity. There are qualities I don't miss (though I'm told they may return), and most of those relate to his profile as a drug user. Right now they are completely absent in Michael. He is patient, kind, loving, and gentle. He is still funny. He is never angry or arrogant. Wow, does this sound like I Corinthians 13....

He is a beautiful boy and I'm grateful for every minute with him, so infinitely grateful for a second chance for his life.

Michael exhibited lots of oppositional defiance and anger in his teenage years, but he had never spoken of suicide. Well, that's not true. He had mentioned it, but never to me, which is still the case, I suppose. He had once talked about it to a previous girlfriend when he had to move from his father's house in Tacoma back to our home in Salem because his dad was moving across the country. The thought of leaving his girlfriend made him desperate. I only found out about the suicidal urges after the fact, but I *had* found out. Why didn't I think of that? It is another "good mother/if only" thought: maybe a good mother would have connected these two occurrences, would have remembered more readily that he suffered great emotional distress when enduring relationship woes. But I didn't. I didn't remember, and honestly I didn't know that he and Kelley were in the middle of a breakup in early October. Probably a good mother would have figured that out, too. *If only.* The devil again.

Hallowed Eve

It is Saturday, a slow day at the rehab facility. Michael had some group therapies this morning and is free for the afternoon. He's had six visitors already today if you count Max and Sasha, which we do, of course. Sasha was so glad to see him she repeatedly licked him all over the face. Ew. He didn't seem to mind as he was feeling the dog love.

Kat and Natalie brought cupcakes and Michael was able to eat them mixed with milk. He has not yet graduated to solids, much as he'd like. Apparently one of the new staffers let him eat some candy from a bag in his room (a gift from a friend's family), and that was a no-no due to his dietary texture restrictions. He incredulously told me, "Mom, they took my candy! On Halloween!" It's now in a cupboard out of the room, waiting for the time when he can eat something besides puree.

Every day his speech is better, which is so great to see (or hear, as Michael would correct). Also every day I see more of the subtle body language and physical personality that I remember as uniquely him. He filled out a "memory book" that will function as his brain while he's here. In it he keeps track of what he's working on with whom and other notes. One section was for personal information, with questions such as, "How would other people describe your personality?" He filled this in with "outgoing, spontaneous and funny." I would say he was spot on. He regularly greets one staffer at the desk with a big, "Hi Karen!" when he moves through the hall. Yesterday she asked, "What are you doing in therapy, Michael?" and he answered enthusiastically, "Kickin' it like soccer."

Each day I ask him if he wants to pray, and so far he has always answered yes. So we share sweet pauses of quiet. This afternoon we sat together and closed our eyes. In my mind I saw Jesus clasping Michael's hand, one revolutionary to another, and I felt a current of strength flowing from him to Michael. When I came around and looked to see where

61

Michael was in his prayer, his eyes were still shut and his face was soft and calm.

When he eventually met my gaze I told him what I'd seen, that I could almost hear Jesus saying to him, "Dude, I'm your brother, and I'm here for you." He smiled.

Sundays have no therapy at all so it will be a good day for visiting. I'll be here in the morning and then will head to Portland in the afternoon for a singing gig. I feel so fortunate that this and one other upcoming musical engagement fall during his rehab stay when I have some flexibility. I'll sing a duet from a Bach cantata. When I looked at the text of the duet I saw the fingerprints of grace on the page, as it speaks so meaningfully to our lives at this moment:

God, ah God, never again forsake your people!
Let your word shine clearly for us;
Although our enemies rage powerfully against us,
Our mouths will still praise you.

Just last night I heard grace described in a wonderful way. I was painting Michael's old room, which is now Kat's room as Michael will be on the main floor upon coming home. It was in definite need of freshening and change, and frankly is no one's favorite place at the moment. However it is now a serene blue color ("mountain stream" its called, though I think it looks more like the ocean), and we are praying blessings over the space. It's interesting how physical places take on energies and personalities, and this one definitely needed cleansing. Rob initiated the process with the monumental cleaning and then continued it by sleeping and praying there several nights due in large part to a cold he was trying not to share before one of my singing performances. While painting I was listening to a lecture by Carolyn Myss, an author from whom I have learned much through the years. She said something like, "Grace is when you do the thing you never thought you could do, when you have always said, 'I will *never* be able to love so-and-so,' and then one day you are full of love for them. Or when you think 'it is impossible for me to forgive this,' but one day you do. These are the gifts of grace, and they defy reason."

I have often looked at parents with disabled children and thought, "That looks so impossibly difficult. God must know that I lack the strength and patience for such a path, and I'm grateful I never had to face it." And here we are, and by grace it is fine. It isn't wrong or right or unfair or just, it simply is, and I know without a doubt we'll all make it. I also know I am not the good one and Michael the problem. I may be the caregiver and he the challenged one, but in essence we are the same: perfect and whole in God, broken and small when left to our own devices. We are all the same.

I see that I'm only strong and safe in this journey as long as I can remain in humility. Otherwise I am dangerously vulnerable. Pride through ego is a relentless assailant, and it is active in me all the time. I feel I have no patience for it, that at some point I should finally be able to rise above once and for all. But it is always there, always asking me which way I will choose: the smaller, physical way of seeing, or the infinite, symbolic vision of the Divine. This seems to be one of the purposes that crises serve in our lives: to strip us of ego and bring us to our knees, breaking our spirits wide open. Without the barriers and interruptions of personal striving, God comes through very clearly. I believe there are other ways to remain in such a constant state of grace, but I seem to need more practice at those.

Back to the "Poser in the Posey" as Rob called Michael, who thought it was funny. He's been making some peculiar sounds as part of his effort to clear his throat and swallow normally, and we've affectionately dubbed him Chewbacca. The sounds are less frequent now, but he just did it again and I said, "Hey Chewy! I think that's who you are for Halloween even if you don't have a suit." He then did a perfect Chewbacca imitation, raising a zombie-like arm and saying, "Arrrarroowwrrerr!" (I had to look up how to spell that on the Internet). What a boy.

All Saints Day

Michael is in his usual place, on his Posey with his computer. It's morning and we've chatted a bit, and Karen, a pastor and former colleague of Rob's, is coming by soon to share communion with us. When I told Michael this he let out a small "oh!" This made me smile. Years ago he and Natalie used to regularly descend on the sacristy after communion services to eat the leftover bread. They were snarfers, for sure.

I've heard it said that the mind gets the day shift and the heart gets the night shift, and the day shift begins about 4 AM. Many of us are familiar with the hour of the wolf, when all that is tidily contained during conscious hours surfaces from the recesses of our psyches. My mind and heart are working overtime right now, filling my sleeping hours with dreams and the waking ones, often in the dark, with thoughts of "what if?"

So I have a lot of time to consider the ways we humans try to make sense of the difficult situations we face in life. I see that for the most part, we approach them with our minds, saying, "there must be a reason for this." We figure if we can only understand the *why* of our plight we'll make it through, or be steadier on our feet, will forgive or accept. I know I rely heavily on my reason when processing anything challenging and do in fact accept circumstances more gracefully when I feel some measure of understanding. I am a college music professor and once scored in the 92nd percentile nationally on the Law School Admissions Test, so I believe my reasoning skills are fine. But the gift of reason is not the same as the grace of understanding. I know I have been unreasonable a lot lately, and I don't mean in terms of being difficult. Michael's circumstance has at times lifted me out my mental field into the realm of grace, and this has gifted me with a glimpse into just how limited I am by thinking. Paul challenges us in his letter to the Ephesians not to live in the "futility of our minds" where our "understanding is darkened" and our hearts hardened, but rather to "speak the truth in love" and to grow up into Christ, primarily by loving and forgiving. In most of my experience, forgiveness is fully illogical. I know I spent many years separated from my faith because I couldn't logically reconcile my mind to matters that seemed unreasonable. I know people who walk away from God because they perceive God to be unfair or unfeeling, as if we set up the divine standard according to the patterns and nature of our human minds, minds that we often elevate to a place of ultimate supremacy.

My mind does not usher me into grace right now, and I don't believe it ever has. Most of my thoughts are not holy. The mind is a beautiful tool, one which helps me make decisions and plan and process, but any strength or mercy comes to me now beyond reasoning. How do we cross this narrow bridge from seeing through the logical prism of our own thoughts into the expansive vision of love? I believe we are gifted with it, often when we least expect it, and then we practice it over time through prayer and choice. Once in a vision in prayer I was led into a room of chaos. It was completely white and all principles of physics were absent. There were tables with two legs on one side and none on the other standing without wavering. There were architectural structures in the ceiling and walls that were clearly optical illusions that could never be built. I asked my guide why I had to come here and she answered, "Because God is here."

I do not always find reasons for why things happen as they do. I can only share my experience, which is that God is fully present in everything, guiding and loving us, especially at the most painful junctures, and that chaos is part of our path. I have seen that one way to open the door for God and receive a flood of mercy is to release my need for explanations and answers. I have witnessed that God can and does redeem anything. It helps if I show up and am willing to participate. I also acknowledge, as Teresa of Avila said, that I know nothing about God.

Chapter 5
Ordinary Miracles

Lost and Found

Michael is in OT right now, and his task is to find things. He has a list of items such as "laundry soap," "fork" and "your room." He has been to each of the items' location before, and he and his therapist are moving throughout the unit to exercise his spatial memory. This morning she worked with him on mental skills, specifically keeping track of two things at once. So they began two games of his choosing, Connect Four and chess, and alternated games between moves. In physical therapy he worked on balance, conditioning, and core strength in the morning and then had a walk outside after lunch. He loves getting out into the fresh air. In speech therapy he worked on muscle coordination, particularly his tongue.

He is on a reduced level of supervision as of this afternoon. They won't zip his Posey bed at night and he's off the 24 hour one-on-one CNA. Instead he has an electronic bracelet that sets off an alarm if he passes a certain point in the unit. His therapy team met this morning and anticipates he'll be discharged toward the end of this week or early next. The primary concerns remain the same: swallowing without choking and impulsivity.

I know I say this like a mantra, but every day he improves. It is amazing and heartening to see the steady progress. Today I was given a beautiful glimpse into just how far he's come by the visit of Chaplain Allen, our friend from the first days in the hospital. Allen last saw Michael when he was still in ICU in a hypothermic coma. At that point we didn't know if he would live or regain consciousness, if he would be in a permanent vegetative state or recover any of his life. Allen was due for vacation and told us another chaplain would be coming on deck but that he would be praying for us. Today I saw him again, jet-lagged, and nearly ecstatic upon seeing Michael walking down the hall. He was *so* happy, so grateful, so thrilled to see the progress Michael has made. The genuine care and joy on his face made my day. He said a day didn't go by when he didn't pray for Michael and for us. I thank God for Allen. I was able to tell Michael about it afterward, along with this story Allen shared.

There was a man who spent three months here at the rehab facility. He had shot himself in the head and no one expected him to live. Then no one expected him to regain consciousness, and finally no one expected him ever to regain cognitive functioning. But as Allen said, they forgot about the "God factor." In the end, the man would always be disabled, as he had reached his plateau in recovery. However, the heart of the story wasn't about what he had lost but what he had found. He birthed a new love and appreciation for life and was regularly cheering up the staff and other patients. He was a floor favorite, as he constantly wanted to give, encourage and love. He had recognized how precious his own life was and shared this joy with others.

As I write these words to all of you, and most of all to myself, I am reminded how we all know the truths this man learned and lived. I believe the wisdom of the saints resides within each of us, but it is simply illuminated to varying degrees at various times. I see that much of my life is given to remembering what I already know, to turning on the light yet again and saying, "Yes, that is true. I will try to remember it more." "The kingdom of God is within you."[1] Yes. The original Greek can also be translated, "The kingdom of God is among you." Yes, that, too. I see God manifest in you, our cloud of witnesses, every day. I thank God for the chance to spend all of these hours and days remembering while witnessing the miracle of life, though I often think what we call miracles are really very normal occurrences if we can only see them through the lens of the Divine. Our human perspective labels things miraculous, and indeed they are. But when we look through the eyes of God, well, I think it must look like this all the time.

Circular

Michael took an assessment in speech that will provide a measurable indicator of his progress when he leaves. They will be working with him on the things he finds "annoying" about his speaking, namely nasality and articulation. He played Wii in PT, both bowling and baseball. He scored 192 in bowling. 192! He'll be outside for a walk again in a few minutes, one of his favorite things. He also took another cognitive test that affirmed his impulsive tendencies are still very strong.

We've had more conversations about using and how he got here. Interestingly he remembers whom he was with but not what he did. We've also talked about what's happening now. I told him God is already using his life to touch others in meaningful ways. We talked about how God doesn't will disastrous things to happen but manages to use them for good purposes. Michael said, "I don't know what's wrong with me. I thought when people had near-death experiences they were supposed to be completely different afterward, but I feel the same." Just then it was time for speech therapy, so we pushed the pause button and came back to the conversation a half hour later. He remembered it, which was encouraging. I asked him if he could think of anything different about himself now and he said no. So I asked about his openness: to prayer, to God, to the idea of something bigger than him working in his life. To this he said, "Yes, it is a big difference.

It feels good." I told him that is probably the most important change I could imagine and that nothing else is needed. I also told him how wonderful it is that so much of him, maybe all, is recoverable, that he is still here and *is* the same. The openness in him moves both ways. He may be letting Spirit in, but he is also letting love move through and out, and it is beautiful to behold. He's demonstrating the nature of love, that it is a complete circuit that requires both intake and output. One thing doesn't work well without the other, and usually a break in the current means both capacities are affected.

Michael announced, "I've gotten lots of compliments on the wooly mammoth." His half-sister Jen gave him this stuffed animal when he was in the hospital. Then his friend Chris arrived and Michael said, "Check out my bed improvement!" He's graduated off the Posey and has a regular bed now. He's pretty excited about this. When a PT assistant came in for his walk and asked, "Do you prefer Michael or Mike?" he answered his usual, "Doesn't matter," to which Chris said, "YONKS!" This is the nickname his guy friends often call him and it brought a huge grin. Michael lights up the most when friends visit, and I'm so thankful for all of them who come and came to the hospital before.

Now, after lunch, he's talking to his grandpa on my cell phone, with more therapies to come. In the past I've reflected how after mountaintop experiences we have to settle back into the level plains of daily living, how most of life happens there in the even places. Now I think about coming up from the deep fissure and crevasse of October toward those same even places in the months to come. Flat side down, round side up.

❧

By this time Michael's girlfriend Kelley was no longer coming by the rehab facility. She was amazing those first days and weeks in the hospital, visiting every day and thinking nothing of repeatedly wiping and suctioning his mucous mess. She would often climb into the bed and snuggle his compromised form with genuine and tender affection. She didn't blink in the face of his newfound disabilities or limitations until one day when another cute blond friend from school visited. There was no way Kelley could have been prepared for the unexpected effects of Michael's injury such as his complete lack of inhibition and judgment coupled with extreme impulsivity. When this other girl visited, Michael pulled her toward him and kissed her on the mouth while Kelley stood at his side looking on. Some days later when Kelley wasn't feeling she could handle her situation with Michael any longer, I told her she should move on without guilt or regret. A brain injury of this magnitude is the sort of thing that puts marriages to the test. I never felt a 16-year-old should have to endure it, especially one who was recently emotionally punished beyond reason through her boyfriend's suicide attempt. A couple of weeks later she came by the rehab facility and gently broke up with Michael. For a while after that I would receive an occasional text message from her. "How's Michael? I miss him." I would say he was doing fine, and that I understood, that we missed him, too, and it was okay.

What Is Ours

Michael and I are on break. It's been a busy day of education. We learned about his tongue muscles and he's done exercises for cognitive processing, balance and strength. His release date has been set for next Tuesday. He was really hoping for this Friday, but his eating continues to pose a major safety risk. He has seen his speech therapist three times today, two for coaching during meals and once for speech exercises. The primary weakness in both arenas is his tongue. At lunch I received training as his eating coach, learning prompts and cautions and when to give the all clear before the next bite. I'll practice again tomorrow.

We also learned that upon release his days will need to look much as they do here in terms of scheduling and supervision. Predictable routines will support his recovery and I'm frequently reminded he will need 24-hour supervision. We'll have a white-erase board where we'll post each day's activities and their times. I know he's very excited to get back to working out at the gym with Chris (though I'll be tagging along) and to other regular activities like going to a movie or hanging out with friends. He won't be returning to school yet as his memory and cognitive skills need further redevelopment before that's possible.

As we continue on this journey of recovery I will begin to limit the personal details I share about Michael. I've watched him evolve developmentally in these past three and a half weeks from infancy through childhood, and what I see now is the beginning of re-emergence into the consciousness of adolescence. As he crosses this bar of self-realization, his story becomes his again rather than mine. Just as very small children originally belong wholly to their parents in terms of safety, decisions, and levels of independence, they eventually move into and claim their separation in the form of adulthood.

Ultimately I can't write Michael's story because it isn't mine, because, as Kat said, our own stories are the only ones we really know. I believe I can continue writing my story, and Michael will certainly be a large part of it for the foreseeable future. But I know I need to allow him his dignity, the choice of what to share and what not to share. It's interesting. In the early days in the hospital he had no sense of modesty or personal boundaries, very much like a small child. This is changing now (which is good!) and I am eager to respect his privacy, both physically and cyberspatially. I certainly will continue to paint the picture of his brain injury recovery, but perhaps without so much of a telephoto lens on him.

Here's what I am learning today from this part of the journey: I see that through Michael's incident and my processing of it I am called into something new. I am trying to let the "unforced rhythms of grace" teach me about that. I am repeatedly reminded that one of the most important things for me to remember is my own smallness. I am safe when small, and run great risk when I stretch into a large personal image or, heaven forbid, supersize. I have great vulnerabilities then, along with a precarious sense of balance. The enlarged volume is too much to manage or maintain, spiritually speaking, and I am quickly poised for a crash. We are all huge in God, infinite even, but that is only in God. We are glorious treasures when divinely expanded, but we can't fully claim the goods as our own. This spiritual wealth is not available for ownership, but its supply is infinite insofar as we are in the Creator, as we are "rooted and grounded in love."[2] How strange to be something but not to have or own it. We walk with one foot on earth and one in heaven, bearing the tension of the duality of being eternal and insignificantly small at the same time. Only from the vantage point of my smallness can I understand my infinity. Otherwise I cannot see it at all, or live it, or share it with others. I do not demonize the material world along the way because so much of what I find beautiful is physical: the human body, color, the sky, a single, lovely note, laughter. What a spectacular world it is. For me the tension of flesh/spirit[3] is borne out more as a matter of perspective.

Once God showed me an image of how infinitely beautiful we are. This picture of our eternal selves was like double helixes of fluid glass, clear, purple and gold, full of jewels and pulsing with light and love, royal creations, each of the same substance. As the presence of God pours through us we do indeed "magnify the Lord,"[4] and we are endlessly and spectacularly beautiful. I often think we can't bear how beautiful we are in God, perhaps because we weaken ourselves by spending so much time focusing on all that isn't of God. This journey moves me deeper into letting go of all that I have held, all that was never mine, so that I might become what I am. I pray to be a lowly lover, walking firmly on the earth with my eyes wide open and my good ear turned toward heaven. Any inner journey is valuable only as far as it moves me deeper into love and service. This is my heartfelt prayer: to offer a bit of salve, or perhaps help build a bridge from brokenness toward joy.

I have held many things in my hands and I have lost them all; but whatever I have placed in God's hands, that I still possess. – Martin Luther

Ghostwriter Wannabe

It's just after 10 AM and Michael is sleeping, resting after morning therapies, his hands folded across his chest. They work him hard here, which is wonderful. This afternoon we'll bring the dogs in for another visit—more pandemonium with fur.

My heart and spirit are still today, perhaps experiencing an unscheduled Sabbath. Or maybe I am ground to a halt by a struggle with my own willfulness. I know I want so much to script the outcome for Michael. I want this to be the thing that changes him, the message that finally gets through, the gift that ushers him into light and the presence of God. I would like for him and those who love him not to suffer so much. But it is misguided to think that either the process or the timing is in any way up to me, as if I am the savior instead of the saved. As a person who has found faith and managed to hold on to it by the grace of God, I can't help but want to share it with those I love because it is so *good*. This faith is the thing that gets me from here to there in every sense, whether that is from one day to another, from a place of darkness to the light of the next spiritual insight, or into the world beyond that we can't see with our human eyes. And yet while I can witness, the only practicing of faith I can do is mine. Not Michael's or anyone else's.

There is no forcing grace upon someone. And when I look at the ways Michael's journey has touched people already, who am I to say what the way should be, for him or for me? God grant me the serenity to accept the things I cannot change, the courage to change the things I can, and the wisdom to know the difference.[5] Meanwhile: O rest in the Lord, wait, wait on God patiently, and God will grant you the desires of your heart.[6]

End of the Week

I see aspects of life-as-usual returning. I've been noticing little signs along the way and lately they have been coming on fast, the way one day in spring the baby green leaves are suddenly everywhere when just days before the branches were bare. Here is a list of some of the indicators that normalcy is on the rise:

- I no longer keep my cell phone on my person at all times, something I realize lots of young folks do but which I have never done before, and my first thought is no longer "emergency?!" when the phone rings.
- I turn on NPR when driving.
- Laundry is back on schedule.
- My legs are sore from a total body conditioning class.
- I ate a bowl of popcorn with cheese for dinner.
- I have watched TV somewhere besides Michael's hospital or rehab room.
- I can tolerate and even enjoy Grey's Anatomy.
- I am tempted again by second-hand shopping.

Michael's release date has been confirmed for Monday,

November 9. He was very excited to see his name and date on the discharge board behind the main desk. So just as things at home are settling into some semblance of routine, I am actively anticipating the upheaval of his discharge. Homecoming is both joyful and scary, bringing up a host of questions and anxieties alongside great relief. I'm addressing many of the questions to the staff here: How will we know when he's ready to go back to school? How will I know when it is safe for him to be unsupervised for small amounts of time? What is the process for determining when he can drive again? We're making strategies for home therapies and safety while understanding that autonomy is of paramount importance to a teenager's emerging sense of self, not to mention his mood. We'll be balancing "You have to come with us when we walk the dogs," with "What's your choice for an OT activity?"

Yesterday, in anticipation of Michael's release, I cycled through some emotions that were not surprising, with discouragement and anger looming large. I remember hearing that most emotions, in their purest form, last one to three minutes. Interestingly, I felt the feelings coming on all day but couldn't name them. They weighed me down with a general lethargy until they drew into sharp focus, at which point they moved through fairly ferociously and quickly. I have learned through time that emotions are meant to be fluid. Problems only arise when they stop up or I repeatedly feed them with thoughts that look backward or forward, particularly of how I perceive I have been wronged or what might go wrong in the future.

Today I thought, "What do I want to put into circulation? What thoughts would God want me to circulate?" There is an endless supply of God, and while all things are possible with God, all things are not yet possible with Christine, as Agnes Sanford would say.[7] I believe we are each allowed the spiritual current that our souls can bear, and God will not try to run stadium lights through a 120-volt connection. Still, the potential is there for each of us to grow stronger in our spiritual strength, and we are given the unmatchable joy of sharing this God-given gift of spirit with the world along the way.

The substance of our sharing may not even particularly matter. It's the giving and doing of it—freely, joyfully, abundantly—that is important. The measure we give is the measure we receive[8] and only in forgiving are we forgiven.[9] Again these truths remind me of the circuitous nature of our spiritual realties, that the reason we remain unforgiven when we don't forgive is not because God is stingily withholding love due to our errors or badness, but rather because we have closed down the circuit and love can't move through. This is a spiritual truth and in its essence it is neutral. It isn't good or bad, it just is. If we flip the light switch at home and nothing happens, we first check the bulb, then the breaker switch, and finally the wiring. It is this way with the current of God's love and light. If it isn't moving, we need to check our circuitry, look for where we are resentful or afraid, closed down or broken, bitter or judgmental, confess it and receive healing and forgiveness, which are often the same thing. The free flowing of love is the sign that we are forgiven or made well (Agnes Sanford again). Finding the circuit break may be our job, but the actual change in us is one of grace.

As I thought about Michael coming home and what I need to circulate I thought, "Patience. Perseverance. Trust." A paraphrase of parts of Psalm 119 came to me in prayer this morning. I remember it from an anthem setting by K. Lee Scott:

Open my eyes and I shall see,
Incline my heart and I shall desire,
Order my steps and I shall walk in the
Way of your commandments.

Blessing Day

This morning Rob and I offered a blessing in every room of our house and every space outside related to Michael's incident, including the empty lot behind us and the deck of the vacant house next door. We claimed and named each area for Christ, praying his protection, strength and cleansing. Rob touched every wall with a cross as we moved through. I felt the Holy Spirit shivers in two places in particular: Michael's old room (which is now Kat's) and his new room, the guest room that has been both Kat's temporary quarters as well as my regular prayer place in the past. It felt so good to pray, to remember that everything belongs to God in the end, regardless of appearances to the contrary.

Praying on the decks was particularly powerful. One of our pastor friends who knew of our plans to bless these difficult places shared a thought with us. She suggested that the decks are not only the places where death reached toward Michael but are also the thresholds of new life, symbols of new possibilities. Praying on the deck of the house next door was probably the most powerful stop in our ritual of blessing and, quite surprisingly, also the most joyful. The focus of the inner vision of that space has continued to change for me over time. Now not only do I see and feel the presence of Christ there in the midst of the darkness of the memory, I see the entire back of the house all lit up, blazing with light and presence and power. "This is the message that we have heard from him and proclaim to you, that God is light and in him there is no darkness at all."[10] I know that this illumination was also the reality at the time, and I am so thankful that God is letting me see it rather than leaving me in the shadow of death. This morning I felt hosts of angels shouting out the glory of God, trumpeting the word of victory of life over death, sending forth the sound for the whole world to hear. I wanted to shout, too. When we got back inside the house we burst into a chorus of "A-a-a-men! A-a-a-men! A-a-men, A-men, A-men!" God is good, *all* the time.

We hope that one day we can return to that deck with Michael. Rob mentioned how powerful it would be to stand and pray with the very alive Michael after praying over and above his lifeless body that night. But that experience might be more for us than him in the end since he still has no recollection of the event, so we will see. I think the lack of memory is a blessing for him and I certainly don't need or want to drag him back into any horror. No matter how horrible that night was for us, I'm sure it can't compare with the darkness Michael knew.

I will remember for each of us that "The light shines in the darkness, and the darkness did not overcome it,"[11] no matter how overwhelming the evidence to the contrary may be. I pray it for each of you. "For I am convinced that neither death, nor life, nor angels, nor rulers, nor things present, nor things to come, nor powers, nor height, nor depth, nor anything else in all creation, will be able to separate us from the love of God in Christ Jesus our Lord."[12]

I realize there is no guarantee for any of us that we will not encounter demons or depths or death, no promise that the physical future will be better or worse than the past. But I am so thankful that no matter what, God is there, is *here,* and showers love on each of us the same.[13]

The grass withers, the flower fades, but the word of our God abides forever. – Isaiah 40:8

Last In-Patient Day in Rehab

Michael and I played Aggravation today, a game also known affectionately from his youth as Wahoo. He and Natalie used to play on a wooden board their Grandma Sharon made by drilling divots for the marbles. I couldn't recall what had become of the Wahoo board, or if we still had it. Michael reminded me that he broke it some years back when he jumped on it. I also couldn't remember the name "Wahoo." I told him he may be struggling with his short-term memory but he has me whipped in the long-term department.

Memory remains one of his major deficiencies, something we're told will continue to improve over time. This challenge has an immediate effect on his sense of encouragement. He can't remember, for instance, that two days ago he couldn't stick out his tongue to a point and today he can. For the most part, he doesn't remember who has visited him. He can't contrast a previous inability to walk or speak intelligibly with his current accomplishments. He lives in the present reality of his deficiencies without the benefit of perspective on his improvements. So I remind him. I tell him how it used to be and how far he's come, and how each of these areas will continue to recover.

Memory is also one of the main components affecting his readiness for education. As he's currently unable to remember most things from yesterday, studying and retaining information remains a way off. He also suffers from cognitive fatigue, a typical byproduct of brain injuries. Right now he works in 20-minute segments in each of his therapy areas. After a couple of contrasting sessions such as aerobic conditioning on a recumbent step bike and a scavenger hunt, he is very tired, often ready to sleep. The fatigue combined with short-term memory loss means it will be a while before he is able to return to school. Upon eventual return, the recommendation is that he start with one class per day rather than a full schedule. His OT therapist thought an optimistic goal might be a single class beginning in January.

Michael will be home by lunchtime tomorrow. I am so glad, so thankful, thankful for every one of you who has prayed and continues to pray, thankful that his spirit remains open, thankful for the care he has received and will continue to receive. So many have asked what they could do, and I say with all sincerity that what you are doing is the greatest gift: loving, praying, holding us in your hearts. We do the same for you, with gratitude and love.

I remember the dedication service for the AIDS orphan

house our team built last summer in Maua, Kenya. One of the missionaries turned to me and said, "These people will be praying for you every day for the rest of your lives." Many people say, "I'll pray for you" and never think about it again. I have been one of these people at times. But these Kenyans really do pray, over and over. Their faith is a powerful witness to God's presence and community. I learned so much from the people in Kenya. Our trip was another one of the markers that prepared me for this past month, for today, and for tomorrow. Kenyan believers know immense joy in the midst of incredible lack. I saw many who understand suffering in ways most of us can only imagine, and yet they forgive freely and fully. They praise God in plenty and in want, and it's mostly want. They are empty in so many material ways that their spirits have immense room for the burgeoning love of God. They are rich in ways we are often poor. I learned much from them. I also learned that ministering to people at the bottom of Maslow's *Hierarchy of Needs*[14] fills a particular lack within me. My ability to give time, labor and money was met with their ability to love, witness, and offer grateful praise. God set up the perfect gift exchange, and I received more than I gave. As I prepare to minister to Michael in basic ways in the coming weeks, I'm particularly thankful for what I learned in Africa. I hope to learn more about being a servant and a vessel for God's love right here at home.

Chapter 6
Home

Reentry

Michael is home. After a few final therapies and discharge activities this morning, we loaded up two carts full of his belongings and were off, pulling into our drive by 10:45 or so. The transition leaves me disconnected. I have grown used to the new Michael at the hospital and the rehab facility, but placing him back into the context of home is disorienting, as though he should be someone else here. So we're both adjusting to the new arrangement, taking it slowly. The dogs, however, made the transition just fine, leaping around with unbridled enthusiasm as only dogs can do, both at seeing Michael and also his good friend Chris who hasn't been to the house in a month. I told Chris it was a happy sight seeing his rear end sticking out of our fridge again.

We are home, and this is an amazing grace. While I may feel disoriented and melancholy right now, I take heart in the sentiment Brenda Ueland expressed at the close of her autobiography, words spoken after the death of both parents, a divorce, and other heartaches and joys:

And it is queer. I have not a touch of resignation or nostalgia or mournfulness for days that are gone. I seem to be entirely cheerful and full of anticipation. I seem to be always holding my breath with suspense, as though something wonderful were about to happen, the next day, and the next day, and the next, and the next, and the next. And I wish everybody in the world could feel this way.

Snoozer

We had a good first night home with Michael. His "new" room is just across the living room from ours. Because of his impulsivity, we placed a motion alarm outside the door, just in case he got a sudden urge to get up and go somewhere in the night. We also placed a baby monitor in his room, with the receiving speaker in our bedroom. His dog Sasha was so thrilled to be able to sleep next to her boy again. The only sound we heard all night long was his gentle, steady breathing. Consequently we got a good night's rest as well. It was a good start. One night down.

This morning I have been putting Michael through his speech and physical therapy regimen, and for his OT activity we played Canfield, a card game that requires keeping track of several things at the same time. He did well. Then Rob, Michael and I took the dogs for our long neighborhood walk. There are some serious hills on the route we usually take, and Michael slowed a bit on those, but otherwise did really well. It was his longest walk since his accident, I think. When we got home he was tuckered out and went to his room and snoozed a bit. It was a big morning. But good.

So let us not grow weary in doing what is right, for we will reap at harvest time, if we do not give up.
— Galatians 6:9

The New Routine

Translucent: 1: permitting the passage of light: clear, transparent
2: free from disguise or falseness

Michael was helping me make dinner last night when I told him we were going to sauté the onions. I asked him if he knew what sauté meant and he said no. I told him to sauté is to cook something in a bit of butter or oil, and when we cook onions this way they eventually become translucent. Do you know what translucent means? "No." It means it lets light through. Like you, Michael, like your spirit right now: open and transparent with light moving through. He nodded and said, "Yes!" The boy is also completely free of the guise of self-consciousness, and I find myself continually reorienting to his honesty and profound presence.

Michael has now helped make Beef Stroganoff, Kota me Kritarakia (a Greek dish of chicken with pasta, seasoned with "generous amounts" of cinnamon, mint, oregano, basil, and parsley), and chocolate pudding. He is a good chef's assistant, patient and helpful. I am still adjusting to this new Michael. The old Michael would not have voluntarily helped cook. The old Michael wouldn't have eaten what I cooked most of the time. The old Michael also had more than a generous portion of oppositional defiance, the complete absence of which is disorienting to say the least. Even the typical childhood/adolescent syndrome of "that's not fair!" has vanished, the steady rudders of teenage righteous indignation and victimhood washed away by injury and recovery. He seems much more content.

I am amazed at how busy the days are. I schedule seven to eight half-hour home therapy sessions each day, modeling them on the exercises and routines we learned at the in-patient rehabilitation facility. In between we do the tasks of daily living: cooking, cleaning, going on errands. Canfield is becoming a staple, as it truly is a champion activity for challenging the player's ability to exercise dual attention. There are four arenas of play to watch, with competitive, reflexive speed being an essential, winning factor. We do physical regimens and speech exercises and even use outings like trips to the store to practice memory: how many items on the list can he (or we!) remember? Cooking and laundry have become therapeutic tasks. I am hearing the rhythm of the days to a whole new beat.

One other blessing: I prayed in Michael's room the day before he came home, on Sunday morning. I usually light candles when I pray, something that has become a test of faith for my family, as I do not have a good track record with candles. This is probably an understatement, as two charred dining room tables and one call to the fire department will attest. Well, when Rob and I went into the room to do a couple of things on Monday morning, Michael's discharge day, one of the candles was burning. I know I had blown them all out, or at least tried, as there had been five lit the day before. The one burning was a three-inch pillar with a matching mate. We assumed I didn't get the candle out, or perhaps it spontaneously reignited as candles sometimes do. In either case it would have been burning for 24 hours and should have been a waxy mess as each of the pair of pillars was already 3/4 spent. But amazingly the candle was barely reduced in comparison to its partner. It was a lovely solitary light, welcoming Michael on his homecoming day. We took it as a good sign. Well, I should say I took it as a good sign. Rob was likely thinking the candle lady was on the loose again.

I have been deeply tired the last couple of days as I let down from bracing against the weeks in the hospital and rehab facility. Today is a bit better. It is good to discover that Michael sleeps through the night. It is good to begin learning new daily rhythms. It is a tremendous relief that some of his impulsivity is beginning to ebb and also that he is able to swallow without choking. It is good to be home.

Below is the text to a beautiful song written by our good friend Bill Carter, a jazz pianist and minister of word and sacrament in the Presbyterian Church, USA. Rob and I have sung it at concerts and communion services, and even at funerals. It's a favorite of ours.

My soul is so tired from the roads that I've wandered,
And hope withers from my despair.
Been so close yet so far as I count broken blessings.
Will someone notice I'm here?

I wait for a light to shine in the window,
I want to hear one call my name.
And I hunger to know if I'm welcome or wanted.
Will someone gather me in?

Welcome home, you worn out and weary.
Welcome home, all strangers of grace.
Welcome home, all hungry and poor,
The door opens wide, find your place.

The table is set, the bread smells delicious.
The wine is poured out for the world.
And I know that I can't ever outrun such mercy;
The Father says, "Welcome home."
God says right now, "Welcome home."
God says right here, "Welcome home."
      – Bill Carter[1]

A New Way to Look at Rocks

Here is an interesting part of Michael's road to recovery. Allen, the Catholic deacon who visited us in the hospital and at the rehabilitation facility, also serves as a chaplain to the State Penitentiary and calls regularly on the lifers and death row inmates. I recently contacted him to see if an arrangement could be made for Michael to visit the man in prison who has continued to pray for him. Such visits are difficult to organize with death row inmates, but I believe it might be powerful for one who tried to take his life to meet one whose life is scheduled to one day be taken from him.

What follows is something Allen shared with us that was written by that same inmate who drew the picture of the child in the hand of God, the picture that was in Michael's room throughout his hospitalization. The inmate's name is Jeff.

❧

LOOKING UNDER ROCKS

I remember as a lad walking along the streamside with my dad, out to conquer The World's Biggest Fish, exploring the universe and discovering the nature of things. My dad would tell me that a person can walk right past stones and never see anything but cold hard rocks, or, you could take the time to pry up the hard stuff to discover little pockets of life beneath them. "Get yourself a little surprise," was how he would put it. Often as not we would look under a few rocks in the mossy areas and scout up grubs or worms for use in our efforts to entice fish onto the hook. When we took the time to look, we found living things under those rocks, worthwhile things alive beneath a surface of cold stone.

Now all these years later and my dad gone, I think of that lesson as I consider this stone cold prison, a rock of perpetual oppression. Society in general, naturally busy with their own lives and routines, pass by this place and give it scant notice. I don't hold this against them—we all walk down paths paying little attention to the stones strewn about the way. In my current state of being, I am like the hidden life beside my childhood streams. I am the one living under the rock.

The analogy of the stone fits equally the prisoner as well as the prison. Public perception, often formed through skewed or sketchy news accounts made at or near the time of trial, often leaves in its wake an image of permanently cold, hard men, men entombed within a time-ticking-away life in a cold, hard place. Men with cold hearts of stone, waiting only the fall of the quarryman's hammer.

Yet something amazing happens when you pry up the rock under which I live. There live thirty-four men on this death row. Recently one of the mainline prisoner self-improvement clubs held a fundraiser for a children's hospital, giving out a small bit of food in exchange for prisoner donations that, for the men on death row, amounted to half a month's prison work pay. Thirty-two of the thirty-four men contributed to the cause. Later, when a mass move to another building within the prison caused us to relinquish our hard-won small television sets, eleven men donated their TVs to a local parish for distribution to poor families, elders in the old folks' homes, or to be added to the charity auctions for children's causes.

Here, these types of things are no anomaly. They occur frequently under my rock, far away from public exposure. Therein lives a truth that might amaze an unsuspecting public. Maybe, just maybe, they could take a minute to stop along their paths, to look under a few rocks in this unfamiliar neighborhood, to hear the echo of my father in a time long ago saying, "Get yourself a little surprise."

Sometimes beneath the hardest of rocks, under the coldest of stones, you can find amazing things. Worthwhile things. Not the least of which are charitable hearts.

JD Tiner
18 June 2007

❧

Practice Makes Progress

Friday the 13th, and what a good day it is! Michael and I are on our regular regimen, though the schedule is a little lighter today since he's chosen to go to The Way for the first time with Natalie and Kat. Between an hour of travel each way and a lengthy, energetic service, it will be a long evening. Two small errands yesterday left him pooped, so I know he'll need his energy for tonight.

I've added one more category to his daily therapies. In addition to OT, PT and ST, he now has SBB, or Spiritual Body Building. Yesterday I shared one of Jeff's writings with him (the inmate on death row), along with an Al-Anon reading on practicing. I thought about all of the things he and I are practicing right now. This morning he re-learned how to clean his bathroom. Daily we go over and over the same speech exercises that strengthen and coordinate his tongue and soft palate. This practice aids both articulation and swallowing and is beginning to bear fruit as yesterday he ate several things previously on the "no" list: salad, hot dogs and nuts.

He and I are lifting the same poundage of hand weights right now, something that never would have happened in the past. So his muscles are practicing strength, as are mine. In SBB we did some exercises for opening our spirits. His hands heated up as he moved through the meditation, a common sign of the flow of the spirit and love of God.

Today we also read a couple of back-to-back stories in the gospel of Mark, both about healing. The first was about the demoniac whose affliction was delivered into the swine herd (I always have felt very bad for the pigs)[2] and the other was of the hemorrhaging woman who touched the hem of Jesus' garment and was made well. I am convinced the very power that Jesus felt flow out of him when the woman touched his hem is the same power Michael felt as heat in his hands when he opened himself to the Spirit this morning. God showed me once in prayer how incredibly powerful that current is and can be, but I could see that it remains a miniscule trickle in me, that my capacity for carrying that healing love needs *lots* of spiritual body building.

So we are in practice mode. Practicing putting one's

tongue toward his nose, time and time again. Practicing the sequences of cleaning. Practicing muscle movements and strength. And practicing the presence of God, over and over and over.

You learn to speak by speaking, to study by studying, to run by running, to work by working; and just so you learn to love God and people by loving. Begin as a mere apprentice and the very power of love will lead you on to become a master of the art. – Francis de Sales

His Yoke is Easy

I've been learning more about anoxic brain injuries, the condition resulting from a lack of oxygen to the brain. Many of Michael's current symptoms are among the most common: short-term memory loss, cognitive difficulties and fatigue, lack of normal social awareness and function. If you saw Michael walking around in public, which some of you have now (one person even commented it was like seeing a person returned from the dead, and indeed it is!), you would think he looked normal. As one of his therapists pointed out, this is both helpful and problematic. The good part is that he is not readily marked as disabled. The challenge is that people will expect his brain to function normally, which it does not. He still does not remember to look for cars before crossing a street. He can't find his way back to a parking place when we've walked through the Willamette University campus. He does not remember why we do certain speech exercises, though every day I tell him how they will strengthen his palate, ultimately reducing the nasality in his voice. He does them patiently and dutifully, though, time after time without remembering why.

I find I am grieving. I am grieving the loss of the person I knew. He is no longer here right now, though many aspects of the person who is here are wonderful. I feel a bit like Angelina Jolie's character in *The Changeling* who keeps insisting, "But that is not my son!" Michael is here, but it isn't the Michael we remember. I know grief will take its own time and run its course, and also that much will continue to change and resurrect during that time.

This morning in prayer I asked God to show me where I am carrying my grief so that I might be able to pray the presence of Christ there. Quickly I was led to my shoulders and the lower, back part of my head. My "*should*-ers," as our language so aptly declares, as in I "should do this" and I "should do that." It is the place we carry our yoke. As God gifted me with this awareness, the scripture "His yoke is easy and his burden is light"[3] came to me, and my first thought was, "But my burden is *not* light!" God eventually helped me to understand that I feel the heaviness because I am still claiming it as mine. The words don't declare, "*Your* yoke is easy and *your* burden is light." So I prayed I might have the grace and courage to let Christ lift the weight and carry it for me, so that it might be light. Light, as in the noun.

Later I found myself looking up synonyms for "yoke." "Burden" comes readily to mind, largely because of its prominence in the verse that Handel set in *Messiah*. And of course Handel playfully set the word "easy" with a very difficult passage to sing. A less obvious synonym is bond, with the yoke being the thing that figuratively holds things together. "He is before all things, and in him all things hold together."[4] I thought of how many connections Michael's story has forged. It has strengthened bonds between those we know well, has repaired other lines of communication and affection that were broken, and has created new contacts with strangers. Just last evening I stopped by a birthday celebration of a friend only to discover that half a dozen people or so around the table, people who until minutes earlier were strangers to me, were among the many who have been praying regularly for Michael.

Life's burdens are not easy for any of us. They simply aren't. How strange that those very burdens become light in

Christ when we walk the way together, when we recognize our ultimate oneness. How strange and true that the very things that bind us together come in the form of crosses—often heavy, wearying, grief-laden crosses—and that as we carry them they become the means of sharing the light and love of God. It's the transformation of energy yet again: the weight becomes the light, the yoke becomes the conduit for grace. I pray for the grace to carry it. Because I believe it is all worth it—every step we take, every challenge that brings us closer together in love and closer to the understanding that we are all the same, that we are all made in God's image and are of one substance with the creator.

Michael has been dozing on the couch all morning. Sunday is his rest day, and I remember the folks at rehab telling me how important rest is for his healing. Max is next to him on the floor, snoring.

Come unto me, all you that are weary and are carrying heavy burdens, and I will give you rest. Take my yoke upon you, and learn of me, for I am gentle and humble in heart, and you will find rest for your souls. – Matthew 11: 28-29

Michael got to know Max when he was a young boy, before Rob and I were married. He was Max's first official babysitter, taking him in at our house for 10 days when Rob was out of town on business. Max was just a puppy, so he needed to go out to piddle in the middle of the night. Though he was only 12, Michael dutifully got up and took him out every night between 2 and 3 AM. Unfortunately, he caught a cold and through the stretch of nighttime vigils he developed a very nasty cough which turned into Whooping Cough, or Pertussis. He had suffered a bad reaction to the Pertussis vaccine when he was an infant, and thus had not been given the full sequence of inoculations. The cough was miserable and Michael was terribly ill, but still he cared valiantly for Max through it all.

Now in his adult years, Max has returned the favor of assuming some of the load. He is often a bellwether for emotional experiences in our house, and the manifestation is always the same. If someone at our house has been going through a stress or upset, suddenly, like clockwork, Max can't pee. He'll go out and try for a long time, dribbling tiny little amounts but never emptying his load. Eventually he'll have a flood of an accident when no one sees it coming. Poor buddy. This is how he absorbs the strain of our sadness or struggle and carries it for us physically. He's had the pee problem again since Michael's been home, and still over and over again he goes and ministers to Michael, sitting by him or lying at his feet, taking on the burden. He seems to know where help is needed the most. Dogs are one of God's most generous creations.

Beautiful Monday

Today is appointment day. Michael had a swallow evaluation at the rehab facility this morning and I'm happy to report he passed with flying colors. We still have a list of precautions and strategies for meal and snack times as the weakness in his tongue persists, but he is cleared to eat all kinds of foods. Hurray! It is clear that even in a short time his exercises for the tongue and palate have paid off handsomely. After he completed one of the motions that was impossible a week ago, his therapist simply remarked, "Okay, that one is fine." Michael and I were amazed. Being cleared on swallowing means he'll move into the next phase of speech therapy—articulation. He is very eager to work more specifically on his speaking.

This afternoon he has two more appointments, one with his primary care physician and another with OT in rehab. In between all of this we squeezed in a trip to Costco where we rewarded ourselves with a lunch of pizza and smoothies. It was a big morning, so he's presently asleep on the couch, even in the midst of Natalie working on a music theory assignment at the piano.

After several days of swirling, the grief fog lifted some this morning. As the haze cleared, my inner eye came into focus and I began to notice beauty again. In prayer I lit candles in lovely, colored glass votives. The play of light as it refracted and diffused into the dim dawn was exquisite. The raucous, blustery wind outside was full of wild pleasure. Michael's docile and patient demeanor struck me as a gift of immeasurable grace. And his sense of humor! He is so ready to laugh and enjoy himself it makes him a pleasure to be with. I see much of the tender thoughtfulness I remember in him as a young boy, and it is achingly sweet.

The inner gray began lifting yesterday afternoon at a classical guitar concert on campus. Michael, Rob and I went to hear Xuefei Yang play a moving and impeccable program and what a balm it was for my spirit. I was reminded of a

Sydney Lanier quote I recently came across: "When I hear music, it seems to me that all the sins of my life pass slowly by me with veiled faces, lay their hands on my head, and say softly, 'My child.'" Perhaps it was my grief more than my sin that passed by, but surely the music anointed me gently as it went.

Michael, Rob and I shared gratitude lists the other morning. Michael's first contribution was, "I'm grateful to be alive." In the years that Rob and I have watched and prayed over Michael's struggles with addiction and self-destructive behaviors, we've often remarked, "As long as there's life, there's hope." So probably the most beautiful thing in my day right now is his life and the hope we all share for it. Thank you, God.

Chapter 7
The Long, Steady Climb

The Next Step

Yesterday was a gentle plateau, a stop at a lovely vista on a long hike. I remember such a place on a climb with Michael and family two summers ago. We were climbing Mt. Buffalo just outside of Dillon, Colorado, and had come a long way when we cleared timberline. There we were afforded a beautiful view back over the lake and town. Up ahead lay boulder fields, lichen, miniscule wildflowers as hardy as sequoias, and successively less and less oxygen. And the summit.

The internal respite of Sunday afternoon and Monday morning let me look back at the larger shape of recent weeks. Michael's hospital and rehab stays totaled a month of tense ups and downs that led to the ultimate release of going home. The first week there was a time of both deep relief and heavy weariness that then eased into a plateau of gentle hope. The level place proved to be a brief respite, however, and the next steps are leaving me feeling like God is an exacting and demanding coach, one who will let me rest long enough to catch my breath but no more. We press on toward the goal.

I turned figuratively from the vista to the next part of the climb in an OT session with Michael yesterday. The focus of the hour was his ultimate assumption of independence and self-sufficiency. This is the purpose of rehab, of course, but thinking on it sent me into a near panic. You see, right now it is all very tidy, if tiring. Michael is under 24-hour supervision for safety reasons, with the primary dangers being impulsivity and spatial disorientation. Either or both of these could lead him to step into the road in front of a car or get lost and not know how to get back. He could leave a gas burner flaming on the stove and walk away. So we are with him. The little alarm is set outside his room every night so he doesn't wander off into harm's way. He doesn't go anywhere unaccompanied. Then I'm not afraid when I can't see him.

But of course the point is to prepare him to go places on his own again, to watch for cars, to find his way around and be independent. And this goal scares me, because he could die. Not from being hit by a car, most likely. I know he will eventually remember to look both ways and be able to orient spatially. His brain is healing, thank God. It is his choices down the stretch that I don't trust. I don't know if his broader choices will lead him to life instead of death. All of these thoughts came racing at me yesterday like a pack of howling animals simply because his therapist began laying the framework for the ultimate goal of freedom. Inside I was yelling, "No! Not yet! I'm not ready. Can't we wait a bit longer here at the plateau?"

One initial way he'll stretch toward self-sufficiency is by working on time management skills. The steps are good, necessary and important. Michael has taken over making his daily schedule. He's following the parameters laid out in therapy, i.e. certain amounts of various ST, OT and PT activities each day. He makes the schedule by 8 PM the night before so that he can know what is coming the next day, just as we all pull out our daily planners or PDA's to see what is on tap for tomorrow. He chooses activities he likes from a list of 30 or so possibilities. It turns out he gives himself a tougher schedule than I do, as he opted for a full hour workout at the gym today. The boy went at it hard. Eventually he'll be allowed conditional, small amounts of time home alone or out with friends, which, as he heals, will move into more time, more freedom, more responsibility. It's the way the dance goes for all parents and children, and we know the drill. So these are all very good steps. That is, they would be if he weren't a young man for whom freedom can mean using and using can mean dying. My job is to help move him toward his freedom, the very thing I fear.

Rob pointed out how in these last weeks he and I have made it out of emotional ICU and now maintain a sort of low-grade fever regarding Michael. This seemed an apt description. Worry is a sickness of sorts and in my experience it is a communicable disease. I, too, have lots of healing to do. In prayer today God was fairly harsh with me as I heard something like, "You know that scripture that says 'my rock and my redeemer in whom I place my trust?' Well that isn't *you*, Christine." I burst out laughing and laughed for a good long while. No, God, I'm not that at all. And I'm sorry for ever trying to be, because those chains of responsibility are heavy indeed, on me and everyone else they touch. God didn't relent as the next words thundering in my head reminded me of the book of Job: "Where were *you* when I laid the foundations of the earth?" "But I'm his mom," I squeak back in reply. "I'm supposed to have his back."

I considered how much my worrying, striving and protecting have helped in the past. Not so much. I do know our vigilance and love have mattered, but in the end, I am neither Michael's rock nor redeemer. It's a tight and intimate dance, the dance of empowerment versus enabling. I re-examined the tools at hand. The two best things I know to help me out of my rat phase where I become stuck in a maze of anxiety are prayer and Al-Anon meetings. Exercise also helps. I returned to the first three of the twelve steps: I am powerless, God is powerful, I choose to turn my life over to God. I considered the alternatives to practicing fear: practicing trust, faith, and love. I remembered that there is another level, a place of higher vibration, for lack of a better way to describe it, where we are safe from the muck and mire of our minds. It is a blessed space and I know how to get there. Twelve step programs call it serenity. Scripture calls it the peace that passes all understanding. It is the place where I am lifted above and offered a glimpse of the divine perspective. I can remember again and again the way to the summit, or at least to the rest stop, where the air is thin and clear and the view is excellent.

Inside Outside

Dag Hammarskjold's well-known quote sums it up for me these days: "The longest journey is the journey inward." It is likely that most of you began reading our updates to keep up with Michael's outward progress, that miraculous motion from death back to life that continues to evolve in astounding ways. Along the way I began following the connection between his external progress and my internal processes, much like a mirror in the mirror. Each new window of opportunity for Michael offers me another reflection on the journey, revealing ever more dimensions.

I am happy to be thinking about Michael's outward progress today. We have a tentative meeting on Friday with faculty and staff at Chemeketa Community College with whom we'll discuss the structure of Michael's education in the coming weeks and months. Looking hopefully toward his future allows me to begin considering mine again, my world that is independent of his. What a good thing! Just opening that window a crack let in a flood of fresh air as I began to consider my job next semester, seeing my students again, and working hard at things I love.

Recently a very good friend of my father's sent me some new music. David is a retired theory and composition professor and was, among other things, chair of the music department at Concordia College in Minnesota where he worked with his longtime friend and my first voice teacher, René Clausen. He recently heard a recording of a colleague's and my performance of Libby Larsen's *ME*, and subsequently sent some scores with the thought that "...it might be time for something unexpected and strange and undemanding to provide a moment or two of distraction." This morning I enjoyed reading through the songs, and one poem in particular resonated well. The poems were written by the wife of a theologian on faculty at Concordia, and only in her later years after having a stroke did she reveal to her children that she had been writing poetry most of her life. Her husband requested some of her poems be set to music for a family birthday gathering in her honor. The following is the latest and last poem in the group David set, poems spanning from 1938-1989.

> *It's only a passing phase*
> *This lethargy, diminution,*
> *This loss of strength*
> *And sense of improper pain;*
> *From agony to alleluia*
> *Somehow.....Somewhere*
> *We'll wake up in the morning*
> *Dancing on the lawn!*
> — *Ethelyn Cantrell Herman*[1]

Amazing Brain

Wow, is the healing of the brain fascinating! Michael is making amazing gains every week. Yesterday I charged him with remembering how to get back to our parking spot from the gym. We parked in a remote lot, meandered to the back entrance of the athletic center, and entered the workout room from a direction we'd never come before. He remembered it all perfectly in reverse. Just a week ago he would not have been able to do that. He also remembered, from a discussion on Monday, that towards the end of the week one of his OT times should include cleaning his room. He made his schedule last night and right there on it was "clean room." This blew me away. Up until now he often couldn't remember what happened earlier in the day, much less yesterday, so retaining this directive for several days and then processing it perfectly speaks volumes of his progress. He's keeping track of the schedule beautifully, often prompting me when it is time for an activity. We just finished an entire game of Canfield, seven rounds, and he is going strong. A week ago two rounds left him fatigued to the point of napping. Sometimes I pause and remember his state when he arrived in the ER. I remember that when he first regained consciousness he lacked the muscle control to scratch his face. Amazing brain, amazing God.

I am reminded of the phases of newborn babies. Just when we discover a schedule or routine, they change, discovering some new skill or need or pattern, and we begin all over again. There is no settling with Michael right now, which is fantastic.

Our education meeting will be next Tuesday. This fall Michael was enrolled in the Chemeketa Early College/High School program. He completed a GED last spring and was poised to begin college level courses in the winter term after taking the requisite trimester of high school classes to provide evidence of and solidify good study habits. He was on task and motivated. We are regrouping now to examine his options based on his current abilities, abilities that will evidently be changing from week to week. The special education director has organized a meeting with the principal, the program director, and the district occupational and speech therapists.

It is difficult to articulate how grateful I am for our education system and all of the people who work in it. I have appreciated the Salem-Keizer school district from many vantage points as my two children have taken vastly different routes through it since we moved here in 1998. Natalie enjoyed a high school experience of wonderful variety and challenge, from orchestra and choir to theater and mock trial, from basic courses to advanced placement classes. She was busy as a bee and loved everything she did. Michael walked a less traditional route, attending four different schools (including one in Tacoma when he lived with his dad) before deciding on and achieving his goal of the GED and early college. Along the way they both encountered compassionate educators who sincerely cared about their success, who met each of them where they were and nurtured them through challenges and victories.

There has been so much love, and I don't say that lightly. I am deeply grateful for our educators and administrators who teach, encourage and love their students. I am also thankful for our society and government and the value we place on education as well as the dignity of each individual, no matter his or her background or abilities. I contrast this yet again in my mind with Kenya where there are no social services or safety nets, and no public education beyond 8th grade. High school is privately funded and most Kenyans cannot afford it. Even to attend primary school they must buy a uniform, a prohibitive hardship for many. I remember Daniel, a painter I worked with there, whose dream was to become a high school math teacher. While the goal may be ultimately attainable, it isn't within any kind of immediate reach for him. He was very interested in geography as well, had never seen the Rocky Mountains, and asked that I send him a picture once stateside. Obviously, he didn't have Internet access.

So here we are in the United States where a tragedy like Michael's is met with a host of helping hands who have the knowledge, capacity and concern to see him through, and a system that supports them in their work. We are blessed, and I am thankful.

Grateful

We've had some serendipitous bits of adult freedom as Michael had his first independent outings. He went to Casey's house. Casey is one of Michael's most trustworthy friends and we know his home is a safe place. Michael played video games there this week, which gave Rob and me the chance for some time out together. Friday night the three of us took in Jazz Night at Willamette where Natalie sang and played keys.

Michael has both a MySpace and Facebook account, with MySpace being his main online hangout site. His current status there says, "Your love is a symphony, all around me, running through me," words from a Switchfoot[2] song Kat recently gave him. I am so grateful for the continuing openness in his spirit. It makes my heart "leap for joy,"[3] as the psalm says.

People often remark, "Be careful what you pray for." I have prayed for years that Michael's spirit would be open to receive the love and grace of God. Over time I learned it most likely wouldn't be me who reached him this way, that something or someone else would bear the word to him. While I'm not a pastor, he was practically a PK (Pastor's Kid) growing up, since my job was full-time employment in church music ministry, and it's a common stereotype for PKs to reject their religious upbringing. So it made sense to me that he didn't want much to do with church. Beyond that, I've known so many wonderful people who have chosen various paths toward the holy that I know it isn't for me to judge another's faith. In the end there are many spokes of the wheel that lead to the center. I have chosen my particular spoke and gratefully stick with it, knowing I will reach the goal more readily this way than if I jump from one spoke to another. So I could handle him rejecting my religion. What disturbed me most was that he actively rejected God or any idea of a higher power with such hostility. His attitude seemed to be summed up in a "believe John 3:16 or you're out" sort of way, and since John 3:16 didn't make sense to him ("For God so loved the world that he gave his only Son that everyone who believes in him will not perish but may have eternal life"), he figured there was no help out there. I confess that verse didn't make much sense to me for a long time, and I had to work my way over and around that and a lot of other traditional language to surmount major spiritual barriers. But that is a different story.

Over and over I found myself at a loss trying to explain my faith to Michael, that it wasn't so much about a single verse as about recognition. There is something bigger than ourselves out there, call it what you like: Love, Heaven, Higher Power, Grace, God, Christ, Spirit, Source, and that bigger thing is *good*. This goodness creates life, holds it together, and animates us from the inside out. I wanted him to know that the unseen world is more real than the seen. That when we believe and trust in this mystery, life is activated in a whole new way. That when we begin calling convergences "synchronicities of grace" rather than random coincidences, we notice them more than we did before, and consequently there is more help available to us. That when we trust a power greater than ourselves we are not only given the strength to persevere but in the process we receive real peace and joy. That when we choose to be thankful in the midst of hardship, something in us changes and reorients, making more room for grace to flood in. That "love one another" is about action, not feeling. That it matters what we believe.

So I prayed, as so many are doing and have done for years now, that Michael would know the love of One whose love is perfect and endless, that his heart would be full of that love and grace so that he might, in that fullness, give himself away to the world. I have guessed that it is for him as it is for so many, as it has been for me in the past, that some pain was too great to bear and the only way to survive was to close down, which of course means shutting out both the good and the bad. I do not believe that God orchestrated Michael's loss in answer to my prayer, that somehow we experienced cause and effect. Michael, like all of us, has free will. But I do believe God took a horribly destructive choice Michael made and paired it brilliantly with prayers we've prayed for years to bring about a fragile incarnation[4], a tender shoot of new life in hope and grace. I am in awe of the grace of God as I write right now, humbled and thankful.

Just today Natalie and I shared a question about the words "fear the Lord."[5] Doesn't perfect love cast out all fear?[6] And if so, why are we called to fear the One who is that perfect love? We talked about how holy fear is more akin to reverence and right perspective, how it recognizes the unfathomable power and depth of God, and that recognition leaves us in our proper place: on our knees, looking up. It is not so much about being afraid as it is about understanding, in our limited human way, how great, good and powerful God is, and how we are not God.

So while I would say I "fear the Lord," I am completely unafraid. I feel the opposite, even. I feel so much loving gratitude that there is no room for fear right now. Because my experience time and time again when I meet God in prayer or worship or in the face of another person, is not one of a harsh or angry parent, but of a loving presence that looks me in the eye, sees all of my faults and flaws and fears, and loves me to the core. Sometimes I can scarcely bear that love, it is so strong and beautiful. Mercy trumps judgment every time, and probably the way I most readily experience judgment is through the natural consequences of my choices: loving choices tend to bring about abundance while selfish, fearful or hurtful choices usher me to hell. Thank you God, that you always call us back from the hells we choose and create, that you never forsake us and never leave us comfortless.

Just as I am, without one plea,
But that Thy blood was shed for me,
And that Thou bidst me come to Thee,
O Lamb of God, I come, I come.

Just as I am, though tossed about
With many a conflict, many a doubt,
Fightings and fears within, without,
O Lamb of God, I come, I come.

Just as I am, Thou wilt receive,
Wilt welcome, pardon, cleanse, relieve;
Because Thy promise I believe,
O Lamb of God, I come, I come.

Just as I am, Thy love unknown
Hath broken every barrier down;
Now, to be Thine, yea, Thine alone,
O Lamb of God, I come, I come.
— *Charlotte Elliot*

An Ordinary Day

It's been a good Monday. Michael's OT time was cleaning and his PT was trips to the big box stores Costco and Winco. In between we had some speech therapy work. It's been a regular day, but that doesn't mean it is without extraordinary gratitude. So here comes my list. I'm thankful for prayer, both the rich blessings that unfold in my daily practice and for the prayers of the people and the power they carry. I am especially thankful for the healing power of love that is borne on those prayers. I am thankful for friends, new and old. I am thankful for our Golden Retriever Max's blondness, as we say, (such *good* blondness!) and the way he lets us bury our faces in his fur, absorbing love like a sponge. I am thankful for Michael's sweet patience and forbearance, his positive attitude and cute sense of humor, and more than anything, for his life. I am thankful for my colleagues and students at Willamette, for their compassion and companionship and the work we do together. I miss them. I am thankful for family, all sorts near and far. I am thankful for the beautiful day today, for sun breaks and interesting clouds and for a view of the stunning end-of-daylight pink/orange glow on Mt. Hood. And I am thankful for this amazing gift of life and the way we are all connected. As one of the Kenyans' favorite calls to worship puts it, "God is good, all the time! All the time, God is good!"

Deacon Allen continued to send me several of Jeff Tiner's writings and pieces of artwork. I received the following words in November, two months before I met him:

LOOKING IN A NEW DIRECTION

When I arrived at Death Row my skewed view of life was both outward-looking and downward-looking. I peered out from my cell, ever at the ready to look down on my neighbors. I would tell myself that another prisoner's crimes were worse than my own therefore I must be a better person. I looked down on the young guy whose combined arrogance and ignorance manifested itself in a motor mouth that never seemed to stop running. I looked out at the psychologically damaged fellow, looked down on him for his foolish behavior. I looked out at the resident manipulator who had to stick his nose into everyone's business, the guy who never met an argument he couldn't start, looked down at him with violent thoughts while thoughts of God never came to mind. Stranded in the quicksand of my own arrogance, I blindly continued to wonder why I could never seem to find a moment of inner peace in the zoo that my life had become. As it turns out, I was an empty vessel, a cargo-less ship sailing in the wrong direction, only looking outward and down.

Then a most amazing thing occurred: I asked God into my heart. I began to look inward and upward. Inward in self-examination. Upward to God for the guidance necessary to my soul. Soon, with practice, I learned that I could consciously make the choice to reject negative thoughts. Instead, I could mentally work to paint others in a positive light while also looking to spiritually better myself. Any one of us can seek this way…through prayer, through holy books, through advice sought from a chaplain, from a priest or from a pastor. You need only look toward God, then look inward and invite Him into your heart. Only by looking in those new directions will you know the Truth. And only in knowing the Truth will you find peace within your own soul.

Perhaps the truth is that I did not stop to see that each of my neighbors was in the same boat as I, that I had no right to judge them. In my self-absorbed irritation at the noisy young man, I had failed to see his childhood beatings and abuse at the hands of traitorous adults which left him stifled of all maturity, forevermore to be the child crying out in pain. In my haste to turn away from the haunted eyes of the mentally ill fellow, I had not stopped to see a string of his forced confinements and anti-psychotic medication at every mental asylum in the state prior to his capital imprisonment that had occurred long before the crack cocaine took over his life and produced an irrevocable dementia. As for the argumentative busybody, I had never stopped to understand that his current acts were a way of making up for a long lack of human contact, that his unsophisticated attempt at social interaction was his way of making up for decades of time lost in the fog of mean-street gutters with only a bottle of cheap wine as friend and confidant.

Looking outward and down upon others, I had blinded myself to the truth of humanity. When I looked inward at my own faults and upward to God for direction, He removed the scales from my eyes and allowed me to look in a new direction, to see in a new way. And therein I found an inner peace. I was no longer angry or vexed by those who surround me. I stopped looking down on my fellow man. I leapt from my self-righteous homemade pedestal and landed squarely amongst my brethren, each of us equal in the sight of God, each of us equally loved by Him.

In the August 5, 1935 entry in her diary, "Divine Mercy In My Soul," Saint Maria Faustina Kowalska wrote:

"When some suffering afflicts me, it no longer causes me any bitterness, nor do great consolations carry me away. I am filled with the peace and equanimity that flow from the knowledge of the truth.

How can living surrounded by unfriendly hearts do me any harm when I enjoy full happiness within my soul? Or how can having kind hearts around me help me when I do not have God within me? When God dwells within me, who can harm me?"

Peace in our own souls is attainable, even in the steel and concrete waiting cells of Death Row. Look upward to God for guidance. Look inward and place His light there, to expel the darkness. And, with Saint Faustina, know that when God dwells within you, no harm may come. Embrace your neighbor's humanity, for it is a mirror image of your own.

– Thoughts from a Death Row prisoner

Looking Ahead

We had an encouraging meeting yesterday at Chemeketa. Michael will be tested to see if he qualifies for special education services based on a continuing health condition. The results of that testing will determine the shape of his educational plan. Meanwhile, he will enroll in one class for the next trimester that begins December 14. It is a newer reading/language class taught through supervised computer instruction that specifically encourages use of both sides of the brain, a perfect therapy for him. If that goes well, we will consider adding a math class. His former algebra teacher has offered to tailor a curriculum to fit Michael's needs and abilities. This is just one example of the generosity and compassion we found around the table yesterday. Indeed all of the people we met with were wonderful, and we came away feeling hopeful and buoyed. Rob got teary several times thinking about how fortunate we are to have such competent and caring people helping us chart this new territory. Michael tracked with us for the hour-long meeting, something he wouldn't have been able to do a couple of weeks ago. The word we consistently hear from those in the know is how swift and remarkable his progress is. He seems to be feeling it too, as in the last few days he has become bored for the first time. What a fantastic thing! Never before have I been happy to hear one of my children say they are bored. So he is really looking forward to getting back to school.

Scheduling is the big unknown, the piece I wish I could push along, particularly as I look toward work next semester. I would be happy to know even a series of likely scenarios but there are simply too many variables right now to make predictions, the main ones being Michael's level of cognitive fatigue (which lessens every week) and the results of the many tests he'll take. So I am working with what I know and lots of what I don't to figure out how much I'll be able to teach in the spring.

This morning I read the story in Mark's gospel about a young girl who died.[7] She had been sick and her father had urged Jesus to come and heal her but he didn't move very quickly. Despite the report of her passing, Jesus continued his journey to her while those around him were saying things like, "Don't bother, she's already gone, you're too late." The door must have looked as closed as it could ever be. His answer, with concision typical of Mark's gospel: "Do not fear, only believe." I found myself hearing these words over and over today, thinking on how useful they are wholly apart from the details of the story. They urge me to both make and fill spiritual space through the absence of one thing and the presence of another. I don't think I was so much fearing today as agitating, ruminating, wanting to know, desiring to see further than my limited vision affords. But there were the words, again and again: Do not fear, only believe. We could replace "fear" with many different words: doubt, regret, despair. Choose your own: Do not _____, but only believe. A person might say, "Believe what?" Believe the way will become clear, and that it will be good. Believe in the power of God. Believe the One we can trust. I have come across similar truths in prayer lately and find myself repeatedly asking, "Is it really that simple? Is that all I need to do?" I believe the answer is yes.

I have learned so many times that the step becomes clear when it is time to take it, but not usually much before. Currently I feel there are steps I need to take, or at least plans to make regarding work, but I feel I lack sufficient information to make an informed stride. Recovery unfolds in real time, apparently, and each day lets us know where we are, but not where we will be tomorrow or next week. And I have to say, now is very hopeful to me. Upon reflection I see that such immediacy is all any day ever offers, but I am used to a much greater ability to project into the days to come. Musicians and professors constantly live with one foot in the future: planning repertoire, rehearsing a certain concert's music for weeks, preparing lectures, making tests. Sometimes such prolonged forward-facing while straddling time zones creates a crick in our mental necks. It occurs to me I am in the midst of an incredible spiritual exercise that requires (forces?) living in the present moment and trusting that "tomorrow will take care of itself."[8] Part of me is immensely grateful for this opportunity, realizing it is finite in structure but endless in potential for life practice. One day coming home from the rehab facility I recognized God's particular, multifaceted gift: I'm able to start again on some very important things with Michael, to spend hours praying and reflecting in writing about what I'm learning and experiencing, to share those thoughts with others. I heard God say to me, "Would you ever have chosen this of your own accord, to spend all of your days care-giving and writing?" I laughed and answered, "No, I can say with certainty I never would have chosen this." But I trust it is good, what I am doing, what we are doing, in spite of the grief and losses. It's been particularly difficult feeling I've abandoned my students and colleagues, though they have in no way placed this burden on me. The words come again: Do not fear. Only believe.

Another Hopeful Monday

It's been another good day. We experimented, changing things up in Michael's therapy routine. His cognitive stamina has made amazing gains in the past couple of weeks so in anticipation of school classes, which will be an hour long each, we are changing the layout of his four hours per day of therapies. Up until now he's been doing eight half-hour segments (1 SBB, 2 OT, 2 PT and 3 ST) with occasional hour-long segments at the gym. Given his cognitive gains I thought it might be good to work OT in hour-long stretches as well in an effort to increase his mental stamina. As I look toward January, I entertain the possibility of three classes a day for him at school: reading/language, weights, and another, perhaps math. If he could handle that I would feel positively elated. Yet again, it would be much more than anyone predicted.

It also occurred to me today that there must be a host of computer games and puzzles online that are designed for brain exercise. *Google* rarely disappoints. We typed in some tags and up came more possibilities than we could ever need. I remember doing my graduate degree a decade or so after my undergraduate one when the Internet was in its baby phase. My bibliography teacher handily dismissed using the net for any kind of research or citation because none of the scholarship was screened. My how things change.

We located a nice site for brain exercises, *Lumosity.com*, that targets all of his deficient areas: memory, attention, concentration and other general cognitive skills related to IQ and reasoning. It offers games, puzzles, IQ questions, etc. So his first hour-long stretch of home OT was 30 minutes of *Lumosity* followed by 30 minutes of Canfield. Michael kept score in Canfield for the first time. Doing math in his head is a prime exercise for him. He is now as quick at simple addition as I am. I still notice some holes in his dual attention capacity in the card game, so I often prompt him there. He is such a good sport, always responding with, "Oh! Okay," or "Thank you," and going happily on.

So today is another hopeful day. His progress encourages me, allowing a preview of future possibilities. I don't know what that future will look like in any specific way, but I increasingly believe it will be good. He gives us many hopeful indicators. Over the Thanksgiving holiday weekend we all watched a movie together, *Management*. It was a quirky, low budget film where Jennifer Anniston left her mark as co-producer and also in the lead role as a not-so-cute, emotionally constipated corporate art salesperson. The plot develops from an encounter she shares with a simpleton who is the son of a couple running a small motel outside of Phoenix. We all thoroughly enjoyed the movie, but the best moment of the evening came when Michael repeated a line. He had caught the subtle irony in it, the humor behind the words that the rest of us had missed. When he quietly repeated it—"Get out of my basement!"—we all burst out laughing. As a friend said today, humor is often complex and subtle, and it was such a delight to see Michael ahead of us in the game.

Rob recently told me about a person who suffered a stroke, the friend of a woman in his congregation. She lost her sense of smell and taste from the injury, and while she regained many things in her recovery, these weren't among them. As is typical for most brain injury patients, her progress eventually leveled off and the changes ceased. She eventually accepted that she would finish out her life without smelling or tasting. But then one day seven years down the road, she woke up in the morning and out of the blue she could taste again. Just like that, it was back! The brain had been working all along to find a new pathway to connect the nerves and impulses for that sense, and one day it made the leap. The plasticity of the brain continues to amaze medical scientists and laypeople alike.

Often I find myself wondering what will bounce back in Michael. Some things already seem very regular to me, particularly physical attributes. The gross motor abilities are the first to recover, so this makes sense. But many mannerisms have become consistent enough that they appear permanent, leaving me to wonder if some things may have already leveled off. He walks differently, with a bit of a "slap slap" as his feet plop on the ground. His posture is also changed, and his hand motions identify him as challenged. His face is much more expressive than before, with his eyebrows grazing his hairline all the time, and funny faces (intentional ones) abounding. Michael used to hide a lot of things, especially internal machinations about using, so he was a master of the passive poker face. Over time we learned the raised eyebrows were his tell, the giveaway that he was up to something covert and forbidden, though he didn't know we knew that. Rob was particularly adept at spotting it. Now those same eyebrows, rather than masking secretive separation, rise up into communicative expression and connection with others. This in itself is a miracle to me, that a motion that once was dishonest could now be so sincere and endearing. His speech is still slow and compromised, making me wonder if the extra expression in his face is an effort to compensate for a lack of verbal communication skills. Whatever it is, it is nearly the opposite of the way he used to be, and, at least for now, surprisingly consistent. I remember his first days after his incident when he woke up, came off the ventilator and eventually sat up. His face hung slack and expressionless, as the muscles were weak from atrophy and unresponsive from the brain injury. He didn't look at all like himself, as the lifelessness changed the shape of his face. Now he looks like a new Michael where the casing is the same but what fills and animates it is different.

I can't help but think of the spiritual parallel. There is a continuing possibility in Michael as there is in all of us. How we animate and fill this space or framework is up to us, one choice at a time. Each choice either sustains the new framework or knocks it off in favor of a different arrangement. Choosing inconsistently makes for a wobbly foundation. Michael and I talked this morning about how faith and spiritual strength are things we practice, how we are all weak and small in the beginning. If we have never lifted weights, 10 pounds can feel like a lot. If we never run, 10 minutes on the treadmill is quite a distance. If we never pray, 10 minutes of quiet can be very, very long. So just like everything else we're doing, he and I proceed in small increments and build up to more.

Michael's questions continue to astound me, as they are consistently keen. Today we were talking about confession as a kind of energetic waste-removal system, a means of letting go of that which is toxic to our spirits. Lots of times we don't even know what compromises us, and I've found a gentle prompt of "God please bring to mind that which I need to confess" works very well. But "confession" is another of those liturgically charged words that is not immediately accessible to the non-religiously minded, so we talked mostly in alternative language: cleaning out, letting go, reconciling, having a shower on the inside, doing a "5th step." We considered some possibilities: the wrong could be toward ourselves or others, could be a self-destructive action or a repetitive, negative tape in our heads. It could be a crime or the constant diminishing judgment of those around us. It could be something we did or something we didn't do. The idea is to let that something go and replace it with something else (confession/forgiveness, surrender/freedom, release/ infusion). Michael considered this and then asked, "So do you have to do it regularly, like going to the bathroom or taking a shower or is it only once?" I loved it. Regularly, for sure, unless you like steeping in your spiritual waste. I can say from personal experience I do not. I suggested weekly. It's so nice to get rid of the refuse and start clean. Like trash day.

Interestingly, Michael almost always puts SBB first in his daily schedule, as though he has an internal compass letting him know which part of his recovery is the most crucial. I love being with him during that time, sharing something that up until now was completely off limits. Amazing grace, yet again.

180

When I was a child I liked to rearrange the furniture in my room. I would do it alone, even at age 10 or 11. I learned early on that brains-over-brawn was my only hope, so I'd take out drawers to lighten the dresser and desk and then position myself for optimum leverage. Often I'd sit and use my legs or stand and use my hips to move the big pieces, inching them slowly toward their new location. It wasn't quick but it always worked.

After writing about confession yesterday I found myself thinking about repentance this morning, another one of those potentially off-putting religious words. I have often heard repentance described as the 180-degree turn we make in response to confession. When we admit our wrongs we're supposed to turn around and go the other way and not do them again. But my experience of repentance is much more akin to a slow turn made one nudge at a time. If I claim that

I've made a sudden turn to go the opposite way, I believe I leave myself open to almost certain dishonesty: "Forgive me, God, for being prideful and judgmental. I won't do it again." Really? Not likely. What are the chances I won't be thoughtless one more time? Or twenty? Or that I won't greedily assert, "Mine!" while forgetting that a huge percentage of the world lives in abject poverty? Not to mention that I often have built up a lot of momentum in a particular direction and it can be difficult to stop the train. Sometimes I'm motivated to pull back because continuing on the current path leads further and further into thick brambles and thorns and eventually I just can't go any more without either exhaustion or injury setting in. Backtracking can be painful. So I find that I repent over and over, slowly extracting myself from an old way of being, sometimes rocking repeatedly against inertia, always with the hope that the many nudges eventually amount to a new arrangement of the furniture in my spiritual home.

When I look at Michael, however, I see a different kind of spiritual motion. It looks as though he has indeed done a swift 180, as if God plucked him up and plopped him down facing a completely new way, likely in a new county. It seems God also rearranged all of his furniture, maybe put him in a new house altogether. I don't sense that Michael is carrying the spiritual weight of his past, which is a beautiful thing. He did write that he was "so sorry" back when he first learned of his suicide attempt and could not yet speak. And that was all that was needed. One sincere apology to himself and God, and the weight disappeared. Granted, memory is one of our major baggage carriers and the holes in his make plenty of room for the load to fall through. And since he is no longer visiting that former land of using, lying and hurting, the burden hasn't returned. Of course it remains to be seen which way(s) he will go in the future, or if he'll find himself carrying that baggage again. But for now Michael will tell a person very matter-of-factly what happened if they ask, carrying no emotional charge in the recounting. "I hung myself" is as ordinary as saying, "I had pie for breakfast."

My first remarkable time of hearing him say this was at a follow-up visit at his primary care doctor. The doctor knew all the details of his case but the nurse did not, so as she did his intake she asked, "What are we seeing you for today?" I answered, "Follow up on a brain injury" to which she responded toward Michael, "Oh, so did you have an accident and hurt your head?" Michael looked at me with eyebrows way up and a "what do I say to that, Mom?" expression, but before I could respond, he looked at her and answered succinctly, "No, I hung myself." Bless her heart, she didn't skip a beat and went right on to the next question.

Michael may be missing some memory and cognitive functioning, but also absent are anger, frustration, impatience and regret. I think about how many times I have recognized and seen that God has the power to wipe our slates clean, to offer us a completely new start free from the weight of our choices and pain, but we simply can't let go and receive it. Why, I wonder. What is so compelling about remaining in our guilt or unhappiness? Is it that we want to keep the door revolving rather than only swinging forward into new life, just in case we want to return to the hell from which we came? It once occurred to me that failing to receive the mercy and love of God when it is offered, which is always, is as great a sin as never asking for it, never acknowledging that we need help. I have asked myself, "Who made me judge?" Why do I think I have the power to say, "No, I'm not worthy" when God says I am?

Michael's uncluttered acceptance of his past choices and current condition inspire me toward a different direction. I see in him a fluid existence where spiritual change happens at the speed of light. I believe this is possible for all of us, and that circumstances and changes like Michael's show us the reality. If I were but brave enough to receive all the love and light God has to offer, I too could take up a newly appointed internal residence in an instant. I think it would be quite lovely there, though not without stress making the move. For now I hope to nudge along a little faster, like stepping onto the moving walkway in the airport rather than only strolling on solid ground, pulling my luggage behind. I'd like to learn to be a little braver. I'd like to lose the baggage. Maybe one day even take off.

Chapter 8
Exploring the Territories

Isn't it Beautiful?

Michael and I decided to have a treat day, so after morning SBB and OT activities and before the afternoon ST appointment at rehab, we went to Costco for another lunch of pizza and berry smoothies. Afterward we ran errands and then went to the gym for our daily workout. When we got home the 50-degree sunshine inspired me to mow the lawn and cut dead flowers. How many times will several days of sunshine appear in a row in December in Oregon, de-sogging grass enough for mowing? I found three beautiful dinner plate dahlias still in bloom, one of which is now on the mantle above the stockings, just below the Christmas wreath. I've had roses in December, but never dahlias.

Once again, I loved SBB with Michael this morning. We have been talking about the healing power of God and how God can heal instantaneously, at the speed of light. Michael couldn't remember what "speed of light" meant, so we talked a little bit about that and how, while God can and does heal that way, most of us can't move at that rate, spiritually speaking, even though the potential is there. Rather we pray over and over and move along in baby steps, repeatedly imagining what our broken places look like when they become as God intends: whole and perfect. Never once did Jesus come upon a sick person and say, "It is your cross that you continue to bear your illness" or "It is my will you suffer." No, he simply healed them, which is why I believe with all of my heart that this is God's intention for us almost every time, though ultimately healing may be completed on the other side. Our job is to continue believing this truth in the face of any and all evidence to the contrary. We keep inviting grace.

Along these lines, Michael and I have been praying for one of his friends. This is a boy I confess I have hated for a long while. A policeman once told me he was a sociopath, and he is the person Michael used with the day of his suicide attempt. At all the worst junctures of Michael's life, whether they involved drugs or crime, this boy has been there. One day I walked back into Michael's room in ICU after a lunch break and found this person standing by the bed with tears in his eyes, silently looking down at Michael's deathly still body. I felt no softness or pity but only a welling rage. "This is what happens to him when you use together. It kills him. I need to ask you to leave." Rob told me it was good he wasn't the one to find him there, as he likely would have decked him. Then we would have had other problems on our hands.

I have pushed and pulled with all my might to convince Michael this boy is not a friend but the unequivocal opposite. Perhaps the boy's parents feel the same way about my son. Michael seems to bounce closer to him every time I speak out, like an elastic band continually shortening and tightening between him and dynamite. The young man is currently in court-ordered drug rehab. He went there upon his release from juvenile detention.

About the time I learned of the incarceration and rehab, God reminded me we're supposed to pray for our enemies. Ouch. I admit that such an approach makes perfect sense, and certainly my continuous animosity has garnered nothing. Haven't I learned that the only way to affect any change in myself or anything else is through love, and even more, that hate is a particularly ineffective agent of positive change? How beautiful to think of Michael, God and me sitting together in a circle of prayer and inviting this boy in. I felt it was important that my effort wasn't singular, that Michael joined in. "Wherever two or three are gathered in my name, I am there in the midst of them."[1] We vowed to pray for him every day. After two days I promptly forgot about it for ten more. I told Michael I was disappointed in myself, knowing this is one of the ways darkness preys on us, through forgetfulness toward loving. I need more spiritual body building, one recollection, one choice at a time.

On the way to the afternoon rehab appointment the sun was setting behind us, a blazing yellow globe. It filled the rear-view mirrors with fire and cast a luminous gold on everything in front of us. It was a beautiful sight. Sitting in the session, listening to Michael patiently complete yet another speech assessment, I heard the quiet voice of someone or something in the invisible host around us saying, "Isn't it beautiful?" Isn't it beautiful, this snapshot of Michael, alive, sitting and answering questions, the infinite supply of God around and within him, traveling his new road? Yes, it is beautiful.

On the way home the setting sun had given way to a rising full moon. Its bossy brilliance dominated the black eastern sky, offering an apt benediction to the day's activities. At dinner, five of us gathered at the table and said grace by each sharing something we were thankful for and Natalie chimed in, "I'm thankful Michael is alive and here with us." And now Max and Sasha are asleep at our feet, the pendulum clock is steadily marking time, and there is a faint thump and boom from the TV show Michael is watching in the basement. Isn't it beautiful? Yes, it is.

Laughing and Learning

Michael and I have laughed a lot today. A friend loaned us a children's book, *George and Martha: the Complete Stories of Two Best Friends* and we've been enjoying it immensely. George and Martha are hippos who share various adventures and ordinary experiences. Sometimes they disagree, such as when they have an argument about dancing. George thinks dancing is dumb, but Martha insists dancing is not dumb and says she'll be very angry if George doesn't attend her dance recital. So George goes, expecting to hate it, though he does wear a nice tie. To his surprise he enjoys it very much, especially Martha's Happy Butterfly Dance (an excellent illustration accompanies this one). In the end George takes up a dancing class of his own, sporting a very sharp black leotard, doing barre exercises underneath a sign on the wall that says, "Dancing is fun." We sat on the couch reading story after story, laughing out loud. Such belly laughter speaks trust to me.

I think we're crossing into some new territory. A couple of times this week I didn't set the little alarm on Michael's room, though I didn't tell him I left it off. It has only blared twice since he's been home: once when he got up to get something to drink and once when his dog decided she wanted to sleep in his room instead of on her dog bed. The problem was she thought of it around 11:30 PM. If I'm honest with myself, I know Michael's cognitive gains mean there is scant chance right now that he'd wander off without knowing where or why. His impulsivity has declined so much I'm not really sure how, if at all, it might manifest, spatially speaking. I do still see it in the way he answers questions without thinking, blurting out a "Yes!" or "No!" and then pulling back and saying, "Well...." My nighttime worries are more related to the old Michael, to past experiences of him sneaking out to drink or do drugs. But he seems so disinclined to do that right now, almost as though such behavior would violate his present profile. Still, I continue setting the alarm for the most part since, as Rob pointed out, Michael might be ready for it to be off, but perhaps I am not, and we all need to be ready.

I had two nights of no-alarm experimentation under my belt when Michael asked a clever question: "Mom, can you take a nap today?" His approach revealed he was thinking on several levels:

1. He wanted to watch a show in its entirety, ending at 11 PM.
2. He knows his mom is not a night owl, is not even remotely related to the species.
3. Mom sets the alarm on the room at night when she goes to bed.

So he was planning ahead, figuring if I were extra-rested he might have a better chance at staying up later. But I had another idea, due to those two successful, incognito alarm-free nights earlier in the week. I told him maybe it was a good time to let him stay up while we went to bed, and he could just get himself there when his program ended. I wish you could have seen his face light up with genuine delight, a huge smile of accomplishment and appreciation brightening the room. It was not at all the face of a nighttime schemer. Nope, just a happy boy.

What We Have

I have learned that every brain injury is unique. Personality changes can result, though they don't always. When such changes do occur they may be an exacerbation or pronouncement of a present tendency or a shift to a nearly opposite quality. So far the latter seems to be the case with Michael. I know I've marveled about it before, but the changes in his demeanor continue to be so striking I can't quite get *my* brain around them.

Today was a case in point. It was Christmas tree day, where we go to Alfredo's lot in West Salem and cut down the tree of our choice. I like it that we've gone to Alfredo for years, and that his tree farm is adjacent to property belonging to friends of ours who have a girl and a boy Natalie's and Michael's ages. Rob likes to speak Spanish with Alfredo, so for a long time Alfredo thought I spoke it, too. When I eventually owned up to my ignorance, he began decorating his English sentences with a few Spanish words, giving me little puzzles to solve. Christmas tree day is a family day, and family days are not something Michael has willingly engaged in for probably five years.

But Michael is different now. Not only does he come along, he seems to enjoy the time with us. He helps, laughs, and most importantly, is present. Michael has spent years trying to be anywhere but here. He has disliked Salem ("So lame" he would call it), disliked family activities, disliked school and especially disliked anything required of him. He would have readily told you all of this had you asked him. I think he was negative about most things, or if not outright negative, he at least maintained an air of critical superiority. I remember when I first understood that criticism and control are both ways we avoid intimacy. This realization shed much light on my understanding of both myself and others. It may have come around the same time I was learning in prayer that surrender opens me to intimate encounters with God. I don't know that Michael meant to be isolated, but he was.

Now he is not only with us but he is in the moment with us. Many have written about the spiritual richness of being present, how it is the only way we can fully experience God. Our spirits are present-time creatures, and while our minds may jostle backward and forward like so many time travelers, our spirits only ever exist in the now. I have thought a lot lately about how present Michael is, and what a holy thing this presence is. I contrast it with his previous, nearly continuous efforts at separation, and I can hardly figure the change. Is it real? Is it lasting? Day after day he is here laughing and being with us, sweet and genuine and open and honest. I have probably laughed more this week than any week in recent memory. Is it possible that such loss and tragedy could engender such joy?

Having nearly lost a child to death by suicide, I find myself thinking much more about what we have than what we don't have. We have Michael here. His life goes on. We have time, laughter and shared experiences. We don't have everything we had with him before, whether good or bad. The other morning I spent most of prayer time in grief again, crying tears that weren't tethered to any specific thought or emotion, just general tears of "He isn't how he used to be." I didn't know what that meant, really, but there it was and it was sad so I let sad come and speak and then move on. It's not even a case of one thing being better or worse or right or wrong. Rather we were there and now we're here and there is no going back to there, no return balloon from Oz and no waking up from the dream.

And I thank God for here, for the present moments shared together. I am so grateful that Michael's oppositional and destructive tendencies didn't become more pronounced, that they went quietly away so that a gentler person might emerge. Every time we laugh together it is like a drink of cool water after a long, hot, dry walk. I don't think I fully appreciated how much I have missed my son these past years, or maybe I simply did as we all do: we get by and we cope however we can. There is no wishing things that are gone into being again, and when someone chooses to leave, there is no begging, pleading or bullying them back into relationship. I remember saying at an Al-Anon meeting some weeks before Michael's incident that I felt I had lost my son, that while he was alive in the physical sense, he was dead to me in so many ways. There was no life between us. And now there is this, whatever this is, however long it might last. It is as sweet as the drops of honeysuckle nectar that we used to glean from the tender innards of tiny blossoms in early Indiana summers. You couldn't be greedy for the goods because there simply wasn't very much there. You would have to wipe out all of the flowers to get any sort of substantial amount. Besides, the sweet was too delicate to think of gorging. But if you could be content with two or three drops from a few orange and cream tendrils, you could enjoy a delectable treat, and every year it would come again.

It wasn't about what you lacked, but what you had.

❧

There was a span of time last year when Michael was particularly removed, relationally speaking. I was missing him, and not enjoying the "him" who was with us. Right about then a young man walked in and took up residence at our house. He was a friend of Michael's who was going through some typical teenage strife that led to friction with his parents. He showed up one day to spend the night, and later that evening as we sat in the living room, he plopped down and gushed that he really appreciated us letting him stay on, that he would help out around the house and only stay until he was 18. Trying to maintain my composure, as though it was completely normal for a boy to come for a sleepover and then move in, I asked him when his birthday was. He said, "January." As in January next year, 13 months away. Rob and I digested his announcement with our internal eyebrows way up, responding that perhaps we didn't need to make any long term plans just yet, but that we were happy to have him, and why didn't we just see how it went? As things turned out, he lived with us for several months. Toward the end of this time he lost a sister to a tragic auto accident. In the weeks following her death he quietly slipped out of our daily lives, and when he resurfaced a couple of months later he was home with his parents. His devastating loss ultimately led to a grace-filled reconciliation with his family.

During this boy's time with us, Rob and I often light-heartedly reflected that we had the son we'd always wished for. He was relational, respectful and helpful. We didn't really have Michael then, though he was physically present, but we had this other young

126

man. Had we been looking only at what we lacked, we surely would have missed what we had. I learned that when I spend my time trying to see what isn't there I suffer a comprehensive lack of vision, a sort of inner darkening resulting from continuous focus on what is missing or invisible. Staring at the blind spot produces blindness, and life in the present disappears from view. I used to have a recurring dream where, try as I might, I simply couldn't focus my eyes. I always knew the intended scene was right in front of me, but it remained effectively out of sight.

Our time with Michael's friend wasn't the way I would have scripted a mother's relationship with her son, but it surely filled a void in me for a while. I find a similar thing in motion now with Kat living here. Natalie is almost completely absent these days. While she lives at home, she spends all of her time everywhere else, which is surely on task for a college student. I miss her. And just as this thought was adding to my funk last night, in walked Kat, another daughter-on-loan, who brings a special, though different type of filial relationship.

So as we move into the holy days, which we commonly call "holidays," I find myself consciously dedicating my time and will to turning from inner blindness to sight. The expansive love of Christ brings great clarity for me, opening my heart to see what is and what can be. I'm grateful for the vision.

Then shall the eyes of the blind be opened,
and the ears of the deaf unstopped. – Isaiah 35:5

❧

But Thou Didst Not Leave His Soul in Hell

This line from *Messiah* came to me this morning in prayer. It is sung in a brief, lesser-known tenor aria that occurs in part two where Handel pieces together prophetic scriptures from Isaiah and Lamentations along with fragments of the Psalms to create an Old Testament narrative of the gospel story. In *Messiah,* Handel uses the text "But thou didst not leave his soul in hell"[2] to evoke the image of Jesus' three days spanning from death on Good Friday to resurrection on Easter Sunday. Interestingly the psalmist wasn't speaking prophetically in the original writing but rather was describing more of a personal experience of rescue by God.

When the line from *Messiah* dropped into my mind, it led me to think on what one of my friends calls her favorite heresy: the doctrine of universal salvation, or universal reconciliation. It's an old idea, one that has been around as long as Christianity itself, and it wasn't demonized for a good six centuries or so after Jesus' death. Universalism has always made sense to me, as the idea of an all-loving, all-powerful God was difficult to reconcile with eternal damnation. Doesn't love always leave the door open for hope and mercy? Why, if we are all God's children, would God abandon some of us to non-commutable sentences with no room for clemency? Why would there be an expiration date on pardon? And why do we think that God's power is only at work in this one, finite physical existence? It is the nature of the human ego to judge and separate people into who's in and who's out, both in this world and the next, and we all like to place ourselves in the "in" group. I cannot prove or disprove a doctrine, but can only speak from my own experience, which teaches me that God is always about inclusion rather than exclusion. Martin Luther once wrote in a letter to Hansen von Rechenberg: "God forbid that I should limit the time for acquiring faith to the present life. In the depths of divine mercy there may be opportunity to win it in the future state." It's kronos vs. chairos again, and once again I am led to buck the linear and limiting vision of chronological time.

All of this is to say that when the words from *Messiah*

came to me I considered Michael and thought, "Thank you God that you did not leave his soul in hell." I believe that, given God's infinite goodness, Michael's rescue could have come in the form of life or death, and I'm so happy it was life. The word "hell" in scripture is often a translation of the original Greek word "Gehenna," which was what the early Jews called their trash heap outside Jerusalem where refuse of all kinds was constantly burning. It makes me think they envisioned hell in a rather broad way, understanding it as a place we all regularly visit. Like most of us, Michael may have visited, but God didn't let him take up residency there. Maybe God simply helped him to throw in his waste without following it into the fire.

On first glance it appears Michael's newly found receptivity to God seems to have occurred without any conscious consent on his part. He was closed to God, underwent a near death experience, and when his consciousness returned his spirit was open. But there was an ellipsis in there, some time where Michael may not have been physically able to speak but likely was having a burst of free spiritual dialogue. Just as our spirits are more open to the unseen when we sleep, I imagined he was offered a soul room with a special view during those early days at the hospital. "I will praise the Lord, who counsels me. Even at night my heart instructs me."[3] I wondered what the conversation might have been like between Michael and God when his body was stilled and unconscious, when his spirit was free to travel and commune unimpeded by earthly awareness or thought. Did he say yes to God's invitation? Or did he simply recognize his true identity and understand his being was of one substance with the Father[4] and no further words were necessary? I will never know. I trust, though, that the invitation was there and the door was open, as it always is, whether he was dead or alive.

I'll close today with the final verse of Psalm 16 that follows directly on Handel's *Messiah* excerpt:

You have made known to me the path of life;
You will fill me with joy in your presence,
With eternal pleasures at your right hand.

Synchronicity of Grace

The testing has begun. Michael's schedule is full of therapy appointments and special education evaluation sessions and home practice routines. I have counted my blessings yet again that I am able to be here for him, to run him here and there, to practice therapies with him or to hold him to his own, independent work. Willamette University has supported me completely in this and I am so thankful. My department chair is also patient as I try to figure out what I'll be able to handle next semester. I'm grateful for that too, more than I can say.

Through all of Michael's paces and my efforts to keep up I continue to learn that recovery from brain injury is unpredictable and uneven. Gains in some areas lead me to think he will progress at a similar rate in all aspects, but this is an erroneous assumption. I'm seeing it is typical for one area of recovery to take an early lead for a while (such as impulse control or spatial orientation) and then fall back to a more measured pace, while a different area makes little or no gains at all.

Memory is one such example. I asked Michael today what we mean when we say the "speed of light," since he and I talked about the concept a week or so ago. He had no recollection of the conversation and didn't know what the phrase meant or implied. Similarly, I asked him if he remembered some specific steps we talked about in praying for healing. Last week he retained the details of the process from day to day, but after two days off from the routine over the weekend he didn't remember anything about it. Clearly memory continues to be an area of challenge. I do think there are gains in his immediate, short-term memory such as from morning to evening or from one day to the next. But retaining the same information in the mid-term range is out of reach for him at present.

Sometimes I have to remind myself that we are only two months in. It is easy to ride the momentum of both his improvements and our hopes and find myself ahead of the curve. After all, what we've seen is nothing short of miraculous. I was reminded of this today by a synchronicity of grace. I called our auto insurance company to remove Michael from the policy. I figured there was no sense paying for a teenage boy whose addition instantly doubled our rates when he got his license. There was some confusion as to which agent I should speak with and furthermore, all of them were busy with other calls. Eventually the receptionist made a decision to connect me to a particular woman's voice mail. I left my message and this afternoon she called me back. I outlined the changes to her, and when I mentioned Michael's brain injury and that he wouldn't be driving any time soon, she said, "May I ask what happened?" A long and lovely conversation ensued. Her son suffered a major traumatic brain injury over a year ago in a car accident. The details were horrific: he endured multiple vertebrae and back fractures, all of the skin on his head was removed and he impaled himself directly between his eyes. He, too, was in a coma. She, too, didn't know if he would live or wake or be in a permanent vegetative state.

She talked about God and how she knew that whether her son lived or died, it would be okay, that life would be good, even. I told her that, to my amazement, I knew the same. To a complete stranger I recounted details of a dialogue with Michael's spirit as it hovered above us that first night in the ER. She said, "It's strange, but right in the middle of that horrible and traumatic time, there was peace. I don't know how else to describe it. A deep peace." I told her I had found the same gift, and that the experience seemed related to how thin the veil was between this world and the next at that juncture. The gravity and intensity of the situation had blown our spirits wide open and God wasn't going to waste the opportunity. She told me she had goose bumps all over.

She also shared how much she cried that her son was not the same. The depth of that grief was one of the more puzzling things to her about the journey. I have known that same loss, and the fact that an auto insurance agent who I had never met was conversing with me about it, well, it was grace. I told her it was no coincidence that we were talking today and she said, "You got that right because your name is not even in my part of the alphabet." She also told me she went through her son's injury and recovery as a single mother. My heart went out to her as I shared how often I have wondered how I would have made it through if I weren't remarried. We usually lived paycheck to paycheck during my seven years of single parenting. Even the college fund that will help foot many of Michael's medical bills exists solely because I was able to sell my house when I married Rob. I remember how tough it was being a single income family in an economy and society that assumes dual breadwinners.

The conversation was another marker along the way, a quick hug from God reminding me yet again we're not alone and there is help all around us if we'll just keep our eyes open. Comfort comes in the most unexpected ways. Imagine the absurdity had I begun the day thinking, "I hope to encounter a stranger today who has been through what I'm going through, perhaps an insurance agent or a bank teller, so that I might have a lengthy and intimate conversation and feel encouraged." It makes me laugh to think on it! Thank *God* the details of my spiritual path are not up to me. How many times have I seen that what God gives me is assurance, not specifics, and that this gift is more than enough, in fact is the most beneficent and practical help I could ever receive? Most of the guidance I receive eventually confirms this generosity, so while I'm often greedily negotiating for more information at the time, God wisely limits me to a simple "Go this way" along with the words, "Trust me." I don't get to know how or for how long, if it will be financially secure or wildly unstable, what the next step will be or if people will think I'm nuts. I continually learn that while what I understand is limited in specificity, it is endless in potential. "I will not leave you comfortless."[5] God's promises are sure, I simply must keep my eyes and heart open to see them. I know that if I miss the blessings, it isn't God's fault. They are still coming night and day. The only thing that changes is my awareness. Today, I saw the gift. Some people might call my insurance agent conversation a coincidence. Not in my book of life. I know it is grace.

I remember a sermon I heard years ago at Grace Cathedral in San Francisco. A woman priest named Hunter was preaching. I noticed her name was near the bottom of the long list of clergy in the bulletin so I figured it was likely that she didn't get a turn in the pulpit very often. She was preaching on the passage from John about comfort, and asked us, "When was the last time you felt comforted? Was it when you saw a beautiful sunset, or shared a good laugh, or when a friend held you when you cried? And do you think God had nothing to do with that?" No Hunter, I do not, not any more. Jesus names the comforter "the Spirit of truth."[6] That Spirit spoke plainly and clearly to me today, and I am so thankful that this time, at least, God gave me the grace to hear.

Grace Is Sufficient

It's been a quiet, off-kilter couple of days, partly because I've been under the weather and partly because Michael and I had our first breach of trust since his injury. He managed to sneak a smoke by me yesterday. Granted, many AA members separate their alcohol addictions from their nicotine and caffeine ones. Most meetings are full of people pounding down coffee and smoking before and after, like chimneys on either end. For Michael's part, his blessed clean times never once included a hiatus from cigarettes. So I understand the fact his nicotine urge is still intact doesn't mean he's headed for a bender. But in this mother's mind, yesterday's scheming and sneaking brought up every possible association with his using days. It's been a lot to process. On went the little room alarm last night.

I remember talking with the hospital psychiatrist during Michael's stay, saying I hoped this was his bottom. She was realistic with me, mentioning that she's been amazed at what hasn't constituted bottom for many addicts. It was a good if difficult perspective to hear, both because it was true and because it reminded me we can never script the future. I will live many, many days to come wondering if this chapter in our lives was bottom for Michael, if it will be the thing that keeps him from using again. One day not too long ago we talked about it, and he said he won't use anymore. I asked him what is different now than before. He looked at me, raised his eyebrows, and said, "Um, I died." There was a slight upward inflection in his answer, like a small question challenging, "Isn't that enough?" to which I wanted to respond, "Is it?"

Alcohol was involved in the insurance agent's son's accident, too. I couldn't help asking her if he uses anymore. "Alcohol?" she asked. "No. He hasn't touched it since that accident. Not an ounce." That was the answer I desperately wanted to hear, because if it were true for her son maybe it would more likely be true for mine. I wanted to make the answer into a rubber stamp and emblazon it onto Michael's forehead so that he might repeat it over and over and over until no other answer can come out of his mouth. I want to speak it for him, to eliminate all other options, giving only the correct answer forevermore, amen, and be done with it.

Traveling down all of these familiar mental streams reminded me of something I know, something I have known for a while. It is this: if Michael were to choose to use after he turns 18 (or after he is able to function independently which, given his injury, could be sometime after 18), I am done. I have told him this before. Even now, given all he's been through, my position remains the same. I will continue to love him and pray for him and believe in him and hope for him, always, but I will no longer pick up the broken pieces, provide financial support, put him through rehab, fetch him from the police station, or offer any other kind of help that comes in response to the messes addicts create. My boundary is clear.

But right now he is my 17-year-old son who very much needs a mom. Last night when it was his bedtime he stood for a while in the little hall between the bath and his bedroom. I asked him what was up and he answered with a gentle confusion, "I don't know what to do." He is a 17-year-old with a brain injury, and I am here.

Even now as I process and recount all of these rather unholy moments, moments where my left-brained, linear understanding of past, present and future impacted my emotions and sent my "what if?" meter into overdrive, God is gently using the very things I've written about in past days to bring me back to center. "Remember that grace is around you all the time, it is only your awareness that changes? Remember I give you assurance, not specifics, and that is enough? Remember I am with you always? Remember that love wins in the end? Trust me." The directive comes no matter what. It is my call if Michael dies or lives a life consumed by addiction or never uses again. I'm thankful that making it through is not a matter of my own strength or resources.

...for I have learned to be content whatever the circumstances. I know what it is to be in need, and I know what it is to have plenty. I have learned the secret of being content in any and every situation, whether well fed or hungry, whether living in plenty or in want. I can do everything through the one who gives me strength. – Philippians 4: 11-14

It Ain't the Heat that Gets You, It's the Humility

Restore to me the joy of your salvation and renew a
right spirit within me. – Psalm 51:12

This line from David's Psalm came to me in prayer this morning and has been weaving in and out of my consciousness throughout the day's activities. Restore to me the joy of your salvation. I felt that restoration this morning after a couple of days of giving in to fear, felt the familiar wave of Presence washing over and through me, reorienting me to what is true. I felt it in the relaxing of tightly wound thoughts that made room for the bounding in of hopefulness. I especially felt it in the return to living in the present moment rather than the non-existent future.

Last night's Al-Anon meeting topic was manipulation. Having just written about the desire to make Michael's choices for him, which would ensure, of course, that they would be the right ones since they would be mine and not his (how arrogant is that?), it was a timely topic. Look for God in the details, Teresa of Avila would say. I think of control and manipulation as front and back covers of the same book. One may be overt while the other is covert but they are the same beast when we are talking about affecting others' behavior. Those of us who live with addiction, or any situation over which we are not sovereign, which would be all of us, I suppose, know all too well the feeling that if the person in question would simply see our perspective and the obvious rightness of it and then do as we say, everything would work out perfectly. This godlike assumption of wisdom and omniscience strips others of their dignity. After all, doesn't God grant *all* of us free will? I am weary of my lack of humility.

Restore to me the joy of your salvation. Humility is the seat of God's saving grace for me, and the only place where I can truly find joy. In Al-Anon we are encouraged always to "focus on ourselves," not in order to be selfish but rather to keep the lens of critical examination turned inward as opposed to outward. Otherwise we could easily spend all of our time focused on others' issues and faults and conveniently neglect our own. We could forget humility.

As I wrap up this missive, the appointments and obligations are now over for the day. Michael's brain is ready for a rest. Today he learned that when people ask him, "Are you getting tired?" they don't necessarily mean sleepy. He has consistently answered "no" when asked, even when his cognitive fatigue is obvious. But for the brain-injured Michael, tired meant only one thing until this afternoon when he was told it could mean another. Once the connection was formed he easily applied it in various circumstances. He crossed similar bridges in several of his therapies today where he couldn't fathom what an answer might be in a certain type of exercise until a new possibility or angle was opened. At that point he could correctly complete the entire series in nothing flat. Watching his brain relearn is amazing.

Restore to us the joy of your salvation. Restore to us the joy of your perfectly and magnificently ordered human brain. Restore us to your intention, God, in body, mind and soul, and grant us willing and humble spirits along the way.

Abundance

It's gratitude day again. This morning I have been in a deep thankfulness for Michael's life. Each time I see him get up and flop flop his feet into the kitchen, pour and slurp his cereal, one huge gulp after another, and finish by picking up the bowl and draining the milk down, I am grateful. Last night on the way to Natalie's choir concert, Rob and I boisterously sang Christmas carols in two-part harmony. As we intentionally sang wrong notes at the end that randomly ended up creating a rather clever modulation, and Michael laughed, I was grateful. When I saw him bear hug his sister after the concert with a big grin on his face, and as he waited patiently without an ounce of teenage "this is so dumb are you through yet?" attitude while I greeted choir members I've sorely missed these past few weeks, I felt thankful and happy. And on the way home when Rob blessed us with a rib-splitting rendition of "Silent Night" sung in his imitation duck voice, and Michael and Kat hooted in the back seat, I was grateful and happy again.

These moments are precious. I have two sets of good friends and one step-parent who each lost a teenage son: one to a grand mal seizure, one when he was hit by a car as he crossed the street, and one to a freak accident of electrocution. All of their sons were extraordinary, wonderful people. Each of the parents' hearts was buried under grief. My heart went out to them before, but does so all the more now. I don't know why Michael lived and their sons did not. It certainly doesn't seem fair. I know that beyond a sense of survivor's guilt, thinking on it makes me all the more grateful for the time we have. I also feel greater compassion for anyone who has lost a child, which I imagine is the worst grief any parent can endure.

Once thankfulness takes hold of a person's heart it has a burgeoning effect, which is why bringing even a small gratitude list to mind can be so healing. Once I got started this morning my heart went leaping and bounding down the blessing byway, thinking on simple things like the beautiful Christmas tree in the living room, to the funny, dumb things our dogs do, to Rob's sense of humor, to music. Music. It was so lovely to hear the Willamette University choral program last night. This would have been my eighth year conducting in it, and I have never experienced it as an audience member. My women's choir made me beam with pride, and the worshipful presentation of the entire evening was a balm.

It was also very odd to think on returning to work in January. Almost all of my work is extroverted, and I am an introvert in my heart. I can be extroverted when needed, so much so that many people would not suspect I'm an introvert. I am learning that over time the outward exertion takes ever more from my inner world, which is probably why that inner world has been so rich during these past weeks. My days have been insulated and insular: tending Michael at home, going to quiet appointments with therapists one-on-one, offering the remainder of my time to the blossoming reflections of my deeper spaces. I am convinced this sheltered existence also accounts for my willingness and ability to share openly. I feel God has used the quiet and relative lack of contact with the outside world to open a path of communication that I otherwise might not have been able to follow or sustain. At the concert I felt God figuratively taking my chin and turning my head with some effort back toward the outward tasks to which I will return. It will be good to be back and to give myself over to external matters once again, though I know it will bring quite a shift.

This is another significant item on my gratitude list: meaningful work to do with wonderful people, and in music, after all, one of God's celestial languages. The choirs last night reminded me of the familiar strain of one of the season's carols. They were joining with the host, for sure.

> *Sing, choirs of angels, sing in exultation.*
> *Sing all ye citizen of heaven above.*
> *Glory to God in the highest!*
> *O come let us adore him, Christ the Lord.*

Chapter 9
Another Day in
Earth School

New Phase

The routine has changed.

Michael began attending two classes through the Early College/High School program at Chemeketa Community College. He is particularly pleased that these periods will constitute his PT and OT for the day, which means there is less to schedule at home. I am happy about that, too, and told him it is wonderful that school will take the place of some of his home therapies. This week is one of his testing grounds. We will see how he holds up with the daily demands of an hour of weights and cardio conditioning followed by an hour of reading/language. How handy that there is only a single week of classes before winter break, forming a perfect trial run period for this phase. I explained to him last week that he'll be in high school level classes for now, which surprised him. This lack of awareness of his current abilities is one of the interesting things about the brain-injured Michael. In so many ways he doesn't know what he lacks or what he's lost. I feel this clean slate of consciousness is a blessing, because greater awareness could certainly mean more frustration and discouragement. He lives in an eternal state of "is-ness" as my mother would say. Only what *is* matters and whatever was, or isn't, holds little sway. I can hardly imagine what it must be like to be so completely untethered to past experiences and expectations.

When I dropped him off at the community college I felt a bit like the mother of years ago when my children first began school. I told him to have a good day and then circled the parking lot a few times, making sure he got in okay and could find his way. He disappeared from view once he was in the door, so I couldn't see a thing during most of the circling and looking, but that didn't stop me from doing it. I wondered if he'd remember who to talk to about his schedule or if he'd find the right person to help him rediscover his locker and combination. I worried that he might get disoriented and then just stand there, not knowing who to ask for help. I considered parking and going in to check, but thought better of it. It turns out he found his way fine, and a couple of hours later he came out the door and found me again straight away. When I asked if he made it through weights without getting too tired he told me they didn't suit up because it was a free day, though they did play some basketball. When I asked about English he said they didn't do the computer program and that the teacher talked for that hour. I remembered how information-laden and non-productive the first day of a term's classes can be. "Talked about what?" "Um...I don't know." A few more questions yielded a bit more information, but I know Michael's aural memory isn't very strong right now. Rather than going in one ear and out the other, most of what he hears just takes a little detour and bypasses the space between altogether.

Michael attempted cutting his hair today. I was proud of him for giving it a go. Before his injury he and I usually shared the job with him doing most of the buzzing and me stepping in for the final check and neck trim at the end. The first time he attempted the task post-injury was a non-starter. This time he completed probably half of it before asking for help. Granted, it's not easily done on the back deck with only the reflection in the window for a mirror. I thought he did really well.

It is strange, going through firsts for the second time

with him. I see there will be a lot of this. Connections have
been severed in his brain, not to mention knowledge lost.
I'm guessing there will be numerous repeats of some of the
firsts we are experiencing now, as many things have to be
explained again and again. God seems to have the same task
with me. Many times I've considered that if I could only
remember what I know, spiritually speaking, I would make
great strides. Instead I seem to relearn what I know over
and over again. Each time I remember a little more deeply
than before. I have reflected that one way to interpret Jesus'
instruction to forgive seventy times seven[1] is to understand it
may take that many passes through a particular issue to fully
let go. Each time we go a little further, release a little more,
see the truth more clearly. It is okay with me if Michael needs
the same instruction over and over. Apparently I do too. Here
we go, Michael. Let's go around again. And again and again
and again, as many times as it takes.

Markings

Today was another milestone. I worked for eight hours on
campus, marking my first full day away from Michael since
October 11. It was voice jury day (finals for vocal music
students) and I was able to spend six of those hours with
my colleagues hearing arias and art songs and sharing our
perspectives on the craft of singing. I work with fantastic
people, so while it was a long day, it wasn't much of a
chore, and I delighted in hearing my students' voices again.
Willamette is a wonderful community.

Michael did his new routine once more while I was gone.
Rob took him to school and Natalie picked him up, and he did
fine in his classes. Working and spending the day away from
him marked his disability with a fresh stroke of highlighter
for me, much like the day we brought him home from rehab.
Just as I had grown used to the brain-injured Michael in the
hospital and seeing him in the familiar surroundings of home
was a strange disconnect, similarly, going to work, doing this

"normal" thing that I haven't done for two months put me in regular mode, so somehow the end of the day brought an unbidden expectation of other normalcy. It was as though the foreign but ultimately familiar rhythm of work rerouted my brain to a previous circuit, and that circuit didn't have any experience of the changed Michael. Hearing his slow, slurred speech and seeing his sweet and slightly vacant expression while his eyebrows went way up was surprising to me, and *that* surprised me since I've been hearing and seeing it every day now for weeks.

I felt my tender places open up through the disjuncture, exposing a fragility that was previously protected, like baring something soft and sensitive to the raw experience of outdoor living. I feel a bit like an animal that has become an indoor pet and now has to make it in the wild. I'm discovering it's winter and I'm unprepared for the temperature change. I'll get there.

I also found myself bridging an internal gap, nurturing a greater awareness of my inner world while working in the outer one. I would pause and breathe deeply from time to time, remembering that the unseen reality I've been so in tune with lately was no less present as I listened and analyzed and wrote evaluative comments. I simply couldn't give it my full attention. The experience reminded me of the feeling that comes after a long vacation when my psyche is relaxed and detoxified from stress. As I return to the regular demands and pressures of daily living the calm quickly recedes. I always sense there should be a way to sustain the peaceful place, a way to remember and live the lack of bodily tension and mental furrowing, but my consciousness always swiftly winds up and recoils into a familiar tightness. The past two months have been no vacation, but they have been a definite break from a particular kind of mental activity, and I have been spiritually nourished in the change. I feel determined to remember what I have learned and to live more steadily with one foot in heaven and one on earth, or at least to listen simultaneously to God and the musical world around me, remembering to give God my good ear.

As I consider the importance of both my spiritual and professional worlds, I feel passionate about maintaining the balance. God has pulled me closer and deeper during this time of waiting and watching, and nothing in me wants to move away from that intimacy. Rather I'd like to bring more awareness of God to all that I do academically and personally. This desire exposes a fearful vulnerability in me. The very thing I want to live seems to have no place in our secular world so much of the time. But even as I say and write that, I know it is fully wrong. Everything I believe and know shouts "No!" in the face of such a distinction. The spiritual life is the only thing that has any firm place in the real world because in the end it is all that survives. Spiritual reality forms and informs the physical, not the other way around. I *know* this truth, that Spirit brings and gives life to all that we do here in the flesh, whether we're singing or playing or teaching or praying. Why do I think there is separation? Why do I live as though there is? What a profound misunderstanding. I pray that God would give me greater understanding and willingness to live the organic, unifying truth of Christ within me, above me, around me, before me, behind me and especially in the hearts of all those around me. Thomas Merton sums it up beautifully in a reflection on Advent, the liturgical season of waiting and preparing for birth: "The Advent mystery is the beginning of the end of all in us that is not yet Christ."

Wonderful Tonight

"It's late in the evening…." (gotta love Eric Clapton), and I intended to write earlier but the day took some unexpected turns. One such detour came as I was preparing to go to my Al-Anon meeting after dinner and something inside nudged me to stay home. I asked and listened, and not ten minutes after making the decision to skip the meeting the doorbell rang and there were four of my lovely students caroling in sweet harmony. Now a couple of hours, bowls of soup and cups of tea later, I'm sitting down to write.

Here is what struck me today: "Your speech may never be quite like it was before." These words spoken gently and helpfully to Michael by his therapist were hard to hear. I realize I have not been considering the ultimate losses from his injury. As long as we're in recovery there is the possibility of regaining ground. The process is long and slow, and it will be a while before we reach the plateau. We don't have to acknowledge any final deficiencies while we're still making the climb. At some point we'll have to make that assessment and come to terms with the results. But I don't like to think about that right now, in fact I don't acknowledge it much at all. So the words jolted me a bit. "Your _____ may never be quite like it was before." The blank could be filled with any number of characteristics: your speech, your memory, your emotional spectrum, your attention span, your abstract reasoning, your cognitive functioning, your social life, your academic potential, your relationships, your world. The almost certain likelihood is of some permanent change, and speech will probably be one such area. Michael is self-conscious about how he sounds, showing reluctance to speak in front of people he doesn't know well. As Rob pointed out, his speech is a noticeable reminder of his injury, much like a scar that he will wear for all to hear.

But somehow the therapist's phrase left me identifying change only as loss rather than simply as difference or even gain. I believe all change does bring loss in some regard, even when the change is for the better. We lose what was and gain what is. Surely this can bring greater abundance as well. So I prefer to "dwell in possibility," as Emily Dickinson says. Possibility is open-ended, optimistic and positive. Possibility, too, invites change if we are ultimately to embrace it's potential. Isn't it funny how often when we consider the future we imagine only negative scenarios? How often do our minds run loose with thoughts of extravagant joy and blessing meeting us around the corner? I would like to think this way more. Isn't it just as likely? I have to say, regarding Michael, the concept of arrival seems rather final to me right now, not to mention laden with potential for disappointment. But then arrival would be a pre-mature birth at this point, so it's good that we are waiting in this extended, pregnant pause.

And for now, Michael is doing great in his day-to-day abilities and functioning. He takes care of his own self-care/hygiene and always gets his own breakfast. He isn't independent in terms of other meals, but he's getting there. His impulsivity is way down, gone really, and I am beginning to feel I can trust him not to float off into random trouble. His mood remains positive. He still has significant short-term memory loss, and lately I'm noticing he doesn't eat lunch or dinner unless prompted. Apparently such lack of initiation is a common cognitive issue related to brain injury. I am reading several books on brain injuries and am learning a great deal from them as well as from his therapists. The information helps me navigate both the individual days and also the larger direction of his recovery. Because I am so glad he is here it is tempting to indulge him rather than push him toward greater independence and self-sufficiency. I have to keep a watchful eye on my inner doter.

It is time to sleep. The fuzzy evening quiet has arrived and I can hear my pillow calling. Life is good, and I am so glad to be living it.

Not Figuring It Out

Michael is laughing in the basement. He's watching something on TV and apparently it is pretty funny because he's guffawing heartily down there. I'm sure I've heard him laugh more in the past month than in the last several years combined. I still can't get over the fact that the only significant variation in his emotional affect right now is an upward one into humor and delight. A diminished emotional spectrum is typical of brain injuries, and while I see this in Michael, I am so glad that his current, limited palate includes happiness. What an incredible blessing.

He's hanging in there with school, though he's had some pretty tiring days. Exercise is often a time of mental rejuvenation for non-brain-injured people, a chance to shut down the internal hamster wheel and glide. But for Michael, physical activity is mentally tiring, simply because the coordination and exertion tax his brain. One morning this week he was nearly zombie-like from fatigue as his weights class left him mightily sore. Thankfully his energy level improved as the days moved along. I remember how tiring the first week of school can be even for normal students (and teachers), so I keep that in mind.

Rob and I are having an adult night out with friends so I have made arrangements for Michael and the girls to go out to dinner together. Kat wanted to give Michael the honor of choosing where they eat, but his decision-making is impaired enough that the task is more of a burden than a privilege. I'm learning this in our daily activities, too. I want to give him choices and let him have some control, but even two options for lunch can be too many. He simply doesn't know how to choose and thus becomes paralyzed with the effort. The learning curve continues around the invisible bend.

I am discovering that while I am learning tremendous things about brain injury and recovery through books and real life experience, I don't have to know everything, nor do I have to have it all figured out. I do have to remain alert and attentive. I learn so many things simply by watching and really *seeing*. In fact, thinking I need to know or fully understand can inhibit my learning abilities. A sense of inadequacy (often magnified by my inner critic) can dampen my intuitive feelers, and I miss things. This is a waste of precious energy, and I see a direct spiritual parallel. While I have many flashes of insight where certain details come

147

into sharp relief, I feel the big picture is always a mystery to me, is always a bit out of focus or too far in the distance to clearly discern the ultimate shape or form. The unknown is always so much greater than the known. However, when I focus on my lack, I find I become lackluster. My spiritual shine diminishes as a dullness born from stinginess of heart settles in.

But then I remember I don't have to have it all figured out. My job is to listen and respond to the daily influx of information from heaven. And how I love it when the volume is loud! But often the voice is still and small, so I'm learning I need to be quiet more often, even in the midst of chaos. I need to remain aware. I feel my job is to keep looking for new and better ways to manifest love and grace, and who knows what form those opportunities might take? The variety is infinite and I don't want to miss the latest incarnation. Isn't it wonderful that so many chances to be the vessel of God's grace do not require any previous job experience? This excites me, this idea of being an eternal student here in Earth School, honing my skills of awareness and my willingness to carry whatever word or gesture God might want to communicate. This is something I feel I can do regardless of my level of understanding: practice awareness, practice seeing God in others and in me, practice knowing we are all infinitely connected and beautiful. Doesn't it sound good?

God's Good Pleasure

Michael went with me to church this morning here in Salem. He didn't want to go but joined me after some prodding. His hunger for and openness to God seem to have lessened in the last couple of weeks. Knowing there are diminishing returns when a person feels pressured or coerced in any spiritual direction, I am not pushing him. I read a fascinating book called *My Stroke of Insight* in which neuro-anatomist Jill Bolte Taylor describes suffering a massive brain hemorrhage and her subsequent eight years of recovery. The hemorrhage effectively shut down the entire left side of her brain. During and after that time she was gifted with a keen spiritual connection, an awareness of being one with the world around her. She was joyful and "fluid," as the boundary between her and others effectively dissolved. She lived in a holy, communal "I" rather than a limited and separating "I" of ego and personality.

Through the recovery process and the reawakening and renewal of the left side of her brain, she realized this particular insight was diminishing but also that she had choices as to how she would respond to the spiritual inhibitions the left side of her brain now posed. She learned she could strengthen the connection to the right side where she had experienced a joyful freedom from the judgments of her inner critic while recovering the brilliant, critical functioning of her left brain. Claiming one side's strength no longer meant canceling out the other's.

As I think about Michael in the early-to-midstream of his recovery, I imagine some similar hemisphere shifting might be taking place. I don't know that he'll retain the consciousness Taylor did of the changes in her thinking and spiritual experience, but I hope, as his memory and cognitive functioning gains strength, he will retain some recollection of his spiritual openness and the possibilities that blossomed there. I feel that even if the door were to close all the way, God has already gotten in. I like to imagine Michael would now be shutting God in rather than out. Who knows what God might accomplish there, incognito, behind closed doors?

Just yesterday I read Teresa of Avila's description of the mental state she achieved in advanced stages of prayer and meditation. She talks about how a person is unable to read in this state, how perhaps one could see letters on the page but would not understand what they were for or what they meant because the mind was elevated beyond reason or critical thinking. This is strikingly similar to the experience

Taylor describes in her book when her left brain was disabled and the right side held supreme sway. Letters were merely "squiggles" on the page that had no meaning for her. She had to relearn what they meant, how to read, and how to write. Language, of course, is a left brained activity. Her injury landed her in a state of altered spiritual consciousness that mystics spend years learning to attain. This fascinated me, particularly as I reflect on the changes I've witnessed in Michael: the blazing, post-injury openness followed by what appears to be a gradual, dimming retreat in recovery.

Reading both of these remarkable women's works has taught me much about my own deep prayer experiences. With practice and by the grace of God, we can repeatedly reach a place of profound communion where we are beyond the confines of language and linear thought. It is peaceful there, and communication occurs not through words but through images and sounds, and through gifts of sudden knowing.

I had such an experience this morning. After some time in a suspended state like a waking dream, I felt the approach of a being. He was small and clothed in white with wings, very quiet, gentle and humble. I was given his name: Geoffrey. And then I understood. He is Geoffrey, a man we prayed with and for in the Methodist hospital in Maua, Kenya last summer. Alice, one of the hospital chaplains, was worried about Geoffrey because she said that he had succumbed to the spirit of discouragement and had lost his will to live. He had been in the hospital for several months already when we arrived. He suffered severe burns over most of his torso and legs in a petrol accident and the damage went deep into his tissues. He was bone thin and weak. We saw many sick, poor and lonely people that day in the hospital, but for some reason God nudged my heart about Geoffrey so I made a commitment to continue praying for him every day.

When he appeared in prayer today I knew he had died. Strong grief came over me as I wept for him and those here on earth who still love him. Then I understood that he visited this morning to express his gratitude for the prayers and love Rob and I and so many others offered on his behalf. I still catch my breath when I feel his humility and tenderness. God was showing me clearly how important our prayers are, both in this life and beyond. Every prayer is heard and answered, and our supplications offered up on behalf of others matter immensely.

I wanted to tell Alice of Geoffrey's visit, but she is far away and without Internet access. I know her heart must have broken when he died. She has a difficult job, spiritually tending the sick and dying, many of whom have AIDS and are abandoned by their relatives and community. I will send her a letter telling her what God revealed, because we all need encouragement, especially when we feel our prayers have failed. But our prayers have not failed, and they do not, because God is hearing and answering them perfectly all of the time. We just can't see such grace with our limited, earthly vision. But every now and again we rise above the fog, like going up in an airplane when it's been cloudy at ground level for weeks. After climbing a while we may be surprised to see that the sun is still blazing away up there, that the rain has simply obscured the light. Geoffrey wanted me to know this truth today. I believe he will bless me with companionship for a while on the next part of my journey.

I share this with you so that you, too, might be encouraged. Your prayers are heard, your prayers matter, and each one is met with a host of help and compassion. Know, too, that someone is praying for you, bringing your name before the throne of God in love. It may not even be anyone you know. And it doesn't matter if we don't know how to pray or what to say. The Spirit "intercedes with sighs too deep for words"[2] on our behalf, like a heavenly translator and decoder who takes our jumbled, half-hearted and misguided missives and hand-delivers a perfectly complete message to the heart of God, likely accompanied with a sublime soundtrack. Oh what Love! We must be patient as we wait for answers, and be willing for life not to turn out how we imagine. God has the perfect vision in mind, and we need to remember it is God's good pleasure to give us that kingdom.[3] Over and over and always.

Making Our List, Checking it Twice

Lists are important for brain-injured people. While we all use lists to organize: grocery lists, to-do lists, and Christmas card mailing lists, those suffering from brain injuries need them even more. The lists can be specific, such as every task required in cleaning a bathroom, or more general. For instance, Michael has trouble initiating things. While this may be common for any teenager, it is especially pronounced for those in cognitive recovery. He even has trouble telling himself to eat. Sometimes his brain doesn't give his body the hunger signal, so he simply doesn't think about it. If mealtime does occur to him, chances are good he won't do anything about it. This kind of inertia regarding the most elemental functions makes motivating to practice tedious, therapeutic exercises rather remote. So this morning we made another list.

Michael wrote down all of the things he would like to see develop or return in his life: driving, more time with friends, going to college, speaking clearly, normal brain function, snowboarding, getting a job, owning a house. Then under each category we listed the daily activities that will help him toward that goal. Under driving we put anything involving physical reflexes, dual attention, and the pairing of motor movement with cognitive function. He regularly avoids lots of these exercises. One item listed under "more time with friends" was "making good choices." Getting a job included tasks such as doing chores and improving thinking skills. This was all in an effort to help motivate him for the daily tasks at hand, which are many and, as he says, "lame." It is difficult for him to connect the practice with the long-term goals. I can understand this, as I often suffer a similar disconnection. And like all of us, Michael faces the compounding issue of simultaneously ignoring tasks while fully recognizing their importance and benefit. Who doesn't do that? "I don't feel very good when I eat only corn chips and cheese dip for lunch but I'm going to anyway," or "I know I want to be in better physical shape, but I'm not going to the gym today. Or tomorrow. Or the next day, either," or "I'd like to have a richer spiritual life but I don't have time. I'm really busy with computer games."

Michael's misalignment of choices and consequences is exaggerated by his injury, so I thought if he could see each of his goals on paper and then categorize the day's tasks it might spur some initiation on his part. "Do you think this will help?" I asked him. "No, I still won't want to do it." But he admitted he might be a little more likely to give it a go with "driving" and "snowboarding" egging him on from the page.

We gave the new system a trial run today when I was out for a bit. We've left him in small increments of time over the last couple of weeks, and apart from scrounging up cigarettes he has done pretty well. He had certain things to accomplish on his own, and much to my surprise he did them all by the time I returned. This is the first time he's been able to complete a list without regular prompting from me since he's been home. Both he and I are weary of Teacher Mom giving him constant assignments and instructions. Turning the table so that the impetus comes from him will be no small task, but again, independence is one of the main goals of recovery. I was particularly proud of myself as I generously re-educated him that it is okay for him to differ with others. Until I pointed out this aspect of self-differentiation to him, it never occurred to him to voice a dissenting opinion. It does now. What was I thinking? But seriously, a person could be at a constant and vulnerable disadvantage in the world if they never knew they could disagree. And like so many aspects of his recovery, once he recognizes a new option, it takes hold and remains. This isn't the case with factual details but it seems to be so with connective thinking. It's amazing to watch.

I began this entry last night and now 24 hours later I'm still not finished. It's a busy season for all of us. As I drove to an appointment this morning, I watched geese flying in the sky above me. While each bunch was going in a single, ordered direction, sometimes with tiny, Swift-like birds in between them, the various groups were heading every which way in lofty pandemonium. Their flight mirrored the town around me where people are scurrying here and there, bustling through a myriad of tasks before they land. One particularly large flock circled and dropped into a field. The descent was beautifully choreographed, a perfect cascade of flapping, gliding wings. Watching the geese was the soft moment in the day. I'll keep looking for more in the days to come, knowing we'll all alight on December 25th very soon. Meanwhile, we'll be checking the list.

Through these weeks, Deacon Allen continued to send me writings by and about Jeff Tiner, the death row inmate praying for Michael. The following appeared in a Catholic paper and tells the story of Jeff's conversion:

Inmates carrying out ministry from death row
by Ed Langlois

From a windowless cell at Oregon State Penitentiary, a Catholic death row inmate evangelizes across the world.

A former white supremacist, Jeff Tiner is now inspired by a humble African saint. He resists publicity for himself, saying he wants only to spread the story of St. Josephine Bakhita far and wide. He uses most of this time and resources to support the Canossian Sisters, the religious community St. Bakhita joined more than a century ago.

At one time, Tiner had other priorities. In 1993 in Springfield, he allegedly shot a man in consort with a woman who wanted the victim out of the house and away from her children. Tiner, court records say, disposed of the body in a remote area of the Cascade Range. He had been in trouble with the law before and bore tattoos of a swastika and the words "White Pride."

Years after being convicted, inmate Tiner was sitting despondent in his cell. A letter appeared under his door. The writer, calling herself his "Swiss Mum," informed him that Jesus, Mary and Josephine Bakhita loved him. Huh?

Tiner tried to throw what he considered a zany screed into the waste bag, but it fell short. He bent over to grab it for another try and it felt as if the letter jumped into his hand. He placed it on his desk and returned to other projects. But the letter nagged him and he felt a small stir of the soul.

Tiner wrote back to the stranger, telling her that he did not know he was Swiss and inquiring about this Bakhita woman.

As time went by, he received more letters and pamphlets from his Swiss friend, a lay member of the Canossian order who had read about death row inmates on the Internet. She taught him about the Sudanese saint.

Born to an important family in the Darfur region in 1869, Bakhita was kidnapped at age 6 by Arab slave traders. Treated brutally, she was sold and resold five times, falling at one point into the hands of an Ottoman army officer who marked her as his with scars and tattoos.

Sold to an Italian diplomat when she was still a teen, she went to Venice and met the Canossian Sisters, an Italian order that had been founded in 1808. Bakhita sought baptism in 1890. A court later found that Italian law did not recognize slavery and so she was freed.

She chose to stay with the sisters. By 1896, she professed vows. She served for years in northern Italy, becoming known for a gentle spirit and holiness. Children called her "Our Brown Mother." She died in 1947 and was canonized in 2000.

"My own story is unimportant," Tiner says, preferring instead to talk about the saint who changed his life. "Her story pierced my soul." After reading about St. Bakhita, the condemned man felt hope.

"I came to understand that I, too, could come back to life, spiritually," he wrote in a 2006 article for the Canossian Sisters' magazine. "I could be rescued from slavery to sin and find redemption and joy in the arms of Jesus and Mary." He felt Bakhita leading him down a path toward Jesus, he says.

"I am no longer waiting to die," Tiner declared. "I am alive in Christ Jesus."

Tiner was baptized in 2005. Because prison officials refused to allow him into the main chapel, the chaplain asked two guards to fill a large laundry tub with water and wheel it to death row.

"There, in shackles and handcuffs, I was baptized in the water that flowed from the side of Christ, made new in the Holy Spirit," Tiner recalls in a letter written to Auxiliary Bishop Ken Steiner.

The summer after his baptism, Archbishop John Vlazny came to the prison and confirmed Tiner and four other prisoners.

For the past six months, Tiner has written regularly to Bishop Steiner, signing his letters, "Mama Mary loves you!" Bishop Steiner admits that he has caught the Bakhita fever. He even wrote his Christmas column in The Sentinel about her.

"I am very impressed with the conversion of this man, especially his missionary spirit," Bishop Steiner says.

Another member of the hierarchy holds St. Bakhita in high regard. When Pope Benedict issued an encyclical on hope this year, he prominently cited her as a role model of the virtue. Tiner sent the pope a letter of thanks.

With Deacon Allen Vandecoevering and St. Edward Parish in Keizer helping, Tiner started the grassroots Bakhita Project to help the Canossian Sisters. The women, who wear simple gray habits, have worked in Sudan since 1996, teaching children who are refugees from the long warfare there. They also provide food and health care for families. Through benefactors of the Bakhita Project, Tiner and his associates have so far helped build classrooms at St. Francis School in Khartoum. They have paid for a brick school and women's center in a desert refugee camp and provided food and supplies for several thousand children attending school in tents. The project is also seeking to raise $45,000 to pay for a new bus to transport students in the desert where temperatures can reach 130 degrees.

Sister Severina Motta, who serves in Sudan, wrote to Tiner a year ago to tell him what gifts can mean there.

"I would have never thought that children can be overhappy with just a few sweets, biscuits, drinks, soap and a little ball," she wrote just after Christmas.

"You must have seen their exploding happiness. They ran along the street carrying the little bag on their shoulders, then they danced and sang under the hot sun."

The lay Canossian and several Canossian Sisters who work in Rome have been sacramental sponsors for Tiner on his faith trek.

"I consider myself very fortunate in being one of Jeffrey's pen friends because of his most edifying spiritual life," writes Canossian Sister Velia De Giusto. "He shows an unquenched thirst for becoming more Christ-like."

One nun in Singapore, moved by Tiner's writings, refers to him as a "lay Canossian brother."

"Has anyone ever done so much and from behind prison bars?" Sister Mary Siluvainathan wrote in her order's magazine.

"These Sisters remind me so of Mother Teresa of Calcutta," Tiner writes in a letter to The Sentinel. "They all refuse to get side-tracked by governmental blather. They crawl right down into the mud to save the poorest of the poor and the little ones."

Tiner's influence has spread on death row. He was confirmation sponsor for Conan Hale, convicted of a 1996 triple murder. It was Hale's sacramental confession to Father Tim Mockaitis that in 1996 was recorded by Lane County jailers, setting off an international argument on religious freedom.

When he met Hale, Tiner could tell the new inmate was distressed, "infested" with demons. Tiner prayed for him, even holding a crucifix up in front of Hale's cell and seeking the help of Jesus, Mary and Joseph. This would be a big job.

The next day, Tiner saw Hale crying tears of contrition. The death row veteran asked permission to teach the faith to the new man. Over time, Hale seemed like a new person. Hale's confirmation was arranged and the presider was to be none other than Father Mockaitis, an arrangement Tiner calls "beautiful symmetry."

Hale, whom Tiner calls "a refurbished soul," now creates and sells art to help support the Canossian Sisters and other religious communities. Three other inmates have gotten involved in the Bakhita Project. Tiner is teaching the rosary to another troubled prisoner.

His fond hope is that the Bakhita Project continues to spread beyond the penitentiary fences. The Holy Names Sisters Foundation printed up a brochure on the project. The flyer is making its way out to Catholic parishes in the area.

Tiner's deep faith, Deacon Vandecoevering says, has granted him a kind of freedom. "This conversion has been an incredible thing for me to witness," says the deacon. "It has been sustained. Once Jeff converted and was baptized, he shed all these layers of sin and became the child of God he was meant to be."

To learn more about the Bakhita Project, go to www.sainteds.com and look at the feature pages. Aid can be mailed to The Bakhita Project/St. Edward Church, 5303 River Road North, Keizer, OR 97303.[4]

❧

Safe in the Flood

Our dog Sasha is really bossy sometimes. She mostly bosses Max, our Golden Retriever, bullying him with growls and woofs and forceful nosing. Sasha is a mutt, and our vet thinks she may have some cattle dog in her. This makes sense to us as she herds every moving thing in sight, and the more warm bodies there are in close proximity, the bossier she gets. She was especially hard on Max this past week since we had family visiting, often turning on him in sudden eruptions of snarling and nipping. So this afternoon when I was downstairs putting my body through some exercise paces and Sasha pounced all over Max again, I gave her a piece of my mind. She groveled over to me, tucked her head in penitent submission and gazed up imploringly with big brown eyes. She's a very cute mutt, after all. Just as she and I were making up, Max let out a "Woof!" right at her and then turned and ran like a rabbit up the stairs. I laughed out loud as she tore after him, realizing how much he *wanted* her to boss him.

Max led me to a grander observation just then: we can't save someone that doesn't want saving, not to mention that our assessment of their peril may be completely erroneous. We may be able to open a person's eyes to how much they need help (Rob insists Max is enough of an underdog that we do come in handy from time to time), but ultimately everyone chooses the help they do or do not want.

I am helping Michael a lot these days. His therapists continually stress the goal of independence, and I am beginning to see why it is so important to keep a tight lead on this objective. Michael often seems less independent rather than more so as time goes by. His friends aren't calling or coming by much now, so I suggested perhaps he call them. Initiation continues to be a major hurdle whether it involves getting up, eating, practicing therapies, or deciding what to do next. Social contact seemed like a good idea, but he simply wouldn't do it. He couldn't articulate why. He said he didn't feel shy or self-conscious, said yes, he enjoyed time spent with friends and that he would like more of it, and absolutely no, he wouldn't call. With his newfound awareness of the power of assertiveness, he flat out refused. My mother's heart aches at his isolation, and in light of his solitary time I realize my fears have shifted. Just a few weeks ago I worried what he might do when he eventually got out more. Now I fear he'll never go. He spends day after day here with his family when he used to be such a social boy. I am learning there is some help we can give and some we can't. And I am beginning to make a regular habit of questioning my wisdom regarding another's happiness.

Of course, sometimes I put the parental foot down, as all moms do. I insisted Michael take a walk with us today, since the Willamette gym is closed for the week and we are off our regular fitness routine. We all needed fresh air. He came and kept pace, albeit half a block behind us. His measured distance reminded me very much of a normal teenage boy who might lag behind to avoid embarrassing familial association. He did catch up when Sasha took a business break, and then happily plop-plopped along next to us the remainder of the way.

Questions and decisions regularly arise as we navigate his recovery: Is this essential help I'm giving? Am I projecting my own goals onto him? Is it better to prod him or wait for him to find his own motivation? Can I help him discover that motivation? Is he ready for more responsibility or is it too soon? These are questions every parent faces in one form or another. And then there is that other, overarching question which occasionally insists itself into my psyche: "Why? Why did this have to happen?" Once I dive into the "Why?" vortex I can easily lose sight of the objectives at hand, spinning deeper and deeper. Why would Michael take the beautiful life he had and throw it away? Why would he attempt such terminal harm? This grief cuts deep. As parents we must feel at times that we value our children's lives more than they do. We incubate them, birth them, tend them, love them, celebrate with them and rear up in indignant rage when someone else hurts them.

I remember when Natalie participated in a school "pageant" and the woman directing the event rigged the results, arranging for her favorite to win. The contest was a fundraiser for a children's hospital, so bringing in money was part of the competition. Since people would be making donations the night of the event, the result was supposed to be in suspense. But at the dress rehearsal the day before I overheard the director saying to another contestant, "Now when they announce your name I want you to first walk this way, and then turn and go there," coaching the young girl across the stage. I was incensed! I confronted her about it and she made excuses and denied it, but the next night when the designated young lady won (as well as the director's son), I felt confirmed and justified in my mama-bear outrage. My anger simmered for a good long while, stoked by repeated mental replays of the injustice, even after Natalie said, "But Mom, it really doesn't matter. The point was to raise money for the hospital, and we did, so it's all good." (Who made my then middle-school-aged daughter more mature than me?). We know it isn't okay for someone to hurt our kids. But where do we direct our rage when they hurt themselves?

I put off praying much of the day today. After a productive morning I did other things, all kinds of nothing, and finally, a half hour after announcing I was heading to quiet time, when I found myself snacking on blue corn chips and playing games on Facebook, I knew I was into some serious avoidance behavior. So I buckled down and went. Once there I quickly came face to face with the object of my avoidance: grief. My beautiful boy, my beautiful, sweet Michael fell deep enough into the well of darkness that he lost sight of the light above and felt the only way forward was to hasten going under. Surely one of a parent's greatest griefs is to see their children hurt. At whom do we rage? I believe the answer is we don't rage at all, we weep. God holds the wreckage of our hearts and heads in strong, secure hands that do not falter or fail. There we cry and rest, and let healing come.

How interesting and utterly human that I would spend a good part of the day avoiding the one place where I might find sustaining comfort. What is so terrifying about surrender, I wonder? Is it simply the posture of presumed weakness or the flood of emotion? Neither is such a monster, especially when I consider the behemoths of pride and emotional sterility. And why would hiding from God seem at all secure? It is an irony to think we find strength in maintaining a tight stillness when such rigidity leaves us brittle and ultimately vulnerable. It is only in the soft, supple care of the One who wrote our names in the book of life before we were in our mothers' wombs that we are safe. I, too, can't be helped if I don't want to be. I can hold tight and brace against love, or I can give in to the wave and be safe within its folds.

Chapter 10
Hope is a Waking Dream[1]

Abundance of What?

It has been an encouraging week. We were given OT strategies to help Michael with initiating eating and we also made good discoveries in the speech department. Up until now we weren't sure if his impediment was due solely to coordination difficulties and muscular weakness or to verbal apraxia.

Apraxia is an inability to perform purposeful movements on demand and brain injury is one of its many geneses. Due to neurological damage, a person may be able to say a word correctly one time but be unable to articulate it the next, thus making treatment difficult. Muscular weakness and lack of coordination, however, respond well to measured practice as well as time in recovery. We are now seeing that Michael can make consistent improvements in the weak areas of his speech which have thus far been resistant to change, particularly nasality and clarity (speed is apparently the last thing to come). This was good news.

I was interested to learn about apraxia because it gave me a word to explain what I heard in Craig all those months ago on the plane (see Chapter 4). I couldn't figure out why his speech was clear one minute and indecipherable the next. I thought maybe he just grew lazy or was inconsistently attentive. Now I understand better. So many brain injury behaviors appear purposeful at first glance, as if the patient is being willfully stubborn, lazy or unresponsive. I am learning

164

much about the complicated issues underlying many manifestations.

We are also encouraged by the changes in Michael's cognitive skills. One area showing improvement is categorical thinking. For instance, if a person were asked to name the states of the USA, he typically might use a strategy such as visualizing a map, thinking alphabetically, or grouping red and blue states in his mind to generate as many as possible. Brain injury tends to sever these types of connections, leaving items in a given category floating unattached to one another and thus more difficult to accumulate. Recovery exercises help re-forge the pathways, making leaps from one item to the next more accessible. Michael took a category test a month ago and again this past week and the scores are moving steadily in the right direction. The progress isn't obvious, especially to him, but as we continue in the long, slow, climb of recovery, it is good to note and celebrate benchmarks along the way.

I find myself wondering about what types of mental skills Michael will have when his recovery reaches a plateau. Will he think analytically in any sort of deep or probing way? I remember a parent/teacher conference a year ago with his English teacher who mentioned that Michael always made intelligent and insightful contributions to discussions. I have always valued intellectual pursuits and have hoped my children might do the same. Both of them have plenty of natural ability, though they have performed at varying levels over time. I recently learned from a colleague that current research demonstrates that the measure of students' success in school is much more closely related to their inclination to please people than to their intellectual faculties. Michael has never been much of a people pleaser (probably a gross understatement).

In light of Michael's current abilities as well as my own reflections on achievement, academic and otherwise, I find myself thinking about what is important and why, which causes me to reexamine what I wish for my children. I remember a friend of mine saying long ago, maybe 25 years or more, "I just hope my children grow up to be good people." I can honestly say I now see more potential for goodness in Michael than I did during his recent drug and alcohol using days. But beyond the question of being "good," which I assume would include behaviors such as being kind and making meaningful contributions to society, what qualities will sustain them through life?

I recently listened to a woman speak on the topic of abundance. She mentioned that many of our minds readily turn to finances when we consider areas we'd like to increase, but she astutely noted that even if we suddenly have more money we still have the same personalities. I had never heard it put quite that way before. She went on to say that if I am a person who visits perfectionist tendencies on myself and the world around me, thus necessarily always focusing on what is lacking, I will still be caught in that same judgmental and limiting quagmire no matter how wealthy I may become. Likewise, if I am a person given to joy and generosity, I will continue that way regardless of the size of my stock portfolio. If we are inclined to melancholy or negativism or anger or silliness or compassion, those qualities will likely continue whether or not we realize our new year's resolutions. She encouraged us to think about abundance in terms of who we are: people who experience more joy, generosity, love, and spiritual depth.

I wonder what ultimately will be abundant in Michael's life. Likely it won't be intellectual pursuit and discourse, but at this point it looks like it may not be toxic criticism and negativity, either. Craig certainly had physical and mental challenges, but he was an undeniably joyful person. So I wonder if my parental aspirations are on target. Am I primarily concerned with how the world sees my children, which, if I'm honest, is more about self-concern than regard for them, or do I hope for a beautiful and generous lens through which they might view life? In the end we are not sustained so much by how people see us as by how we see the world. It is not what goes in that defiles, Jesus said, but what comes out.[2]

On the occasions in prayer when God has blessed me with an encounter with what I have come to know as my soul, I am always astounded at her joy and vivaciousness. She is a being of great wonder, exuberance and love, fully unbounded by earthly concern. She is (I am?) always the same. When I look through her eyes at people around me, I see as she sees: past another person's (or my) pain or limitation to his or her ultimate goodness and abundance. While I can't begin to live consistently from such a perspective, I know we are all capable of more frequent visions such as this, because each of us holds within us the same rich store. No one person is special or set apart in this regard. The particulars of our treasure trove may be different, but every one of us is infinitely beautiful and free because we are all made of the same substance, which is ultimately one of love. Surely the soul is a window through which we see clearly, a vantage point of the collective, egoless "I am" that is holy rather than the small and limiting views of our individual personalities. My glimpses tend to be partial and brief, but this doesn't limit them in truth. Heaven is both already and not yet, and I am so grateful for God's generous sharing of already. This would be my truest hope for my children and all of us: that we might have both the abundant vision and experience of God's love, however God might choose to manifest, whether in brilliant intelligence, compassionate service, quiet contentment, or unbounded joy.

Off the Ladder and into the Dark

This morning Michael stood just inside the bathroom door for about six or seven minutes. He didn't turn on the light, didn't move further in or back out. He just stood there, occasionally glancing in the dim, grey mirror, sometimes looking out toward me in the kitchen. I've come to recognize this particular stall, so I said to him, "Are you working up to it?" He smiled and said, "Yep." He was going to have a shower, and he seemed clear about that, so the hesitation wasn't due to lack of a decision. It was just that initiation piece again. Even when a decision has been made, setting it in motion seems to require a Herculean mental effort on his part. Eventually he made it all the way into the bathroom, closed the door, and a minute or so later, on came the water.

According to one of his therapists, he's no longer allowed to answer, "I don't know" to questions. This default is a reflexive response to almost every inquiry. But, given time, his brain will actually dig up and bring forth a real answer. Getting to that information requires a fair amount of time and thought on his part, but he eventually arrives. Just like the shower.

Yesterday we worked on simple multiplication and division problems: 48 times 7, 69 divided by 3, stuff like that. Michael didn't remember how to do any of it, but after I walked him through a few problems his brain reformed a groove fairly quickly. I'm sure he'd need another reminder today of how multiplication works, but I also see that a more secure grasp isn't too far off. If I weren't reading so many informative books on brain injury I'd be more freaked out about all of the knowledge he's lost. But so many of the situations I read about are so much worse: a neuro-anatomist who has to relearn what "edge" means in reference to a puzzle piece, for crying out loud, or a woman who is still incontinent and on a feeding tube upon release from rehab, or the patients who spend weeks in comas. I see that already we have it pretty good. And without exception each of the people in the books made amazing recoveries, both of knowledge and ability. Where they were right then was not where they were to be. It took time.

I'm reading my third brain injury book: *Brain, Heal*

Thyself. It is written by a woman whose friend suffered a massive aneurism. The two of them met in AA, and the author becomes the caregiver for her friend. It is interesting to watch her apply the twelve steps to both her daily tasks and her recurring fears. At one point, when the friend is still in a coma in the hospital and the "what ifs?" are having a heyday with her anxieties, she tells her sponsor something like, "I don't think I can do this. I can't take care of a vegetable the rest of my life," to which her sponsor replies, "How long have you been in this program? Are you taking care of a vegetable today? How do you know what God's plan for you is? Your life is none of your business!"

Well put, and to the point. It made me laugh. And still I see that alcoholics and al-anonics are different in some basic ways. The old joke about al-anons is that our tombstones could read, "She's Finally Minding her Own Business" because we tend to be chronic worriers and fixers of others. So when we spiral onto the mental hamster wheel, we can help ourselves off by focusing on ourselves instead of the problems and issues of those around us. Otherwise we might suffocate people with help. AA members typically have to exit their spiral by looking outside themselves and doing something for someone else. The issues are flip sides of the same coin, but I have to say when I read the line "Your life is none of your business," it reminded me of how many things we all pick up, carry, and rent-to-own which do not belong to us, including ours and everybody else's futures. Honestly, I've learned so many life skills in Al-Anon I feel it is a program that could benefit anyone, whether or not they qualify by being "bothered by someone's drinking."

My home group's meeting topics this week are "Take what you like and leave the rest" and "The God of our understanding." While all 12-step programs are spiritually based, no one there ever tells another what to believe. In fact, we're expressly forbidden to talk about non-program agendas. This makes for great harmony, because the things that divide people never make it to the table. How often, when someone shares an opinion, point of view, or statement of faith, do we feel the need to draw the lines, to mentally note where we agree and where we feel they are wrong? How often do we think, "This is how I would do it or say it," or simply dismiss another's perspective or faith as invalid, inferior or downright intolerable because it doesn't fit with our understanding? Whether we voice our opinion out loud or not isn't the issue. It's the life of the inner critic, the need to be right, that's so wearying. This reflexive judging is the age-old need of the ego to define itself in relationship to others, and as someone recently pointed out, there just isn't much room on any given rung of the ladder for a crowd. Everyone else always ends up above or below.

One of the beauties of Al-Anon is that the only thing we agree on is that alcohol has made our lives unmanageable and that we need God to help us out of that chaos. Of course, over time we come to see that all kinds of things make our lives unmanageable—brain injuries, for instance, or recessions or broken relationships or a thousand other life surprises—and we need God to help us sort out all kinds of confusion. Then we are blessed to be able to "practice the principles we learn in all of our affairs."[3] One of those principles is the blessed neutrality of taking what we like and leaving the rest. I may be completely inspired by one member's sharing and totally put off by another's, but I am not asked to buy into everyone's opinions. When are we ever, really? And yet we continually invest so much daily energy in either refuting or supporting another's position. Why is it so difficult just to let howling dogs lie?

I've often thought I could never be a courtroom judge because I'd have such a difficult time making a final pronouncement. What if I was wrong? What if there was something I failed to consider? I'd wonder who made me God, even in this authorized, limited arena. We have a little magnet on the fridge that describes both Rob and me fairly well, though thankfully we're plagued with this predicament primarily in our personal rather than professional lives. It's an ape putting his hand to his forehead, exclaiming in dismay, "I used to be indecisive, but now I'm just not sure!"

So Michael has my sympathies. I figure he can stand in the bathroom doorway in the dark for as long as he needs. Since I tend to vacillate between snap, ladder-placement judgments and paralyzing considerations, perhaps a measured, directional approach isn't so bad after all.

P.S. Michael just listened in as I read this entry to Rob, smiling and chuckling at the parts about his indecision. That boy knows how to laugh at himself. Earlier today I told him one of the things God has given him through this ordeal is joy, amazing as that may seem. It brings to mind a phrase Rob is fond of sharing: *The reason angels can fly is because they take themselves so lightly.*

Mind You

The human brain surely is a fascinating thing. Michael's testing was completed this morning and it is so interesting to see more clearly his post injury assets as well as a more specific picture of his holes. He has lost IQ, not an uncommon effect, but he has retained the ability to process and relearn things. A psychologist friend of mine told me this means his chances of regaining the IQ points are strong. Apparently an inability to process can make retrieving intelligence more challenging. Yesterday in OT we talked about abstract reasoning, an area of weakness. When pressed to take a guess at what "abstract thinking" meant (after first answering with the forbidden "I don't know"), he came up with "thinking outside the box." When challenged further to describe "thinking outside the box," he eventually offered an apt description, which I no longer recall. What initially appears to be an absence of ability might be more accurately interpreted as a reduction in pace when his brain is given time to get there. Granted, he doesn't get all the way to the "there" he used to claim, but still I am encouraged that he can find his way eventually.

One hopeful marker is that his reading skills are fully intact. He's lost vocabulary, but this is a relatively easily batch of information to retrieve, given time. I can see that the challenge of his education team will be to pinpoint and address the holes. He'll need basic relearning in some areas but not in others, and I'm guessing he may progress fairly quickly. I feel encouraged today.

I learned from one of my brain injury books that it is important to surround myself with optimists regarding his recovery. The word from my psychologist friend was so helpful, another timely drop of encouragement from God's well of supply. I regularly tell Michael that he'll make it back to college one day, that he'll drive again and meet his goals. Why should we believe otherwise?

Brain, Heal Thyself is teaching me about appealing to the subconscious mind to assist recovery. The strategy suggested is a combination of advertising and 12-step techniques, and one aspect includes using visual aids. Advertisers do this all the time, presenting images of our subconscious desires (beauty, security, wealth, power) and then pairing the images with their product. Apparently the technique works, else we wouldn't be bombarded with its manifestations day-in and day-out. So my ideas ran something like this: Last summer, the day that a friend of Michael's was killed in an auto accident, Rob saw him having a seriously bad day and offered to let him drive his cherished classic BMW M3 convertible to cheer him up. As we picked Michael up from some time with friends, Rob got out of the car and said, "You've had a really tough day. Why don't you drive?" handing him the keys. Michael, recognizing the obvious joke (he was 16 at the time), said, "Yeah, right," and headed toward the back seat. When Rob countered, "No, really," Michael's face lit up in a combination of disbelief and excited anticipation. Mind you, Rob's own daughters were never given the opportunity to drive this car, and for my part, I knew our relationship had turned a corner the day he first handed me the keys. I recall there was another extenuating circumstance that day as well, which, oddly enough, also involved the end of someone's life. So this was a big deal, and we took a picture of Michael at the wheel. I plan to pair that picture on a poster with the checklist of tasks on his daily list that are meant to help him return to driving, a sort of "Dual Attention Exercises = Picture of Michael in the Beemer" message. Another poster may include a picture of him partying with his friends (he has several of those tucked away on his computer) next to a big equal sign and then another picture of him lying lifeless hooked up to the ventilator at the hospital. A third poster might include a picture of him in his cap and gown at the graduation ceremony after he completed his GED next to a list of OT or ST exercises, anything to pair the particulars in the present with the goals for the future in his subconscious store.

Tonight we're off to watch a friend of his play in a high school basketball game. Michael has put on his chain necklace and pierced crystal stud earrings for the outing. He may not recall what "a rolling stone gathers no moss" means, but he knows what it means to dress for a night at the game.

Karmic Revolution of Grace

"The measure you give will be the measure you receive."[4] These words make sense to me on an intuitive level, and along with "Cast your bread on the waters for it will return to you,"[5] they are as close as the Bible comes to preaching karma. As I think on the message, though, I am struck by how much we tend to think of equal measure as situationally specific: This person should care for me as much as I care for them. A dollar's worth of investment should yield a dollar's worth of goods. Tit for tat. I scratch your back, you scratch mine.

But the heavenly flow of grace doesn't seem nearly that tidy or particular to me. For instance, right now we are on the receiving end of a huge imbalance through our health insurance coverage. Michael's medical bills well exceed $100,000 and the vast majority of those costs will be paid by Blue Cross Blue Shield. How many years would I need to pay his monthly premium for the insurance company to recoup their expense? The answer, of course, is that it doesn't add up. Insurance is a shared risk venture and we are currently receiving the benefit of the "shared" part to Michael's "risk." Thus some of us receive help with bills we could never hope to pay, while others make premium payments for years without cashing in on their value.

What strikes me is that, much like insurance, life is a shared risk venture, but a risk in one area doesn't mean a return in the same. I believe it was Teresa of Avila who said that she felt she should always patiently and humbly bear a wrongful accusation because she had committed countless other errors or injustices which had gone unnoticed. She never felt entitled to righteous indignation in the overall scheme of things. I think of how Michael and our family received and continue to receive hundreds of prayers, prayers that we will never be able to repay one for another. These prayers infused a bleak situation with life and hope. I find myself with an urge to say "Thank you!" to each of those pray-ers, though I don't even know who they all are, and I surely would be hard-pressed to pray in return for all of the specific needs in each person's life. I also feel inclined to thank the thousands of others subscribers to Blue Cross whose investment in shared risk gave my son the care that saved his life.

Kenya comes readily to mind when I think of what a society looks like without investment in social and shared risk services. There, health insurance for an entire family costs $11 a year, but almost none can afford it. Often getting sick simply means dying. A situation like Michael's, in most places in Kenya, would have meant certain death. And of course many Kenyans don't deal in currency at all. They barter and exchange goods and services, or the miniscule amount they collect goes immediately for their daily bread. I will never forget the little boy walking several miles to town holding a single sheet of paper in hopes of selling it so that his family might have something to eat that evening, perhaps a yam or piece of field corn to share.

While we may have woes in our health care system, I believe it is important to regularly offer gratitude for what we have. And of course I am one of the fortunate ones who can afford to buy insurance policies for my children, so I have even less room to complain. "Don't talk with your mouth full," Rob's mom would have responded to complaints about problems in our culture or government as they emerged from the mouths of some of the most richly blessed people in the world.

I believe we are blessed in life even when situations or relationships are unequal, perhaps especially when they are so. How often do we truly receive the same amount of care and love as we give to someone else? If we are very lucky, we may find such a relationship with a spouse or very close friend. But even those very healthy and balanced relationships often slip out of equilibrium when job, health or personal concerns make one person the primary giver and the other the receiver. If we are waiting for matching income and expenditure columns in any specific situation, whether the lines are mental, emotional or financial, we may wait a very long time.

A better option seems to me to give and receive graciously without keeping score. Why, for instance, should a parent continue loving an addict who has given them nothing but grief? Is it out of a belief that one day the addict will come to their senses and turn the karmic spinning wheel the other direction and finally even the playing field by giving generously to the one who has loved them through their extended scourge of selfishness? I don't believe that's why. We keep giving, loving and hoping because it is what we do and because it is the right thing to do. And, if we are honest, we really can't help ourselves. Loving always seems better to me than the small, suffocating alternative. I don't suggest that we should repeatedly set ourselves up to be victimized, abused or used. That wouldn't be loving. I do believe we should give without strings attached, and be willing to receive when someone gives to us the same in kind.

God has been gracious with this daily manna in our lives lately. I can't begin to tally the number of times a bill has arrived and within a day some source of income or gift appeared which literally matched the amount due. Countless words of encouragement have shown up when they were needed the most. One of these recently came from my brother, who has borne a lifelong struggle with addiction. For years I didn't know if he would survive, and once when I was on the phone with the police in his hometown in Colorado, frantically asking if they'd found any unidentified bodies in ditches, I realized I had reached the point at which I had to detach and turn away. I couldn't take the pain of loving up close any more, so I quietly removed myself emotionally and vowed to pray and hope for him at a safe distance with no personal contact. When he figuratively came back to life a few years later it was a prodigal story of such inspirational and profound proportions that I wished I had my own great big fatted calf with which to celebrate.[6] So when on the phone the other day he mentioned that he can now envision the day when he will no longer battle the addictive demon, I felt humbled to my knees by the grace of God. I really never thought he'd make it, and now his spiritual light is shining so brightly he runs the risk of singeing anyone within his immediate vicinity. He said that the urges to use are still there but they are so faint and weakened by the spiritual substance that grows stronger every day that he can now anticipate a time when the one will fully cancel out the other. That word came to me on a day when I felt deeply discouraged about Michael's battle with substance abuse.

There have been so many other instances of timely encouragement. My only response can be one of gratitude and praise to God for such blessing and generosity. The abundance inspires me to give what I have without attachment to effect or outcome. I am learning yet again that the point is to give freely and fully, whatever we have to give.

In Kenya we gave a sewing machine to a woman whose house had burned down. When she tried to thank us she couldn't speak for several minutes. She was beyond words, as she would have had to save her shillings for years and years to buy another one. We also built a home for a family of AIDS orphans. Through our labor and the generous giving of people here at home we gave them a gift they could never have procured by their own efforts and can never repay. Rob's CPR, your prayers, and the hospital's care gave Michael his life (and, of course, the angel who held him up). We can say, "These are good things and we are grateful," but I think it matters that we take it a step further. I prefer to call the service we offered in Kenya and the miracles we have received here Grace. Grace gave the orphans a home. Grace gave Frida a sewing machine. Grace arrived in the forms of timely donations and encouragement. And Grace gave Michael his life. One might say this is just a matter of semantics, that we may call it what we like. But that would discount the power we reveal in claiming and naming the grace of God. Faith activates God in our lives and grace is one of God's most beautiful manifestations. I hope always to see it more clearly. As I sat between Michael and Rob at Natalie's concert at the university last night, I was struck again with profound gratitude for both of them: the one that helped give the other life and the one who is on the receiving end of a gift he can never repay. But Michael can offer what he has in countless other ways, and like each of us, that is more than equal measure. By the grace of God, it is enough.

The Times, They are A-Changin'[7]

It's time for a progress report. Next week brings transition, so I'm pausing to take a look back at where we've been as well as to survey the road ahead. Yesterday in therapy Michael listened to a recording of his speaking voice made on November 2nd when he was in residential rehab. Hearing the recording was a great encouragement for him as he regularly tells us he can't discern any improvement in his speech because he has no memory of what it was before. But he could readily hear the difference between that tape and another made on December 31st. In fact he was amazed at the change. Hurray!

I am reminded I need to provide him with audible and visual benchmarks of his recovery so that he can experience the encouragement the rest of us feel.

I recall that when he was discharged from in-patient rehabilitation his OT suggested that an optimistic educational goal might be one class per day in January. Michael has been doing two thus far and appears ready for more. He's been tracking and rating his mental and physical fatigue every morning and afternoon so that we might get a picture of his stamina. Both challenge and rest are equally vital components of recovery. The fatigue levels are improving rather than declining, which tells us that he may be able to handle three classes in another week or two. This is nothing short of amazing. Even though his progress is slower now than during the first dramatic weeks, it still exceeds the expected pace of recovery. His OT will put him through the driving assessment test later this week, checking areas such as reflexive response time and dual attention levels. The fact that he's even taking this step blows me away. I said, "Michael, that you could go from dead to driving in a matter of a few months astounds me." He liked that.

I'll meet with Michael's educational assessment team on Tuesday of next week to receive a report on his testing and to synthesize his educational plan. I find myself excited about the meeting, not because I'll hear about what he's lost since

October 11 but because I can see such gains since October 12. This will be where we lay out the road map for the next part of the journey. Perhaps most importantly, I know he feels optimistic about his future. I am continually amazed that he is undaunted by his cognitive limitations. He is where he is and plans to be beyond it in the future. What a wonderful attitude.

The big, anxiety producing "what if?" in my mind is considering Michael's increasing freedom to explore social relationships. Interestingly, he is still avoiding them for the most part. In fact he immediately blushes a bright red whenever he comes into contact with his peers (he's had a couple of coincidental encounters this past week). He said he doesn't know why he feels shy and embarrassed, but there it is. I see the blushing and accompanying bashfulness as strong and welcome deterrents to pursing old, destructive friendships with drug-using friends. It's as though God has given him a little protective impulse to inhibit the magnetic attraction he has always held for those who use. Granted, the impulse is non-discriminating and affects all of his relationships right now, but until he gets his sea legs back in the social ocean, I'm thankful for a slow and cautious testing of the waters.

I've been thinking about ways for Michael to give back or pay it forward. Tonight he's working on a letter to Jeff Tiner, the death row inmate who began praying for him in the early days after his injury and who wrote him. I hope he'll continue the correspondence. Michael and I spoke again yesterday about how he and God seemed to decide rather specifically that his time on earth wasn't finished and that he had more to do here. I told him that the two of them will have to figure out together what that "more" looks like, what his purpose and gifts are to share. He nodded, seeming pleased at the thought of his whole life lying before him like a present: hidden, full of potential, and wrapped in a second chance.

Hey Jeff.

Deacon Allen gave you my name and you prayed for me because I hung myself. I just wanted to say thank you for praying for me and for the picture you drew and, well everything. My recovery is moving along pretty quickly is what I'm told, although to me it feels like it's going slowly. One of the things I've noticed was affected is my ability to keep a conversation going or just knowing what to say in general, so this letter may be very short.

– Michael

Holes

I learned something from the letter Michael wrote to Jeff. I have noticed how quiet he is most of the time, answering questions with one word or minimally developed sentences. The thing I didn't realize was Michael's awareness of the change in his conversation. The good news is he can expand and articulate conversation upon request, but not without a good deal of encouragement and prodding.

So I've added dialogue to his list of therapy exercises. He has to both initiate and respond to conversation. We vary the routine by pretending I'm one of his various buddies, and what would he say to me if I were so-and-so. It is challenging for him, so we've had to brainstorm a list of conversational starting points. These could be a particular friend's interests (golf, basketball, a boyfriend) or something more general like movies, music, or pop-culture trends. The interesting thing is Michael can't remember anything that he and his friends ever talked about before. Granted, this could be because much of the conversation wasn't very memorable, but how do you rehabilitate a person into bantering about nothing?

Finding the holes continues to be a fascinating exploration, and just as interesting is discovering the "wholes," or extant areas in his brain. For instance, he took the general knowledge portion of the driving assessment in OT last week, receiving a near perfect score. This portion included recognizing and understanding signs as well as written navigation of very specific traffic situations with complicated diagrams and "what would you do here?" questions. Michael always loved driving and clearly values it, and that information has survived. He has yet to test on the divided attention, reflexive response and vision portions, but it sure was encouraging to see both his common sense and informational store intact. How far he is from putting that information into practical use in real time remains to be seen.

He's had more mixed success on some other common tasks he's encountered. Today I had him mail two packages through the automated postal center at the post office. I stood by and let him work his way through, and it turns out the most difficult juncture was getting started. He didn't remember (or ever know?) that packages have to be weighed to determine postage. A pre-brain-injury Michael would have figured this out from the set-up at hand, but post-injury Michael stood and looked at the collection of surfaces and screens with no idea how to proceed. Once he got going he was fine, and by the second package he was moving along seamlessly. But who could have guessed he wouldn't know mailing packages involved a scale, or that you couldn't put both items on the scale at once? Or who could have known that when the orthodontic assistant told him he could rinse his mouth after having a mold made for a new retainer he would swallow the water after swishing, not realizing the point was to spit out the particles of goop? And who knew he *would* remember what "plagiarized" meant and also that he did it (with an ornery twinkle in his eye) when providing a written answer for his OT on what causes earthquakes? Sometimes I can't keep up with what needs re-learning and what doesn't. There are no predictable patterns or categories to map what is in or out of his brain, or if there are, I haven't figured them out yet. Rather, we respond to each blank spot as it appears. Holes here, retainers there, and the package is in the mail.

Straight Street

It was a dark and stormy night ... just kidding. Well, it *was* dark and windy last night, which meant that this morning there was trash all over the street. Rob found it as he headed out to work and returned briefly to report that the lid on our big blue recycling bin had blown open and papers were strewn about. So I announced to Michael that for his daily morning chore we would clean up the street.

I had no idea trash was so recognizable, or rather not. Michael and I headed in opposite directions and both knew within picking up two pieces each that the trash wasn't ours. I guess garbage is more personal than I thought, which makes sense. It just looks so impersonal and anonymous when jammed into bushes and clogging gutters. We didn't know whose mess this was, but we knew it wasn't ours. But there we were, the debris was an eyesore and we had the time, so we finished the job.

Michael continues to have a pleasant, helpful attitude about almost everything, even about picking up someone else's garbage. Previously he would have balked with indignation upon discovering the mess wasn't ours, as if the deal was only valid according to the original parameters and now that the contract had changed he should be off the hook. But he's different now. He plugged along without complaining, scraping up wet newspapers and even soggy Kleenexes from the street. After about 20 minutes, as we were finishing up, one of our neighbors came out to retrieve his recycling bin saying, "Wow, what a mess, huh?" I was happy for the conversation, relieved even, because we were caught in the act. You see, about a year and a half ago we had a falling out with almost every neighbor in our area, save one who never gave up on Michael or us, and probably some others who were blissfully unaware of our circumstance. Michael and some friends had visited crime on nearby properties when drunk, and we were quietly shunned for a long while after. Folks who previously held pleasant, neighborly dialogue with us now looked the other way in silence. It was awkward, to say the least. I found myself wanting to mount a defense, to say, "We're not bad people! I understand how you feel, and I wouldn't want my son living on my street if I were you, either, but that doesn't mean *we're* bad!" But there was nothing to say, really. It's difficult to apologize in general for something you didn't personally do. It's awkward to explain that you didn't raise your child to be a criminal while crossing paths on the way to the mailbox.

Anyone who loves an addict eventually learns there is nothing you can or can't do to prevent him or her from using, nor can you avoid all the havoc that comes in its wake. We call it the three C's: We didn't cause it, we can't cure it and we can't control it. But that doesn't mean we don't suffer when the addicts in our lives visit their malady on others and us, and Michael's offenses had been serious. Couple our neighbors' unhappiness with my self-consciousness about Michael's behavior, and it was an icy scene. So we went quietly on through those months, walking our dogs or working in the yard, silently stomaching people's suspicion and judgment.

Which was why the sidewalk conversation today was so good. It was normal, quick and easy, and it seemed to signal we were no longer the pariahs on the block. I answered, probably a little too quickly, "Yes, we thought this was ours but it isn't. Oh well, it looks better now!" I knew I cheapened our effort by highlighting our good scout behavior, but I couldn't help myself. There was redemption on the rise, and I wanted to bask in it just a bit.

On the way back into our house I explained to Michael how this had been a neighbor who formerly wouldn't speak to us because of Michael's illegal activities that one summer night. I told him how ashamed I'd felt, how almost everyone quit speaking to us, and how we no longer went to the neighborhood ice cream social or Christmas tree lighting because it was too awkward. "But that part is over now. And not only that, we've done our good deed for the day, haven't we, Michael?" Understanding he had moved from bandit to good Samaritan, basking in the glow a bit himself, he looked at me with a big, closed mouth grin, and nodded, "Mm hm."

Chapter 11
High Life, Low Life

The Promise of Living

Michael passed the rest of his driving assessment today. He was well within range in all categories. Apparently patients with much lower scores than his are cleared to drive. His wallet was lost the night of his incident, so after an intervening trip to the DMV he'll be on the road again. I can hardly believe it.

One area that showed great improvement on the test today was depth perception. His vision was tested when he began outpatient therapy and his depth perception was dismal, almost non-existent. Now it is completely normal. I told Rob that watching the miracle of his recovery almost compensates for some of the suffering last fall. Every week we receive surprises in the form of recovered abilities. It's like a birthday that goes on and on. Michael was *so* cute this evening upon arriving home with his news. He was radiating happiness and excitement, beaming from ear to ear—for a long, long while.

Michael has had a good week. He was approved for special education services on Tuesday, which means he'll receive the benefit of that structure and support at school. I thought the picture that the district psychologist painted of Michael's strengths and weaknesses was astounding in both depth and accuracy. The thorough testing and analysis offered us a good roadmap by which to proceed, and already he has begun the journey. Yesterday he dropped one class from his schedule, replacing it with another, more demanding one. He added one other, bringing his total to three per day. I recall that when he was discharged from in-patient rehab in November, we were given an optimistic estimate of one class per day come January. Yet again, Michael is moving through recovery faster than anticipated. I feel like leaping around!

Because, in addition to the wonderful news for Michael, all of this means I have been able to resume my full load at the university. It has been so good to be back teaching voice lessons and conducting rehearsals, connecting with students and colleagues. I feel my job is a meaningful, good fit for me, and I'm thankful.

As I drove to pick Michael up at Chemeketa yesterday I headed smack into one of the brightest rainbows I have ever seen. The eastern sky before me was a deep, dark gray and the sun behind was blazing low. The resulting huge column of color standing in front of the massive black shadow of clouds was so brilliant I could hardly bear to look at it. And it lasted and lasted and lasted. I gratefully received the blessing of this symbol of hope and promise, remembering our saying that "Every day that is a good day is a *good* day."

> The promise of living
> With hope and thanksgiving
> Is born of our loving
> Our friends and our labor.
>
> The promise of growing
> With faith and with knowing
> Is born of our sharing
> Our love with our neighbor.
>
> The promise of loving
> The promise of growing
> Is born of our singing
> In joy and thanksgiving.
> – Horace Everett[1]

Humble Thyself in the Sight of the Lord (Or Someone Else May Do it for You)

I remember when Michael first walked again. He was off-kilter, fairly weak, and tended to career around his room and down the halls of the hospital. "Slow down, Michael, not so fast!" was a mantra. It was as though he had no inner brake to regulate his speed. I used to wonder where he was going in such a hurry. And of course it wasn't about where he was going at all but simply that he was on the move. He apparently liked being in gear, but unfortunately his brain was always a few clicks behind his body.

Well, today I discovered Michael's driving is much like his early walking. He doesn't speed, exactly, but he does career around as though his foot is a little unfamiliar with the brake pedal. To his credit, he didn't endanger anyone on his first venture out. He stopped immediately at a yellow light, and made it safely to and from our destination. But his driving isn't quite right yet. His brain lags behind his truck the way it used to trail his body.

So I told him he's not cleared to drive alone yet, and that we'll add driving practice sessions to our daily list. Though he's been very eager to return to driving to school by himself, he answered in his usual sweet and compliant way: "Okay." I thought of how disappointed he must feel. It's hard on a boy's ego to see his former freewheeling independence remain just beyond reach. And as if to add insult to injury, when we were sitting in Dairy Queen, our destination of celebration for returning to the driving world, in walked a friend of his with a girlfriend in tow. This friend had been one of Michael's closest, and he warmly greeted Michael with the usual hand sign/handshake ritual and a gentle, "How are you, man?" Michael answered briefly while blushing and then sent out the silent but clear signal that he didn't have much else to say. Watching the awkward conversation, I thought of another hit his ego was taking just then: he was at the DQ with his mom. He pulled his keys out of his pocket and set them on

187

the table, a gesture surely intended to let his friend know he was back at the wheel. Without words he managed to communicate, "I may be sitting here with my mom, but at least I drove her down here!"

Michael has taken lots of ego hits. He has a speech impediment. He is slow in conversation, mentally as well as physically, and he doesn't come up with any clever or cool things to say. He no longer has a girlfriend. He can't drive by himself. I think he is brave to be carrying on so well.

As I considered the mantle of humility imposed on Michael, I realized my ego suffered a little bruising today, too. I set myself up for it perfectly last night with a quiet, prideful moment. I was reading a section in a book about envy. The author was describing how destructive envy is, how it can consume us once we are in its grip. She asked us to think about who or what we envy and why, and how we feel toward the objects of our envy. I thought, "Gosh, I don't really have a lot of problems with envy. I think I'm fairly envy-free most of the time." That little prideful puff set me up for a thorough thumping into humility today. It came in the form of recital program notes where a student gave greater recognition and thanks to another teacher with whom she studied for two months than she did to me when I had instructed her for more than three years. While I wasn't feeling envy so much as wounded pride, my less-than-humble thoughts about envy surely set me up to be reminded of how much I have to learn about humility.

It is easy to look at a disabled person and feel superior, to notice the things that we have that they lack, to realize the abundance of our normalcy next to their oddities. It is easy to look at anyone this way. And we are wrong when we see this way. *I* am wrong when I see this way. I am wrong when I place others below or above me on the ladder. I have found that almost every time I feel the chaffing, vulnerable edge of superiority I am poised for a swift return to the painful but welcoming softness and safety of humility.

Michael used to scoff at the kids who rode the "short bus," i.e. the one for special education kids. Now he's scheduled to ride one. Life whittles each of us down to size in our own special way. I have to confess I am always sort of relieved when I am delivered from an indulgence in pride. I'm not sure why pride is so uncomfortable, even when it feels satisfying in a shallow, temporary way. Arrogance is instinctively violating to the spirit, I suppose. I am thankful for this recognition, and for opportunities to learn. Pride goeth before my falls[2] over and over again, but at least I'm familiar with the warp and woof. I'm praying toward the day when I'm content not to climb the ladder at all, when it no longer holds a draw, and eventually disappears from the landscape completely, when my lion lies down with my lamb without appetite, by the grace of God.

Dear Jeff,

My name is Christine, and I am Michael's mom. I believe Deacon Allen shared Michael's recent letter with you. I, too, appreciate your prayers for him, as well as your writings and artwork that Allen has shared. Thank you for your powerful witness in God's name.

I'm writing to see if Michael and I might be able to visit/meet you sometime. I know Michael would like to do that. I'm not sure if he'll be approved on a visitor's list as he has a juvenile record, but we'd like to try. He's a minor so I understand he'd probably need to be accompanied by a parent. Allen has mentioned we'd need to fill out a form. If you are interested, you can mail it to us.

On another note of interest, I also know your friend Sheila. Her best friend Barbara is a good friend of mine. Barbara shared our blog with Sheila who then surmised that the death row inmate she was reading about must be you. Sheila and I had a wonderful conversation a few weeks back where she told me your conversion story as well as more about the project you spearheaded in Darfur. We were amazed by the connections and synchronicities and especially by the power of God's grace. She is a neat lady.

Thank you for your prayers for Michael and for us. He's come a long way, and his recovery will continue for a while more. Given how long his brain was without oxygen, he really shouldn't have survived, medically speaking, and if he did he shouldn't have been much more than a vegetable. But, as Allen said, doctors often underestimate the God factor. Michael is here today by the grace of God, and while he isn't the person he was before (both for better and for worse), he is alive and has a second chance. I can't help but think that he and God decided he had more to do on earth, because he was really gone there for a while. It would have been a hard, hard way to lose him, to the finality of suicide. Every day is a gift.

Blessings to you and to your ministry through prayer.

In Christ,
Christine Elder

Love Hurts

On our way home from school yesterday I asked Michael if he ever talks to any of his peers during the day. "Nope." I asked if that's how it was before his injury, if maybe he didn't talk to too many folks last fall and he answered, "No, I used to talk to people." Now he chooses to sit outside for lunch so he can avoid conversation. It's a catch 22: He wants more of a social life but at this point the cost in awkwardness and effort is greater than the reward of trying, so he keeps to himself.

We practiced conversation again on the way home. He had to ask me questions as if I were one of his classmates, and when I asked him a question he had to give me more than a one-sentence answer. I wondered if his lack of social interaction was as painful to him as it was becoming to me. I resolved to keep trusting in the recovery process, to continue practicing with him, drawing dialogue out of his brain which seems to hoard information and words with a miserly zeal, and to wait.

When we got home he had mail, a three-page letter from Jeff Tiner, the death row inmate. I was surprised at how positive and upbeat the letter was. It wasn't just the words, but the feeling that came with the pages through phrases like "Greetings, my brother!" or "Right on!" This was Jeff's encouragement to Michael for going to community college. I don't know how to describe it other than to say I knew right then that Michael had a new friend, and a pretty good one at that. Here are some words from Jeff's letter:

"I am really impressed with you, Michael. Clearly, God favors you for some special mission in life. He only let you stretch your neck so far, then said, 'Ok, dude. That's far enough,' (hand-drawn, bewildered smiley face goes here). We're 'birds of a feather,' tho—I had to come all the way to death row before I opened my eyes and heart to God. I'm thinkin' me and you—we're stubborn. HA HA

"It's a miracle, and wonderful, and amazing, and holy—how you've been given a great opportunity to live your life anew. I've said many, many prayers of thanks to Father God, Jesus, and the Holy Spirit for you."

Michael read the letter all the way through standing just inside the door. It came with a visitor request form that we'll fill out and send back, and the instruction to "share this letter with your mom." The approval process for visitation takes about six weeks. Jeff also included a lot of information about his "main focus" during his daily 22 hours of cell time, which is to "...aid the Canossian Daughters of Charity in Sudan and the war refugee kids they teach and care for." He included a brochure about the Bakhita Project (see the featured page at www.sainteds.com which includes the article "A Roof for Bakhita" to learn more about the project). He spoke of the issues they face including extreme poverty and high infant mortality, and he described the 700-student vocational center where girls and women are taught marketable job skills. Over 1,300 girls attend St. Francis School and Jeff has taken it on as his mission to write letters on their behalf to increase awareness and solicit prayers. Then, as he says, "God touches hearts and folks chip in and good stuff happens." The more than 4,000 missives he's written from his cell have helped to rebuild six classrooms at St. Francis School in Khartoum, among other things. All of this is from a man who was once a white supremacist.

It seems a great blessing for Michael to begin forging this unlikely friendship. I immediately felt a resistance to it, and not for the obvious reasons, but because I realized I might come to care for this man, that in some way I already do (doesn't every mom have a soft spot for those who help their kids when they're down?), and that caring could likely mean facing loss. I have to remind myself that fear of grief is never a legitimate reason not to live life fully, and it certainly doesn't excuse rejecting the love of Christ.

Later in the day another surprise friend appeared. Justin is a male acquaintance of Natalie's who decided he'd come and hang out with Michael for the evening. They watched TV and talked, and a good deal of laughter wafted up the stairs. It was a heartwarming sound.

I'm not sure who was comforted more by these two serendipitous gestures of friendship, Michael or me. I do know this is how God works in the world, through people showing up and meeting us where we are hurting or lonely or lost, one situation, one person at a time. It might not be in the way we imagine, but it is more than enough. God uses each of us the same way: nudging us and asking us to be there for one another. When I say to Michael, "God loves you," this is what I'm talking about: love with skin on that meets us where we are. Thank you, God, for Jeff and Justin and the way they tended a mother's heart and a young man's loneliness. Thank you for letting them be your hands and feet, and for asking us each to be the same.

I have found the paradox, that if you love until it hurts, there can be no more hurt, only more love. – Mother Teresa

The Knee Bone's Connected to the Thigh Bone

As I sat down to begin writing about the amazing connections we've discovered in this part of our life story, I found an e-mail from my new friend Sheila. So apparently it really is time to write about synchronistic grace!

I first spoke with Sheila a month or two ago. Up until then I'd only heard about her from Barbara who lives in Idaho. Sheila is Barbara's best friend, and Barbara had shared with her about Michael's situation, asking for prayers. Eventually Sheila began reading our postings, and when we first wrote about the death row inmate who shared his prayers and artwork with us, Sheila knew it had to be her friend Jeff. Sheila met Jeff through an editorial she and three others had written to the Oregonian newspaper urging people to come to the aid of those suffering the humanitarian crisis in Darfur. God touched Jeff's heart, which was already primed by a spiritual connection he had with that part of the world, so he contacted her to see what he might be able to do to help. They became friends through the correspondence, and eventually Jeff enlisted the aid of Deacon Allen to spearhead his fundraising efforts. "Guess what? God just made you a missionary to Sudan!" Jeff said to Allen one time when he visited, and to Allen's "eternal credit, he didn't skip a beat, just replied, 'Cool! Where do we start?'" On yet another level of connection, Rob knew Allen through a mutual encounter with congregants going through the death of a loved one whose family members were both Protestant and Roman Catholic.

As I think on this intricate and divinely engineered web, I, like Sheila, see the fingerprints of God's hand all over it. The delicate sinews and strands remind me of how infinitely bound our lives all are to one another. In the end, I think we are much closer than six degrees of separation, and these grace-filled moments of awareness point out the larger truth. Sure, we can trace the threads, as in "I, Christine, am now connected to Jeff on death row who already was connected to Michael through prayer and to Sheila through friendship, who is connected to Barbara, who is connected to me and Rob who was already connected to Allen who became reconnected with us that first night in the hospital and who already was connected to Jeff who now is connected to Christine..." But eventually we see the connection isn't linear at all but circular, or maybe a better way to say it is enmeshed. We are all enmeshed in God as the body of Christ, and the body is one. We could trace the path from any one cell in our body to another, and while it might take us longer to travel some routes than others, we would get there eventually. It reminds me that when I look at someone and see them as "other," I'm seeing what is true but also what is not. I am Christine, not Barbara or Allen or Jeff. We are each unique and glorious creations with individual gifts to give the world. But at the same time, we are all the same, no one more important than another, all of one substance with the father, bound in the grace of love. I find joy in both things—the infinite variety of each individual creation and the amazing sameness and interdependency of humanity.

Sheila told me that day we talked that one thing she learned from her encounter with Jeff was to do what you can do and not worry if it is grand or earth shaking or significant. Simply do what God gives you to do. In her case, she wrote a letter. Someone she didn't know read it and had an idea, and another agreed to help, and now thousands of girls in Sudan have benefited. As Mother Teresa said, "None of us can do great things. We can only do small things with great love." Sometimes we humans severely limit ourselves by thinking we need to be God. We weary our hearts by thinking if we can't save everyone from poverty or disease or abuse, or right every wrong or at least bring some closure to a crisis, that our efforts aren't worthwhile. I believe God sees otherwise, since eternity never arrives, never wraps up neatly at points of closure. Rob once helped me see that the biblical concept of "end time" is more accurately translated as "the fullness of time," a much more expansive rather than linear idea. Angels cheer on every good and grace-filled choice, and each selfless deed moves the world closer to Heaven. Even in the midst of an overwhelming sea of suffering, our drops of compassion matter. When we are content to be who we are: small, insignificant creatures who hold the boundless glory of all creation within us, then we can join with others in becoming a bright cascade of light, and beautiful things can happen indeed.

I've Seen Fire and I've Seen Rain

The light bulb came on. Michael has rounded the corner into dawning self-consciousness. This new bit of inner illumination changes things, because his growing awareness is of his limitations. For weeks he's gone along so evenly, happy and content. We knew this easy phase couldn't last indefinitely because the truth is there is a hard road ahead. We knew he would eventually see the road more clearly, that the landscape around and within him would come into sharper focus and he would realize just how far he has to go before his life feels like his own again. We understood that his one-dimensional, happy demeanor was due in part to a lack of comprehension of his limitations. The good news is his understanding is increasing. The bad news is this understanding discourages him.

We were told to watch for this shift, that it would come and that likely he would need help navigating it. I find myself considering mental health resources and options. Michael *really* doesn't like talking about his inner world, even more so now than before. And of course his resistance to communication ends up increasing his isolation and discouragement. But God keeps reaching out to him one invitation at a time, asking him to move out of his comfort zone toward more companionship.

An hour or so after Michael and I talked about how he's feeling, a conversation which literally caused him to break into a sweat, another young man called him to ask him to coffee in the morning. Michael resisted, making excuses about not knowing where the coffee shop was, etc., so later I found myself telling him the story of the man in the flood. The tale is familiar to youth group types, and while he'd heard it before he didn't quite remember the ending. He smiled at all of the familiar parts of the story, which goes something like this:

A massive flood was sweeping the land, so one man decided to pray to God to save him. First some neighbors came by in a vehicle that had high water clearance. They offered him a ride out and he declined saying, "No, I'm praying to God and I know God will save me." The rain continued and the water rose, turning the streets into rivers. His living room was now a lake, and more people came by, this time in a boat. "Come on! You've got to get out *now!*" they cried to him, and he said, "No, I'm staying here. I know God will hear my prayer." Finally the waters swelled so high his house was nearly covered. He took refuge on the roof, praying fervently. Along came a helicopter offering him a rope but he refused the help saying, "My trust is in God. I will be safe!" Off the helicopter went, and the waters rose, sweeping the man away to his death. Upon arriving in heaven he railed at God saying, "I believed in you! I had unwavering faith and trusted you would save me! Where were you?" God answered, "I sent you a car, a boat and a helicopter. What more did you want?"

I told Michael that God must have some pretty special consideration for him since over and over a hand of encouragement reaches out right at the very moment of his discouragement. It is as though God keeps saying, "I know this isn't easy, but you're going to make it and I'm right here with you. See? Here I am again." It seemed clear to me Michael had better reach back and take the hand rather than repeatedly opting out of salvation. But then that would be me telling Michael what he needs and how he should handle the social challenges of his brain injury recovery. Did I mention I am al-anonic?

Obviously I had a bit of work to do on myself around this issue, because my first response to Michael's discouragement was a still, throbbing anxiety mixed with grief, and close on the heels of these feelings was the urge to fix things for him. What if he heads down the dead-end road again? What if he turns to alcohol to self-medicate? What if there is nothing I can say or do to help him? *I* know! I could start by organizing his social life! These were all useless thoughts, and more than that, they were harmful. Thoughts such as these knock me off center and leave me fighting to regain my balance. I "hate them with a perfect hatred" as it says in Psalm 139. The Psalmist is referring to those who hate God, but I find my tightly wound mental tracks of fear and worry to be as anti-God as anything I ever encounter around me. I knew I had to tend myself quickly, sort of like staving off the flow of blood from an injury. I needed to stop the emotional bleeding before I could dress the wound. I went to my quiet spot, read a couple of centering entries, and waited. Eventually I asked Rob for help, telling him I needed help moving, both mentally and physically. We went to the gym and worked out, and I began to relinquish my internal vice grip on Michael's world and return to my own.

You see, I find I really get things for a while, have some

keen insights, even, and then I feel at a complete loss to understand even the simplest truths. I vacillate between profound trust and deep uncertainty. Thankfully I'm not alone, as something I read this morning reminded me. I'm in the middle of an unlikely project at present, going through a "red letter" version of the bible and reading only the words Jesus spoke. Just this morning I was reading the story in Matthew's gospel where Simon finally identifies Jesus as the Messiah and Jesus encourages him by telling him how right and smart he is, so smart that he is given a new name. He calls him Petrus (or Peter), meaning rock, and pronounces, "On this rock I will build my church."[3] Jesus goes on a while about how good Peter is, and I imagined how special Peter must have felt. I can almost hear him thinking: "I'm the one who got it! I'm the one who understood and had the smart thing to say, who saw and named the truth." The thing is, the next words that Jesus speaks just a few verses later are "Get behind me Satan!"[4] and he directs them to Peter who is missing the boat so hopelessly that Jesus has to forcefully thump him down in front of everyone. Immediately prior to this rebuttal, Jesus is giving the whole crew of disciples a similar verbal reprimand, wondering how they possibly could be talking about not having bread when they recently witnessed Jesus feeding five thousand people with five loaves. Hello, were they not paying attention? Jesus must have wondered how he could possibly be any clearer.

This is me. Didn't I witness God saving Michael's life? Haven't I witnessed my human efforts falling short over and over while God's providence comes through sure and secure, whether it is through emotional, financial or spiritual support? Why can't I remember what I know? Why, when the first sign of distress bubbles up, am I so willing to toss my serenity out the window in favor of buying a bunch of trouble I don't own and can't afford?

I take heart in reading about the disciples who were right there with the Master and still repeatedly missed the boat, even with the truth staring them in the face. I'm grateful God is patient with my lapses of trust and understanding. I also believe that God will help Michael through this next part of the journey, and that I might even be one of the ones offering him a figurative lift out of the flood, perhaps toward someone who specializes in these kinds of natural disasters. I won't be passive, but I won't be God, either, and hopefully I, too, will recognize the hand of God when it reaches out to save me, which it has done, over and over again.

You Shall Know the Truth and the Truth Shall Make You Odd[5]

God is good, all the time. All the time, God is good. I have updates today.

Driving: Michael is driving to school now. He's been at it for a week, and so far so good. His return to driving meant we had to find a different vehicle for him as the '86 Nissan pickup truck he'd previously driven wasn't safe. I discovered this in high relief that first evening I took him out for driving practice. It turned out the defrost and heat no longer worked, so as Michael was managing the multiple attention demands of driving (including a stick shift, no less), he was also repeatedly wiping the windshield with his sleeve. His Parkinson's-like hands would fly from the stick to the wheel to the windshield in jerky, uncertain spurts. This freaked me out completely. I couldn't see a thing through the foggy mess, and right then and there I decided that with all of the current strikes against him, he absolutely needed a completely safe vehicle to drive.

It turned out an older but fully functional, airbag-equipped Mustang was still for sale by one of my associates at Willamette, so we turned the deal and brought it home. Michael was ecstatic, giving us another shining display of that ear-to-ear grin with the staying power of the Energizer bunny. What teenage boy wouldn't be happy with a sleek black Mustang? But here is the odd part. Kat struck up a conversation with him later that evening, mentioning that she'd heard he could drive to school again and wasn't that great, etc. Michael talked about his accomplishment with her at length, all the while making no mention of the car. It was sitting in front of the house and she'd seen it but didn't know whose it was, and Michael never thought to mention it. Shouldn't he have been boasting about his latest windfall? What teenage boy doesn't brag about a new set of wheels? It's clear Michael's ego is still partially out of commission, reminding us things aren't yet normal in his brain.

A follow up in the social arena: I encouraged him to make the morning coffee date while thankfully managing to let go of the outcome. I realized I needed to trust Michael's own sense of what is good for him and what isn't. He didn't go, and that was fine. And then to my surprise it turned out he had made a plan with the same fellow for later in the day. That plan didn't quite materialize due to a miscommunication of some sort which left Michael waiting alone at a coffee shop for 45 minutes, and what emerged from that misstep was a trip to the pool hall Friday night. Whoa. I have been praying, "God, please let him have a normal social life and have something to do in the evening besides watch TV. But please don't let him have too much of anything!" And then here it came. I was simultaneously thinking, "Hurray!" and "Oh crap!" He was so ready to flex his independence muscles he didn't even consider asking about going, and he wouldn't have told us where he was headed had I not pranced around and prodded him with questions. And then off he went. The young man who invited him is on the reputable list of friends, so that was fine.

But the pool hall? Isn't that where teenagers gather and do things teenagers do, like make plans for other things where they feel their oats and get bad ideas? Oh crap, indeed. And won't Michael be the only one there with a brain injury, and how can he possibly navigate such temptation with any hope of coming out unscathed? More bother! The thing was, in addition to being worried, I was also really excited for him, so excited that as he headed out the door I forgot to mention when he should be home. This didn't occur to me until about 9:30, when, unfortunately, I was watching *Grey's Anatomy* which included a panic-inducing scene where a woman wakes up on the operating table while her insides are completely open to the outside. The next scene featured a teenage boy with unidentifiable abdominal pain who ended up having a heart bleed. These were not good things for a mother to watch while worrying about her intellectually compromised son who had *driven* himself to the pool hall, for crying out loud, without a curfew hanging over his head!

Well, it all worked out fine. Michael walked in by 10:00 and was sober and happy. The little stinker had been smoking again, though, and I realize there will be no battling that particularly tenacious addiction in him, especially since in a few more months it will be his own legal and stupid choice for the rest of his life. He managed to play pool okay. He had a good time. He had toppled out of our little nest yet again and floated out onto his wings without flailing or crashing.

What struck me was how desperately I wanted to make the plan for him, to make sure it worked, and to see that it was tidy and safe (aren't coffee shops much less threatening than pool halls?). Along the way I also wanted to spare him the pain of social discomfort and loneliness. My mom and I were talking just yesterday about how much parents want to spare their children pain, whether the pain be small and insignificant or huge and life-shattering. But by protecting them from life's disappointments we do them a disservice, because every life has great disappointments, and learning to protect and nurture our hearts through heartbreak while remaining open to life is a skill we all need to hone. It occurred to me that while I must keep vigilant watch over Michael for any depression that turns inward to the point of destruction, discouragement is a natural and even appropriate response to the circumstances he now faces from choices he made.

Michael is busy learning the way teenagers do, the way we all do, I suppose—by experience. Another case in point: When he began driving again I noticed he didn't turn on his headlights in daylight fog. So we talked about how he needed to do that for safety, and how it's harder to remember to turn them off in the day, and how his car likely didn't have a reminder beep to alert him if he forgot. But even as I reviewed this with him I thought to myself, "Probably the only way he'll ever really remember this is if he kills his battery." It didn't take long. It happened today, but he navigated the inconvenience well. He found someone at school with cables and got a jump start. And, of course, the good news was that he had remembered to put his lights on in the fog in the first place. Even with the after-school snafu, he still made it to his afternoon speech therapy appointment on time. He might not have the memory he used to have, but he is responding well to the issues raised by the deficit. He gets kudos for good problem solving with no harm, no foul. Along the way I am learning to let him learn more on his own, with support, but without interference. I literally helped hold him up in the hospital when he first began walking again, and now my job description is more akin to a distant safety net.

It has been strange to watch Michael revisit the various phases of childhood development as he's progressed through recovery. He was like an infant when he first regained consciousness, with no ability to speak and completely dependent on others for things such as food and basic hygiene. His motor skills were so rudimentary that when he moved his hand to scratch his nose he would frequently miss, just like a baby who lacks the eye-hand coordination to connect with his intended target. Since then we've witnessed a fast-forward repeat of every step of childhood including learning to eat and walk, and even enjoying children's books together. He's come an amazingly long way. It both pains and encourages me to say it, but I think he is an adolescent once again.

Chapter 12
Finding North Again

Diamonds, Brilliant and Clear

Michael has had a good day. Or maybe I should say I have had a good day being around him. Here is something amazing. His speech homework now includes tongue twisters, some of which are quite extensive, as long as good-sized paragraphs. Listening to him go through his paces on these blew me away, because just a month ago he was having trouble with rudimentary processes like nasal and non-nasal sounds, or navigating Ls, Ds and Rs. He was struggling simply to make words sound normal. Articulation and clarity have come so far that he is now working on inflection and speed, two of the later aspects to be recovered. It is exciting to see and hear.

I also put him through a short set of math problems after dinner and was happy to discover he now remembers how to do multiplication and long division. I realize these are 3rd or 4th grade level skills, but that really isn't the point. The point is he couldn't do the problems earlier, and then he couldn't recall the skills even though he'd relearned them, and now he can. Woo-hoo!

There are so many positives in Michael's recovery and I love celebrating each one. I also am reminded that the ultimate meaning in the end of this story, if there is such a thing, isn't about where Michael lands. I have come to understand that the "success" of all of our praying, hoping, hurting and celebrating is not dependent on a happy outcome, because each moment in life is fully meaningful in its original context in time. Events don't garner meaning only by being contingencies for other, future moments. If God has answered our prayers for Michael's life and recovery with reckless and generous abandon, which I believe God has, the grace of that gesture is not undone if Michael were to choose to throw hope down the sewer of addiction again.

This is a lot for me to digest. Because it seems only fair that if we hope and pray and work this hard, and God meets us and even encourages us on, that we should be able to cross the finish line in glory with an outcome that everyone can look at and say, "Oh yes! Isn't it good and wonderful how all of that worked out?" This is my fervent, daily hope, of course. Yet I am convinced that the measure of success is not in the final turn of events, but rather in how well and how deeply we love along the way.

I thought about the myriad of ways we can love in the world. In my own life, these include teaching, singing, writing, praying, conversing with friends, and being present with my family. We can love by speaking truth or by quietly remembering that sometimes it is more important to be kind than to be right. All of these things are good and worthy, but none of them guarantees outcomes. We love because loving is right, not because it gets us to a certain climactic high note before the curtain falls. We love because in so doing our spirits are transformed to the likeness of the substance from which we come.

If Michael were to die from a drug overdose tomorrow or at some future date, our prayers, effort and support would not be in vain. Because in loving, in giving ourselves away, we are changed, as is the world around us. We can do nothing more beautiful than pour out our spirits as living sacrifices in service to the endless and saving love of God, God who meets us with both grand majesty and perfect gentleness, taking the clay of our substance into the crucible of the divine heart where we are formed and forged into diamonds that shine like stars.[1] Each gem holds the light of eternity within, endlessly burning with the inexhaustible supply of God's presence, mercy and strength, becoming more brilliant with every acknowledgment of this truth. When we love, we become more love. This is why we do it, this is why we love, because something essential in our spirits longs to become and return to that which we recognize as home. We want to be *who we are*. Tragedies and celebrations don't change our being. Only loving brings us into greater focus, whether the end of the story is a tearjerker or fairy tale happiness.

There is tremendous freedom in entering this crucible, because our lives are no longer our own. We have more responsibility, yes, but we also are free from the human tendency and desire to control and understand. We simply surrender to life in love and recognize that God has the final word, and that word is *good*. God showed me an image in prayer this morning of Michael walking happily off into his life, though whether in eternity or into adulthood on earth I don't know. He was free and healthy and on his way. He is God's, as we all are God's, and I will continue to take heart in loving as we travel the way together. Because loving brings me closer to home, and home is where my heart knows the truth of who I am.

And this is my prayer, that your love may overflow more and more with knowledge and full insight. – Philippians 1:9

I Wanna Sing You a Love Song

Michael sat and played his guitar the other day for about two hours. He was playing again this afternoon and I was astounded at how much he has recovered in the past couple of months, all without touching the instrument. When he first picked it up in rehab he could only remember three or four chords and not a single one of the melody lines he used to play. He was discouraged enough that he didn't even want to try, even with the nurses repeatedly begging him to play.

Now, after a cold-turkey hiatus, he's playing several complete songs and a good-sized handful of the riffs his uncle Tim taught him last summer. Today he played and sang a song called *Warmness on the Soul* by Avenged Sevenfold. His deep baritone voice was gentle and perfectly in tune, just like I remember it from before, and his strumming didn't miss a beat. The lyrics are about romantic love, but when I looked them up online I couldn't help seeing them through a different lens. Here is part of the text:

And we have gone through good and bad times,
But your unconditional love was always on my mind.
You've been there from the start for me
And your love's always been true as can be.
I give my heart to you,
I give my heart 'cause nothing can compare
*   in this world to you.*

When I heard these words today they sounded like a love song to God. As cheesy as the sentiment may sound in pop lyrics, it is true for me that nothing in this world can compare to the infinite love of God. That love nearly undoes me sometimes, because the tenderness and intensity within it is so concentrated and pure that my less than lovely spirit can hardly bear it when I meet it face-to-face.

Once at the Goodwill I found a gemstone ring. When I bought it I couldn't tell the color of the stone, it was so covered over with grime and filth. But I brought it home and cleaned it, revealing a beautiful, clear light blue stone set in gold with a few clear crystals on each side. I think entering God's field of grace is like this. We come not even knowing or understanding the depth and clarity of our own beauty, but in God's gaze we are transfigured and revealed. And so we give our hearts in return, because nothing else can compare.

Restoring the Balance

Healing from a brain injury requires constant adjustment to change. I watch regular shifts in Michael as newly recovered skills emerge and come into play. One good change this past week is that his doctor cleared him to go snowboarding. This has been one of his main short-term goals, primary enough to warrant its own motivational poster on his wall which encouraged him by keeping the steps toward the prize in mind. So on a Saturday sometime soon we'll head up to the mountain. Like his return to driving, he'll need to approach the sport as though he's learning it for the first time. While he's recovered most of his strength, his coordination still lags a bit behind. So he'll be feeling his way down the mountain, seeing how his body responds, and I'll be there next to him on skis, making sure he isn't seduced into trying black diamond (advanced) runs or jumps promising lots of air. But wow, he's going!

His teachers are talking about getting him back into Algebra for the third trimester. His body, as Michael says, is "swole" again, primed with muscular bulk and definition. He's reading novels and poetry and participating in discussions. And yet he still couldn't understand or follow my verbal instruction of how to nick the top of a banana crosswise to open up a resistant peel (physical demonstration was necessary). Yet again I expect cognitive repairs in one area to bring similar, parallel progressions in other areas, and I am reminded that this just isn't the case.

Sometimes the changes come quickly and we move rapidly through new territory, sometimes we plod evenly along, and sometimes we just tread water. My own world demonstrates similar ebb and flow, the familiar play between balance and relative imbalance. I remember someone once saying there is always at least one area of our lives out of whack at any given time whether it be health, finances, family, work, relationship, or spirituality. Rarely does everything line up in simultaneous abundance and harmony. This has been a very busy work week and weekend for me so I am a bit off-kilter, internally speaking. When these periods come, my strongest craving, apart from unfettered time, is for a strong connection with my inner, unseen world. Martin Luther said that he always prayed for one hour every morning unless he had an exceptionally busy day ahead of him, in which case he prayed for two.

This morning I was finally able to give myself wholly to prayer rather than only going through the motions, and for the first time all week I felt the familiar settling of Spirit and Presence. I have missed my good companion. God is always palpable when I show up wholeheartedly, and doubtless God patiently nurtures me beyond my awareness in between when I am distracted or only partially present. I don't like it when I'm away, but I recognize my spiritual absence as part of the balance. Dry periods regularly appear, sometimes for very long stretches, and abundance and harmony always return as well. I have learned that I have to intentionally revisit what is most important to me or the business of life will regularly rush in and take up primary residence, as if my spirit erroneously hangs out a "vacancy" sign. I also have learned that the base of equilibrium in life is not my relative busyness or stillness, or even my general state of peace or disruption. The only two constants are change and God, and God, who is always the same, is the grounding in the midst of both chaos and tedium. I'm grateful God always awaits my recollection, opening the floodgates of insight and connection at just the right times, even though I often feel impatient and fussy in the waiting period. I remember that silence doesn't mean absence, and as Augustine said, if we desire to see God, we already have faith. We're so much closer than we know most of the time.

Dear Christine,
    Greetings, Michael's mom! ☺ God bless you and all

you love.

I think our "ships passed in the night"—I sent a letter to Michael with visiting forms, next day I get <u>your</u> letter. It was nice to hear from you. God's rescue of your son, it's quite an amazing grace, a real example of the Divine Mercy of Christ. I'm very happy for you, that you still have your baby boy to hug....

Finally, I wish and pray for all goodness through God for you and your family, and special graces for your husband's ministry and holy vocation. Write any time, and I hope to meet you and Michael.

Your brother in Christ,
Jeff

❧

On the Mountain

The mountain was beautiful yesterday. It was a perfect day to ski and board. Fresh powder fell the previous couple of days and then the sun came out to play. Michael was raring to go. We planned an early departure so that we could get in a full day. We didn't quite meet our 6:30 AM mark, however, because I failed to take into account the planning and organizing deficiencies of a brain-injured boarder. We talked about packing up our gear the night before, at least a couple of times, and we had *just* made a trip to Sports Authority early that evening to get Michael new bindings with his Christmas money, so I figured he was on it. I should pause here and say that the fact he even *had* that money is a small miracle, as he has never hung on to any wad of cash for more than a week in his entire, pre-injury life. It's nice to celebrate the unlikely blessings of his altered brain.

So there we were in the morning, Natalie and a friend already in the car, boards loaded in the back of the old SUV, food prepared and packed, and Michael was nowhere to be found. After a bit I went back into the house to look for him. He was standing in his room, surrounded by a sea of half of the contents of his dresser and closet along with piles of dirty laundry and other debris, looking bewildered. "I don't have any warm socks." Apparently a conversation I had with Natalie as we were loading the car reminded Michael that he hadn't brought cold weather socks along. Which then led him to realize he didn't have gloves, which then made him consider that he didn't know where his helmet was. I had forgotten that, due to his injury, he still needs very specific and concrete instructions. To him, "Get your gear together the night before" only meant "Have your board and boots ready." And to that end he had gotten his board and boots out and expertly attached the new bindings without any assistance, appearing fully competent and prepared. Sigh. At this point we went through the list of items one by one. We searched for the helmet, finding only a large, child-sized one designed for skateboarding—even though we saw the snowboarding helmet earlier this season...*somewhere*. We realized that the hat he was wearing with the big fuzzy ball on top wouldn't work underneath the snowboarding helmet. We found one of Natalie's hats: bright orange! Good! It would be readily identifiable on the slopes. But bad! The helmet was too small, sitting perched atop his head like a big, black maraschino cherry. He'd need to rent one. Forty-five minutes later we were finally pulling out of the driveway.

On our first run down the mountain I thought of sea turtles. We swam with them once while snorkeling in Hawaii a couple of summers ago. On land their movements are awkward, slow and labored, but underwater they become breathtakingly graceful. The utter perfection of their bodies gliding and turning in the water is one of the most exhilaratingly beautiful things I've ever seen. This was how Michael looked to me on the mountain that first run. He was coursing seamlessly and effortlessly down the slope, his body turning and swaying without any of the Parkinson's-like symptoms that are visible on flat land. I remember my father, a retired neurologist, telling me that the parts of

Michael's brain in the basal ganglia that died from his injury might produce lasting change in some physical motions and coordination. It's true that he lacks the smooth grace he had before his injury. He was so physically beautiful and easy, relaxed and incredibly coordinated and strong all at once. Now the simplest movements are uneven and halting. But all of that disappeared on the mountain. He looked like I remembered him, and it was beautiful.

Until the second run.

My family skied every year when I was young. We would spend two separate weeks on the slopes of Summit County in Colorado, running hard all day long for six or seven days. My mother always talked about "getting your confidence back" those first few trips down the mountain. Since we lived in Kansas, the stretches between ventures were lengthy. So we'd take it easy, finding our rhythm on the slopes and letting our assurance rise with the success of several gentle runs before we took on the terrifying thrill of the black diamonds. Well, Michael was really ready to go after that first trip down a green slope (green = beginner, blue = intermediate, black = expert), so we headed to a blue. And suddenly he moved to a new sport. Instead of boarding, he was tumbling.

It began with a wrong turn, or rather a late one. Just like Michael's speech where his brain gives the signal but the muscles can't articulate the information at normal speed, his brain told his body to go left but it didn't respond in time. He ended up in a mess of powder. There was no emergency, no threatening close call, he was simply in the deep. And as any boarder knows, once you are buried up to your thighs in snow it is a long haul getting free. Even with the help of my ski pole and repeated pulling and heaving, it still took him 20 minutes of intense effort to break out.

His temporary imprisonment in the powder shook his confidence, not to mention that the hard work was exhausting. After that he tumbled regularly. It got worse through the morning and then was much better in the afternoon. This surprised me, as I thought he would become more tired as the day wore on, but then I discovered a missing puzzle piece: He hadn't eaten breakfast. You would think I would remember by now that some aspects of his daily life simply are not normal and need regular prodding, but I'd lost track of his food consumption in the 45 minute delay while we searched for cold weather gear. He had much longer upright stretches after lunch.

I brought up the rear on each run so that I could keep an eye on him. After particularly bad falls where he tumbled a good while, he'd often sit still for a minute and eventually say, "......Ow......" to which I'd respond, "Are you okay!? Did you break anything?" Eventually he said, "Mom, I fell, and it hurt and it's fine." Just like the doctor said, he was learning again for the first time, and new snowboarders fall a lot. Oddly enough, I realized I had been thinking, "Well, if you broke your arm, that would be okay. As long as you don't hit your head!" So I relaxed a bit, letting him tumble without commentary, and then when the falls became obviously more frequent in the later afternoon, I asked if his legs were tired. He responded with an emphatic, "Yeah!" So we headed down the mountain one last time toward a reward of hot chocolate. Knowing when to start or stop activities, whether they are physical or mental, is another weakness since his injury. But he didn't need much persuading when the time came to call it quits. I was glad for that.

All in all it was a grand day. The snow was good, the sun and clouds wonderful, and no one broke anything. Then God showed off with a pretty sunset on our drive back to Salem. Michael has now met three of the initial goals he established in recovery: driving, spending more time with friends, and snowboarding. Still on the list are speech (which has shown great gains but may never be fully normal), going to college (good strides in this area, too), getting a job, and living on his own. As I consider the list I see he has now met all of his short-term goals. We'll keep at it for the long-term ones.

For my part, the day at the mountain produced a welcome change in my internal soundtrack. It relaxed my mind in a deep way, something I noticed upon waking this morning. My thoughts were reluctant to wind up to their usual speed, as though they lacked the familiar spring toward motion and volume. Rather they were drifty, soft and yielding, sort of like the deep powder, but in a good way, as if I landed there and it was okay to sink in and rest in the quiet with no need to get back on the run.

Chapter 13
The Insatiable Beast

Barbed Wire

Is there something in your life that is very difficult or challenging and simply won't go away? I'm guessing your answer could be yes. No matter how blessed our lives may be, there always seems to be a "thorn in the flesh," as the apostle Paul called it,[1] and that thorn is often persistent and painful. For some it is a health issue, for others a grief, for another a difficult colleague or work situation. The challenge might be financial stress or relationship woes, and try as we might to rise above or heal or change, the issue simply remains. Mostly we learn to live with it. If we're lucky we may eventually move beyond it, but more likely it simply becomes part of us in a new way.

Rob once told the story of a tree that sprouted next to a barbed wire fence. When the young sapling grew close enough to touch the fence, the wire cut into the tender bark, leaving the flesh open and raw. But over time and through steady growth, the tree eventually enclosed the wire, taking it deep into its trunk as the years added layer upon layer. Though the barbs now ran right through the center of the tree, they no longer cut the way they had in the beginning. The wire had simply become part of the tree, which was tall and strong.

I have been internally disrupted the last two days. The disturbance came on yesterday and I couldn't shake it, a low level anxiety that left my chest feeling tight and my limbs feeling weak and disconnected. I felt a soft "no, no, no" welling up, but I didn't know what I was addressing. No, *what*? I've come to recognize these intuitive hits, and they frustrate me. Often they provide just enough information for me to know something is amiss but not enough to name anything specific. I find myself thinking it would be easier not to know anything at all.

This morning I was tending to domestic details before work. I balanced the checkbook, which requires a computer for online access and a calculator. My laptop doesn't have a number keypad apart from the row at the top, which I find tedious. We have an old desktop unit that does have a full keyboard, and usually I hook that keyboard up to my laptop when it's time to do anything with numbers. For some reason today I thought, "Oh I'll just use the old computer." When I tapped the space bar to wake it up, I found it was on Rob's screen, and just then school portraits of Natalie and Michael in bygone years cycled through his screen saver. When I saw Michael's picture I burst into tears. And then I knew: the anxious disruption had to do with him. I didn't know why, I just knew it did. I am amazed how God leads us in such quiet and non-obvious ways. I believe God knew this was a connection I needed to draw, and I am grateful.

A mother of a private voice student of mine asked me thoughtfully this afternoon, "How's your son?" I told her I didn't know, that by all outward appearances he was doing really well, but that I felt something was off. His newfound, increased time with friends was nagging at me, among other things. "Oh, a mother's intuition..." she said, with knowing foreboding.

The energetic disruption continued when I got home, growing stronger. Michael had called my cell to say he was going somewhere with friends. Rob and I walked the dogs before dinner, one of our best times for good conversation. I told Rob it seemed odd to feel so off-kilter the last two days when I have been feeling so steady and good for a while now. The resulting verbal processing led me to a decision to use one of my home drug testing kits on Michael when he returned. I figured if I simply faced the doubt head on I could either A) set my fears to rest or B) have some concrete evidence on which to proceed.

Suffice it to say the thorn in my flesh continues to be Michael's addiction, and my intuitive suspicions were well-founded. He's now lost every privilege I can think of, given that his last substance use left him for dead. According to Michael, this latest relapse came about because, as he said, "I guess I didn't think." After talking with him, it is clear he doesn't experience the same connection that we do between his using and the destruction it causes. Addicts often fail to connect these dots, at least consciously, while those who love them cannot help but see and suffer from the obvious relationship of cause and effect. It's one of the great injustices of the disease.

So now we know. We know that the devil inside is still after him and that it has a foothold, even after all he's been through. God how I would like to shake it loose and fling it to hell forever. I do hate it with a perfect hatred.[2]

My vague though intensifying anxiety instantly gave way to a sick stomach and sharp pain in my head the moment I saw the positive test result. And now that the scores are in, the little physical eruption of my intuition volcano has subsided. What remains, and will remain, is to figure how we can best help Michael while maintaining rich and meaningful lives for ourselves. It's amazing how the beast of addiction can suck the joy out of a room in nothing flat. And damn it, I want my joy! I will not give it over to the beast for feasting.

I will fight like a wild animal to help Michael get and stay clean, but I will fight with just as much vigor to live in joy and gratitude, no matter his choices. I will not give up my life. My life is God's, and God does not give it to hell.

Help Is On the Way

Michael and I had a good talk on the way to school this morning. He's not driving for a while, so we are afforded more "car time" together, which I have consistently experienced as some of the most fertile ground for connecting with my kids.

We talked about how occasional slips are part of recovery. I remember a stray cat that was adopted by a drug treatment center. They named it "Relapse" because it kept coming back. We talked about the relapse cycle, how he'll need to trace his steps backward and see where the weak link first appeared, because the initial chink in the sobriety armor always occurs long before the actual use. We talked about how the urge to use is part of him, will be part of him, and how he has tools to use when it comes. When the desire comes to fill up some space with drugs, or to create a diversion from boredom or part of life that is difficult or simply not compelling enough at the moment, he could ask to be filled with something else. I asked him, "What would that prayer sound like to you, Michael, in your own words? What would you say?" He said, "God, help me." I told him I pray the "help me" prayer all the time, and the amazing thing is, God does help. Our willingness to ask for assistance opens the channels for grace to move through, and failing to acknowledge we need help keeps those same channels shut tight. I told him try as I might, I can never really get there ("there" being patience, strength, peace, compassion, self-control, etc.) on my own. I always need God to help me complete the journey or process. And likewise God doesn't usually finish the good work begun in us without our participation. It's not that God can't, it's that the laws of the universe God created allow for free will, so when we turn toward God, God responds in kind. When we don't, well, God just lets us go our own way. We can walk alone, but it's much harder that way. While God is all powerful, it seems much of the time God chooses not to force things upon us without our consent, and likewise we can't complete them on our own without God's grace and strength. It's another complete circuit.

I recounted my anxious, intuitive hits of the previous two days to Michael, telling him that his guardian angels must be determined, because my discovery of his recent use helps him much more than it does me. The information was given to me not so that *I* could be okay, but rather so that I could help *him* toward okay. Someone up there really wants him to thrive. God keeps extending that hand to him saying, "Come on, dude. You need to meet me half way here. I can't do it for you. Go with me on this one."

God was every bit as kind to me in prayer this morning. After just writing about thorns and barbs yesterday, the readings I encountered were all along those lines. Here are two quotes I came across, the first from Marie Noël:

"The best and most nourishing souls are made of a few great and radiant acts of goodness and a thousand, tiny, obscure miseries which feed their goodness like the wheat that lives from the decomposition of the soil."

The second came from Pope John Paul XXIII who would often say during times of trial, "I am a little bird singing in a thorn bush." As I read and prayed these words this morning, I noticed there was a songbird just outside my window. It was warbling boisterously, oblivious to my contemplation, and I loved it. It was the divine accompaniment to my silence, and about the time I finished praying I noticed it concluded its song. We are meant to be observers of grace. The more we see, the more appears, and indeed the more blossoms into being.

And then as if these gifts weren't affirmation enough, I found that in my continuing journey through the "red letters" (Jesus' words) in the Bible, I had just come to the parable of the sower in the Gospel of Mark where Jesus talks about the fate that befalls various seeds that fall to the earth. I thought about the seeds choked by weeds and those that grew up "among thorns," which Jesus explained to be "the cares of the world, the lure of wealth, and the desire of other things."[3]

God was LOUD. Yes, Christine, there are thorns and barbs. Yes, there are a thousand small miseries. Yes, the miseries and thorns are part of life, but how are you going to *respond*?

I thought about Jesus' description of the seeds as the word of God. What, exactly, is that word? The gospel of John says, "In the beginning was the word, and the word was with God, and the word was God."[4] That word, the seeds that fall, are the presence of God. And what are the things that choke us off from that presence, or distract us, or try to convince us, like a dementor in the *Harry Potter* series, that we can no longer remember what is true, or why life is good or how much happiness we know? What is it that keeps us from growing stronger in love?

We each have our own answers to that, and I think that our struggles can either become weeds and thorns or fertilizer for the blossoms of faith. Let's face it, flowers really do bloom bigger and brighter when fertilized, and, frankly, fertilizer *stinks*! I know God blesses me by using my struggles in this fruitful way, and the fact that God gifts me with strength in the struggle, well, I believe that is something I'm meant to share. Because no matter what we're given, whether it's wealth or talent or laughter or joy or insight or compassion or courage, I am convinced that it grows in the giving. Likewise, in hoarding we begin to wither away, much like the parable of the talents.[5] I believe I am called to write about this because God is showing me a way through, and I'd like to share that vision with others, knowing full well that each path is unique. No matter the struggle, there *is* a way through, there is a compass and that compass is God, the presence that stands with us and makes the long-lived barbed wire through our middles bearable. And it is right in the heart of us, right in front of our very eyes, communing with us *all of the time* whether we know it or not. Life is what it is either way: full of both joy and pain, triumph and hardship, for every one of us. The difference is in the quality of the journey. For me that journey is made not only bearable but truly joyful when I acknowledge the presence of God, the source of all that is.

So today I praise God with all of my heart and soul and voice for abundant blessings, with joy and gratitude. God is good, all the time. All the time, God is good.

Jeff Tiner and I were now maintaining a regular correspondence. We wrote weekly letters and were beginning to get to know each other. Most of our writing covered spiritual topics, and he frequently included others' writings and reflections in missives he sent me. Below is one such letter in its entirety. The day after he wrote it I was given an image in morning prayer of a little bird. She was small, plain, and black. I had asked God how to proceed in sharing Michael's story beyond our immediate circle of friends and family, to give it wings of flight. I wrote in my prayer journal: "I'm small, but the point is not to be earthbound.... I'll be brave enough to go where God leads, for the sake of love." The next day, in the morning before Jeff's letter arrived in the mail, I wrote "I see the little bird again. It's flying east, and as it goes it becomes clear. The light moves through, diffusing and magnifying and showering. Oh I pray God is indeed calling me to be that little bird, to help share and spread the light." After these images in prayer, the following letter arrived:

Dear Christine,

Peace be with you. ☺ I was reading some poetry from "The Selected Poetry of Jessica Powers" (ICS Publications, 2131 Lincoln Rd. NE Washington, DC, 20002, $11.95, 800-832-8489). I came across

220

her work "The Legend of the Sparrow" and thought of Michael and his unique path to sanctity. So, I copied it down and enclose it for you here.

As for the book itself, if you never read a book where nearly every poem has you saying "wow" over and over, I encourage you to get this book. It plumbs the depths of spirit and Christian faith in awesome and often sublime ways. And who knows….perhaps these writings will inspire Michael in his Am. Lit. [American Literature] class, get him to open up through creative writing.

I also enclose a small copy of a recent portrait I drew in pencil - - my great sisterly guide St. Josephine Bakhita. May she shower your family with love from above. ☺

Have a blessed day.
Your brother in Christ,
Jeff

The Legend of the Sparrow
(For a child who dreams of sainthood)

There was a sparrow once who dreamed to fly
into the sun.
Oh, how the birds of earth set up a cry
at such imprudence in a little one
when even eagles dared not venture near
the burning stratosphere.

"She will come down within a mile or two,"
they prophesied with dread.
It was, of course, most pitifully true.
Scarce half-way up the mountain overhead
she crashed into her feathers, as they said.

But when her wings healed, up she shot again
and sought a further bough.
She was more humble and more cautious now,
after a brief novitiate of pain.

Three times she rose; twice the wind brought her down,
once her own weariness.
At last she clutched a branch in her distress
and cried, "How can I ever hope to rest
in the sun's downy nest?
I faint; I fall whatever way I go!"

But then she turned and saw the home she left
unnumbered miles below,
while just beyond her lay the mountain top,
a kerchiefed head of snow.

Nobody told her and she never guessed
that earth's last height was all that she need seek.
All winds blow upward from the mountain peak
and there the sun has such magnetic rays
that in one moment she was lifted up
into his tender blaze.

Down in the valley there was such a stir:
A sparrow reached the sun!
Why had the wind and weather favored her?
What had she ever done?
Yet since they must, they spoke the praising word,
measured her flight and paused to gasp afresh.
What was she really but a little bird,
all feather and no flesh?

Only the sun knew, and the moving air
the miracle thereof:
a bird that wings itself with resolute love
can travel anywhere.
   –Jessica Powers, 1946
   –(Sister Miriam of the Holy Spirit, OCD,
     1905-1988)[6]

Too Much Heaven

I learned something this morning as I processed through some thoughts and feelings about Michael. I learned I have held on to an anchor of sorts in the form of completely fabricated perspective, and this little reality I have created has maintained the balance until now. I have thought, "Well, all of this loss, of Michael's intelligence and personality and abilities, of thousands of dollars, of two months of work, of time and heartache and effort and hope, all of it is worth it since this tragedy will be the thing that brings change, as in the change I want for him, namely that he will be freed from the scourge of addiction, and therefore so will I."

Over and over I have written and said that there are no guaranteed outcomes, that success isn't based on the story turning out how I imagine, that the truth of God's goodness and power isn't manifest only if Michael's life has a happy ending worthy of a Hollywood feel-good flick. But still I have held on to an expectation for an even exchange: my suffering for a preferred outcome. If truth be told, I would rather end up with an advantage in the bargain, maybe even a significant one. Unfortunately, his story isn't an escape from reality but rather a dive into it. So I realize in some ways I am feeling our losses more keenly and deeply now, because the carrot I was dangling in front of my nose was just snatched away by his recent relapse, and I feel I may be without compensation for a very long time.

I have had countless thoughts of, "What can I say to Michael? What can I do? What have I forgotten to say or do that could be helpful, and how can it be that I can't come up with a single thing, positive or negative, that will convince him not to use?" He's been through in-patient drug treatment rehab twice. He's followed up with outpatient drug counseling and countless twelve-step meetings. We've used chat therapy and behavioral conditioning techniques. Where is the answer? Once again in the whirlwind of my ferocious mental efforts I've forgotten the first step: "We admitted to ourselves that we were powerless over alcohol (or drugs) and that our lives had become unmanageable." I have admitted this reality repeatedly and willingly, only then to deny it time and time again, as if through sheer determination I can change a cosmic, immutable truth, namely, that I am not in control.

What are *you* powerless over? How tired are you of trying to control it?

I needed a new anchor this morning, because as much as I know my pretend anchor wasn't reliable, my invention of it was pretty convincing there for a while. I thought on these words:

"All God can do is give his love, and suffering never comes from God. God is not the author of evil; he wants neither human distress, nor wars, nor natural disasters, nor violent accidents. God shares the pain of all who are undergoing times of trial and enables us to comfort those who are suffering.

"God wants happiness for us; but where is the source of such a hope? It lies in a communion with God, alive at the center of each person's soul."—Brother Roger of Taizé, *God is Love Alone.*

This hit home for me in prayer as I remembered again *the kingdom of God is within.*[7] I know this communion, and I know that when I am in it, I am indeed content. I may weep on my way there, but each time I discover its truth I know that being in communion with God is a complete answer, and it truly does dry my tears. I wrote these words in prayer today:

Deep inside of each of us is an opening or a threshold to the kingdom within. Beyond the opening is the vastness of eternity. As we bring forth that presence, or rather welcome it in the finding and naming, it floods us from within. It moves outward and courses through every cell. This is communion with God, this enmeshment, lack of distinction, fullness of being in oneness. So often I go to Michael and try to bring things *to* him. This never works. God also comes to him from within.

Circumstances, whether good or bad, do not bring happiness, peace, or contentment. Only knowing God and living in the knowing does such. As I give up my attachment to life's circumstances, to events, people, outcomes, work, and processes, I'll lose, but I'll gain so much more. I'll gain the kingdom within.

The day before it occurred to me that our little spirits really can't handle too much heaven, at least mine can't. In prayer I had been practicing gratitude for what I have rather than focusing on what is broken or missing, and it was a powerful exercise. The cascade of words I was recording on paper built into quite a crescendo as I listed everything that came to mind: the beautiful day, the ability to teach meaningfully, my love of music, Michael's life, deep time with the Spirit, my husband, my possessions, and so on. I am rich. The wave of gratitude dislodged something in me and I felt awash, disoriented. So I wondered: Is it possible our spirits can't handle too much of the higher vibrations of thanksgiving, hope and peace? Are we actually disoriented from joy? Do we have to return to the heavier frequencies of fear, worry, anger and judgment just to feel some sort of safe, familiar grounding in earthly concern, as if too much heaven would undo us? Will I lose something of the earthly attachments so dear to me in the change, even if the attachments bring suffering? I am sounding much like a Buddhist about now. I love truth no matter the source.

Today I choose not to believe the lie that I need my fear, worry and suffering to feel safe. I will grieve my losses honestly and deeply without undercutting the presence of whatever emotions may come, but I will not claim those places as my spiritual home. I can almost hear angels cheering me on. I will shed this old, dark, reptilian self and walk in the light, with the presence of the kingdom within radiating out through every breath, simply because it's who we are, who *I AM*.

Unlikely Places

I am going to the prison on Saturday. I have been approved to visit Jeffrey D. Tiner, State ID #12004798. Michael won't be with me this time as he has one more hurdle to clear in the approval process, namely receipt and authorization of the notarized form I mailed this week stating that I am in fact his parent and that he has my permission to visit. So I'll go on my own first. I think I am in for an education.

For instance, I asked the woman who schedules visits if there is anything I should know. "Oh, have you never been to prison before?" No. "Well, don't wear blue or denim." This would be what the inmates wear and we're going for distinction. "Don't wear anything see through or revealing." Check. "And don't wear a bra with an underwire as it will set off the metal detectors." Hm. I forgot that they even make bras without underwires, and it occurs to me I am on a lenten shopping fast. Thank goodness for sports bras tucked inside exercise clothes. Here is some of the latest news from letters from Jeff:

- He shared some thoughts on how I might encourage Michael away from junk food by equating eating with the progress he hopes to see in his weights class.
- He responded to some of my thoughts about engagement with God and God's will, naming discernment and openness as key ingredients.
- He will be sending me a cut from the $24 he makes each month serving food and cleaning the tier with the request I forward it to the Maua Methodist Hospital we served in Kenya last summer.

This last is because of a story I shared with him that I heard via e-mail from the missionaries with whom we worked in Africa. Their recent letter recounted the plights of three women who are patients in the burn unit. One is there because her brother-in-law was having a dispute with her husband, and in response to that disagreement the brother raped her and then set her skirt on fire. She suffered major burns and disfigurement. The other two both have epilepsy and had fallen into open fires where they were cooking when seizures came on. Seizure medicine is free at the clinic but simply getting to the hospital, much less getting treated, is a stretch for many in ways it's difficult for us to fathom. Due to their incapacities, two of the women have been deserted by their husbands, which means they now have no family, no work, and nowhere to go since, according to cultural custom, once a woman marries she becomes part of the husband's family and is no longer claimed by her family of origin.

Jeff was moved by their stories and was particularly incensed at the rape. He said he wanted to go "Rambo" on the perpetrator, but knew the right thing was to pray for him, as well as for the woman. I felt his heart was sincere and compassionate, and this is the only Jeffrey Tiner I know. I don't know the man who was convicted of murder. I don't know the white supremacist who spent years being "covered over by ever deeper layers of sin through drugs and crime," as Deacon Allen once put it. I know the man who is a new creation, for whom the old life is dead and gone and a new life has begun.[8] I know the man who has been praying for my son and asking others to do the same, who has raised over $100,000 for poor women and children in Darfur by hand-writing over 4,000 "beggar letters" from his cell. At least I am coming to know him. And I know that God changes lives. Love changes people.

I realize my trust might appear glaringly naive. Don't lots of death row inmates find God behind bars? There's an old saying in the military that there are no atheists in foxholes, and another saying among inmates that lots of guys find Jesus in jail and then leave him there when they get out. For my part, I figure I have nothing to lose by giving Jeff the benefit of the doubt, and much to gain by exploring this new friendship.

Jeff is allowed two visits per week, and a visitor must call a few days ahead to request a time. He said if his allotment is already met for the week they will "reject you right there on the phone," but not to worry because that almost never happens to him as he has very few visitors. I thought of how many people he must have alienated throughout his life, how many bridges he's burned. He has written me that it took him 50 years and landing on death row to find his way to the light. So in his words, I should "Give Michael time. He'll come around." I think he meant to encourage me, but given his address, I'm not sure the words had the desired effect. Besides, he seems to be referring to God's timing rather than mine.

My correspondence with Jeff began on Michael's behalf, and for the first time I begin to consider its reciprocal nature, not just for Michael but for me as well. We are clearly in the circuit with Jeff, that circuit of Love that flows both ways, or more accurately, all ways and always. "Lord, when were you sick or in prison and I visited you? The King will reply 'I tell you the truth, whatever you did for the least of these brothers of mine, you did for me.'"[9] Surely someone on death row is about as low as he can go. And yet this man creates beautiful art, sends his pennies off to help those less fortunate, and is a spokesperson and solicitor on their behalf. I think again of Brother Roger's words: "Happiness is found in the humble giving of one's self for others." Love changes people. I see Jeff offering prayers, encouragement and hope to Michael, and we are giving friendship and prayers in return. He's now in our bundle, and we're in his. Isn't God found in the most unlikely places?

Here is a prayer he shared with me, which he prays daily:

> *Come, Holy Spirit, enlighten my heart to*
> *see the things that are of God.*
> *Come, Holy Spirit, into my mind that I may*
> *know the things that are of God.*
> *Come, Holy Spirit, into my soul that I*
> *belong only to God.*
> *Sanctify all that I think, say and do,*
> *that all will be for the glory of God.*
> *Amen.*

Moving on Up

I have saved the last eight text messages Michael sent me before his suicide attempt. Most of them came that day, a couple the day before, and all of them were completely normal.

"Mom, I'm going over to Chris' house for a bit. Just wanted to let you know."

"Have you thought any more about the no sleepover rule?"

"Ok."

This was the last message I received from him at about 9:45 that night, maybe 30 minutes before he hung himself. It came just after he had texted me he was going to "stop by Kelley's for a minute" and I had responded, "Ok, you need to take the garbage out when you get home because it's trash day tomorrow." "Ok." These are my last communications from the pre-injury Michael, and I don't know when I might ever delete them. They are a tiny piece of before.

I have also saved a recent voice mail from him for a different reason. This one I keep because I think, "What if he tried to kill himself again and we weren't able to stop it? I want to have his voice." I've had enough thoughts like these that they are becoming normal for me now. I realize that once a person attempts suicide, those around him live with the possibility of a repeat action for the rest of their lives. He not only thought about that line, he crossed it, and like so many boundaries, once the threshold is broken it is easier to cross it again. So I save the message.

Oddly, we don't have any pre-injury recordings of Michael's adult, male voice apart from one song he sang and recorded with his sister. I had a video camera when the kids were little but after the third time they broke it from neglect and abuse, once after a $300 repair, I decided not to invest in one any more. It is strange to have no audio record of his speaking voice from before.

Michael has been depressed lately which has led me to

consider morbid possibilities as more immediate threats. Between the depression and the recent drug use, which I now know included more than one infraction and more than a single substance, fear has been a regular companion. As I visited with one of his teachers about my concerns, asking her and others to keep an eye on him, she asked me, "Doesn't this make you afraid?" I could only answer yes.

But I know my fear doesn't help Michael. Surely it is a natural response and not one I will circumvent any time soon, but again, it's important I don't set up camp there. It simply doesn't help any of us. This is what God is teaching me. We are all vibration, as in there is no solid object in all of creation, appearances aside. We are moving, vibrating collections of atoms, and we are also spiritual vibration, which is why we can become more light (or grace or love) than matter as we grow in spiritual maturity and endurance. I see that I am continually presented with choices: small, very significant choices. Where will my spirit reside? The lower vibrations include fear, jealousy, anger, judgment, and hatred, the higher ones peace, gratitude, joy, compassion and love.

We all are attuned to these differences. We can feel someone's anger when they enter our space, before they speak. We notice if a room has a good feeling or a bad one. Another person's optimism and joy can be contagious. And I see that God is showing me I can make choices at every juncture. The problem isn't so much in the thoughts that come into my mind as in subscribing to the belief that they are true. While I can't choose not to feel fear when it comes (and fear can be an incredible blessing, a great gift when it alerts us to danger), I can see it, name it, and then choose to remain in trust instead. There is a fundamental difference between the intuitive, anxious disruption I felt before discovering Michael's drug use, which was a genuine alert, and the daily worry I can easily overfeed with anxious thoughts.

I feel this as an amazing spiritual exercise, and I

acknowledge I am learning it because it is a survival mechanism right now. But unlike childhood survival mechanisms that are necessary at the time and then become outmoded liabilities in adulthood, this is a skill that will serve me, God, and others for my entire life. I am amazed that Life, the Universe, God, could come up with such a beautiful internal process in response to an unwelcome and very difficult challenge. Isn't God amazing?

I recently read about a man who was engaged in a 21-day negativity fast. He committed to starving his negative thoughts toward himself and others including anything judgmental, critical, shaming, selfish, or anxious. I loved this idea, and while I wouldn't say I'm on a fast, I think I am holding an ongoing vigil. Already I can more readily identify the lower vibrations when they come around my internal corner. As they move in to take up space and eat the groceries and drink the wine in my spiritual home, I can look and say, "Oh, there is worry. I'm going to usher it out and return to hosting trust." So today I found myself filled with gratitude for the way God is using this challenge to help me to mature spiritually. I *want* this, I want to commit to moving "from light into light."[10] I want it not only for myself, but because I believe the more grace we have in our consciousness and the less fear and hate, well, the more light there is for all of us. No good thing (and no darkness) is ours alone. Perhaps, true to the laws of abundance, as I come to better know and remain in these light frequencies that feel so weightless, joyful and peaceful, I will be able to give more away, and there will be more to go around. Like virtual loaves and fishes.[11] I believe I have more than I could ever ask or imagine in God.[12] I just hope to put it into practice.

Prison

The first thing I noticed was the grounds. Daffodils, forsythia, and manicured lawns lined the long walk from the visitor parking to the administrative building. As I neared and passed under the guard tower, three flocks of geese rose up from behind the prison, flapping and honking in cacophony. In short order they formed a trio of 'V's and took flight. I thought of the trinity.

Once inside I followed the well-marked, short route to the visitor area. There was a waiting list for visitation so I dutifully entered my inmate's name and sat down in the room with 15-20 others. After a minute or so they called an inmate's name. Another couple of minutes and they called "Tiner," which was mine. The man motioned me to the counter and said, "Did you schedule a visitation?" "Yes." "Then you don't need to wait." I was learning already. I told him I noticed that the posted list of contraband included sunglasses and that I had some in my purse. Was that going to be a problem? "You won't be taking your purse in." Oh. Right. "Where am I going to put my purse?" "In one of those lockers," he said as he motioned to a wall of little square metal doors with numbers. They reminded me of the ski lodge. He told me to go ahead and take care of that now as the metal detector monitor would be calling me in soon. I put my stuff in the little cubby, locked it up after another visitor pointed out that I needed to put a quarter in the slot *inside* the door (which I don't think I ever would have found on my own), and got in line behind two soft spoken, elderly ladies.

The first of the two kept setting off the alarm on the metal detector. The scanner is very specific and indicates which area of the body is offending. The problem was around her chest. "Are you wearing an underwire bra?" "No, I'm not!" she said, communicating that she had come prepared on that score. "Well, maybe it's the hooks on your bra. Lots of women wear sports bras because they don't have any metal." Suddenly I felt rather smart, if only due to dumb luck. "I can't imagine what it would be!" "Well, you can't go in if you can't pass the metal detector." "Can't you just pat me down?" "Have you ever visited prison before?" "Yes, but not this one." "Well, unless it is your very first visit to a prison in Oregon, I'm not allowed to pat you down. If you've been before, even somewhere else, you have to make it through the metal detector, and you only get three tries." "I just want to see my son." She said this last word more in quiet disappointment than rebellion.

The dialogue went on a bit longer, revealing that she had undergone breast cancer surgery and sometimes small metal plates are inserted in the procedure. "But if that's the case we need a note from your physician." Meanwhile the woman with her made it through the scanner without alert. They were sisters, and they decided the non-alarming one would go ahead and visit on her own. The two of them looked like church ladies, the ones who might bring the cookies on Sunday or play bingo on Friday nights. Their bodies were soft and round, their hair short and their faces non-descript, if a bit worn.

I went in with a group of four or five who had passed muster. When we first checked in at the counter and presented our ID they had stamped our hands with an invisible ink. Now as we passed through the first round of barred gates, they scanned our hands with an ultraviolet light wand which lit up the word "access" (I think that was it) in an eerie, orange glow. Two more sets of metal gates closed behind us and we went down a hall. I was reprimanded for not obeying the "To the right!" command, which I thought meant we were supposed to turn soon. No, they needed us in single file on the right side of the hallway so that the guards at either end maintained an unobstructed view the length of the corridor. I had been wandering to the left.

We went through another locked steel door and arrived in the visiting area. It was roaring with conversation from the four, long double rows of chairs spanning the length of the room. One row filled with inmates faced another row which held the visitors. Everyone had their chairs pulled up knee to knee with their respective partners, shouting while leaning forward so they could hear. There wasn't an empty chair in the place, and there were probably about 100 people. I found myself standing next to the aunt whose sister didn't make it in, looking over the room in bewilderment and saying, "I don't know what my inmate looks like." She replied, "I don't either!" She enlisted the help of a corrections officer and shortly thereafter another guard approached me and said, "Are you here for Tiner?" "Yes." "This way. He's actually a pretty good guy. I've gotten to know him some." He led me to one of the little booths with plexiglass and phones that you see in movies, and our visit began.

Jeff had just come from Mass, something they celebrate only twice a year, though just that day they talked the priest into coming four times a year. He said, "So now we get Mass four times a year, and you're here...it's a good day!" Mostly we talked about Michael and spiritual topics. He is a fellow seeker and believer, a voracious reader, and is devoted to prayer. He rises at 4:30 AM every day so that he can pray in the quiet before the block wakes at 6:00. He has several prayer times throughout the day, not unlike the liturgy of the hours in monastic settings which includes Compline, Vespers, Evensong, etc. By his own admission he is an "unintended monk." He never sleeps more than 39 minutes at a time as the guard check happens every 40 minutes, day and night. An inmate two cells down talks loudly to aliens from 6 AM to midnight. "I really crave solitude, but then I realize I may be the only person praying for that man."

I found talking to Jeff much like talking to one of my brothers. It was easy. He and I share the same love of God which opens up all sorts of common perspective and vocabulary. So it was familiar to me in a new way. We spoke of abundance and how when we have communion with God and give freely of what we have it comes back to us a thousandfold. He experiences the truth of this mystical law even in his prison cell. I told him I felt we'd already been introduced by the Holy Spirit but that now we were getting to meet face-to-face. He told me he appreciated some of the blog entries I'd sent him and that if I didn't mind, he'd like me to keep those coming. He said, "Well, if you weren't already married with kids and all, I think you'd make a good mother superior." I laughed at that, telling him I'd always felt an affinity with nuns. But I made a quiet mental note that it was him, not me, that said, "Shall we have a prayer?" when I first sat down.

I look forward to taking Michael to visit. I believe, for whatever reason, God put it on Jeff's heart to care for Michael, and he takes that call very seriously. Oh, and I was reprimanded yet again on the way out as I talked with another newbie visitor. There I was, veering left again. Amazing that I could get in trouble twice on my first visit! "Oh honey, you'd make a lousy inmate," Rob said to me that evening. Let's hope so.

All God Can Do is Love

I love it when the grace of understanding illumines my field of perception and something that I didn't know before suddenly becomes *clear*. I don't think or work my way there, I simply look around and notice I've arrived at a new vantage point, and am grateful.

I have been thinking about Michael a great deal, of course. His oppositional defiance has returned with a vengeance, meeting almost every approach or word I share with an immediate resistance and dismissal. Sometimes he's outright rebellious, other times quietly defiant. But it is back, and oh so familiar. The good news is this means his brain has healed yet again in a new way. The bad news, of course, is obvious.

So Michael can't really hear or receive anything I offer right now, which is typical for his developmental stage. What teenager thinks their parents are smart? An apocryphal quote attributed to Mark Twain sums it up so well saying, "When I was a boy of fourteen, my father was so ignorant I could hardly stand to have the old man around. But when I got to be twenty-one, I was astonished at how much he had learned in seven years." It's just that Michael recently *was* receptive as he traveled through various developmental phases for a second time in brain injury recovery. What a gift those little open windows and doors were. I'm thankful they came, and will now batten down the hatches against the onslaught of the arrogance of teenage ignorance.

Understanding what I *can't* do for Michael leads me to think on what I *can.* "All God can do is Love." I recently came across these words of Saint Isaac of Ninevah, a 7th century Christian thinker who spent years studying the gospel and meditating on the words "God is Love."[13] It occurred to me to question why I think I should reserve a power for myself, namely to control outcomes, that God doesn't seem to claim. Why isn't it enough for me to set about doing what God does, *all* that God does in the end, which is love? God respects each of us enough to grant us free will, and in my experience divine guidance is almost always gentle, soft and unassuming. God never insists that we choose the loving, less painful, or more joyful route. Why do I think I should exercise greater influence than God?

This thought struck me like a bolt between the eyes. Once again God revealed my misguided arrogance, which had sneaked past my awareness bundled in my needs, particularly my need to avoid pain while helping those I love as I see fit. I have much to learn from this lesson. Thank you, God, for the grace of understanding. I pray I might understand that doing only that which *you* do is enough, and that therein lie all of the treasures of heaven.

When Michael was small his dad and I had a strange premonition. We both thought he would die in childhood. Neither of us mentioned it to the other right away, but eventually a passing conversation unearthed our mutual fear. I wondered if the thought had to do with how Michael came into the world.

He was always a bit fragile as a tiny one (aren't they all?), beginning with a difficult and lengthy birth in which he aspirated meconium and was born with pneumonia. He had to stay in the neonatal intensive care unit for a week on IV antibiotics. The day we were to take him home we hovered around him until 10:30 PM when the last drip of the medicine made its way into his little body and he was cleared for release. The nurse went to pull out the catheter (the IV inserted directly into his umbilical cord), but encountered some trouble. "Huh. That's odd. Usually they just pull right out." She gave another tug and part of the plastic broke off, creating a direct opening for a gushing vessel. A bright red fountain of blood squirted out onto his little belly with every heartbeat.

Thankfully the NNICU doctor lived only two minutes from the hospital so he was called while the nurses escalated into full-blown panic right in front of us. The doctor was there in minutes and with some fine finagling managed to get the little broken piece out. He mentioned he'd seen this happen once before but that the extraction required surgery. That doctor was a saint. Michael had made a big mess during all of the screaming and stressing (both his and the nurses'), and without missing a beat the extremely well-paid physician cleaned Michael's dirty bottom, diapered him up, bandaged his little belly-button wound and delivered him to our arms for homecoming.

When Michael was a toddler he was hospitalized again, this time with the flu. He had become severely dehydrated after a several day bout. His inability to retain fluids left him so weak he recoiled from our touch, reminding me of a wounded animal who retreats and hides to die. That night at 11:00 I called a friend of mine who also happened to be our family physician. I described Michael's condition, how his eyes were glazed and could no longer focus and how he reflexively pulled away from all sensory stimulation including touch. She said, "You'd better take him in." I asked, "Do we go now or in the morning?" "I'd go now."

That hospital venture was shorter lived. When he arrived, Michael was so listless he made no response when poked and prodded, including when they inserted the IV. But the following morning when he spied donuts going by his door in the hallway he got up, held on to the crib rail and began jumping, pointing and chanting, "Doh! Doh! Doh!" Just then the doctor came in for morning rounds and said, "I see someone's feeling better!" We witnessed the miracle of hydration that day.

As Michael grew older and his dad and I were no longer together, my mind developed its own, specific version of the childhood death fear. I kept thinking, "If I can just get him past age twelve I think it will be okay. I don't think he'll die after that." Perhaps my fear was focused on his smaller childhood years. I was relieved when his 13th birthday came and went, but in later reflection have considered that was the year Michael began using drugs and alcohol. I realized that I did lose him then, just not in the way I anticipated. And here he is, 17 going on 18, still alive, but with an acute pass through the valley of the shadow of death forever in his history book. I'm still working on fearing no evil.[14]

Death to Life is a Two-Way Street

I have readjusted so many of my hopes and goals for Michael over the years. I remember when I moved from wanting him to graduate high school and go to college to simply wanting him to survive and not suffer or cause any serious bodily harm. Oh yes, and I was hoping for no more visits from the police on his behalf.

I have revisited and revised my aspirations for Michael yet again. I have moved from "I sure hope this ordeal represents bottom for him and brings the change we so desperately want and need" to "I'm sorry, God, for trying to assume a control that even you don't claim." I move from specific hopes for Michael to a simple desire to set him free on his own, free from my rules and influence, free from the jurisdiction of the parental police, free from the restriction of my mold. His opposition to all that I am wearies me. I'm sure that he desires freedom from perennial evaluation by my standards as well. So my goals are to continue nurturing his healing and to help him get a job so that, God willing, when his 18th birthday comes he can set out on his own and begin to learn the only way he ever will, by experience.

Our briefly re-forged connection has ended for now. We no longer share Spiritual Body Building time, and we aren't enjoying funny stories together or teasing around the table. But oh my goodness those were a couple of enchanted months. What a gift God gave me in that time with Michael, and what a sweet glimpse into the softer, safer-feeling Michael who doesn't need to bury his vulnerabilities behind the steely shields of fear and distance. I won't forget, Michael. I remember who you are in there, even if you don't.

And still, stepping back and looking at God's broader brush strokes, I am reminded that we all must grant one another the dignity to choose our own paths, whether they be roads that lead to life or to death. And I don't mean only the choice of life or death in the ultimate sense, but rather all of the little choices along the way, ones that either infuse us with inspiration or suffocate us with smallness and pain. I remember that as I navigated the roads of adolescence and young adulthood, I first had to learn who I was *not* in order to understand who I *was*. Perhaps we all have to go through the refiner's fire[15] where the dross is burned and blazed away. And boy is it hard to watch those we love take the heat.

While birthing always seems to bring monumental disruption, there is still so much blessing in the change. I trust the pangs, even though the labor is long and the immediate outcome fraught with concern. I know there is glorious life in the midst of this challenge and that every day is a gift. I often think of the enormity of that gift when I see Michael. Nothing is ever only black or white, only good or bad. As frustrated as I am with his choices lately, as angry and betrayed as I often feel, I also still feel a rush of affection for him when he gets up in the morning and his speech-impeded self is all groggy and cute. I appreciate that when I need to follow him to the gas station to make sure the money makes it into the tank instead of some other sinkhole, he turns and says, "Thank you, Mom, I'll see you in a couple of hours." I will continue loving and letting go as best I can, receiving in the midst of it every unlikely blessing God offers.

I am about to do a new thing;
Now it springs forth, do you not perceive it?
I will make a way in the wilderness
And rivers in the desert. – Isaiah 43:19

Chapter 14
Taking it as it Comes

We Don't Get What We Deserve

Deacon Allen, who introduced me to Jeff Tiner and who was such a gift to us during Michael's first days in the hospital, posed a question in a recent correspondence. He wondered who has been on the greater journey these past months, Michael or me. He went on to say that in the end it probably doesn't matter, but that one major difference between Michael and me is that I have had the benefit of a longer life with God and thus have learned to "work with God and not against him."

I thought that was a beautiful way of describing something we learn in the walk of faith, which is that peace and contentment grow out of how we respond to the challenges in life more than from events themselves. I am coming to know in an organic way what I have believed for a long time, that circumstances are not the source of our joy. Nor do the particular ins and outs of our days produce happiness or abundance. These qualities are found only by knowing God in the midst of every part of our lives, both our trials and our triumphs. Peace is not an absence of struggle, but rather a state of being within the struggle. This has always rung true for me intellectually, but what a gift to have the real power of it sink into my cells and sinews and become more of a living force than simply a good or right idea.

I believe God first gives us thoughts that make sense or

seem plausible and then enlivens them in our spirits over time. If we're not paying attention we might miss their advent, and maybe that is fine too. Maybe the Spirit infuses us quietly most of the time, and then one day we notice we have more courage and trust than we did before, or something we formerly only heard with our ears we now know as truth in our hearts with the knowledge only faith can nurture. Allen put it this way: "...by placing your trust in God, He is blessing you with an ever deeper faith, which leads to understanding. So many people think they must understand God before they can believe, which doesn't work, but that is a topic for another conversation."

As I thought about this, I realized how grateful I am for an opportunity to learn and live in a more potent field of grace. As I give up looking for joy and peace in circumstances, in things being "right" or without pain or difficulty, a tremendous freedom opens up within. In a way it's like finally laying down my burden, the burden Christ has been carrying all along. And it feels good to lighten the load. I think that, like so many, I simply won't set it down until it becomes too much to carry. This can be one of the gifts of the burden. We are forced to surrender out of a need to survive. I think it is possible that I would not have reached this deep well of blessing were the challenge not so great. I might have been able to carry on, resisting acceptance of such an outpouring of grace through my imagined ability to take care of myself without God's essential care. I could have fooled myself longer. I could have been the self-reliant, strong woman who all the while misses the very cornerstone of her strength. It has been good to feel the tremors of this internal earthquake so that I might learn what truly stands in the end. All the rest is rubble.

My trust in God, in life, in the goodness of all that is has only grown through these months. And it has deepened most profoundly in the darkness rather than in the light. I now trust much more deeply in God's providence, plan and power, for me and for all of God's children. I realize such trust might not make sense in any logical way, but this understanding has become one of the truest things I know. My vista has opened and expanded, and I don't think I'll return to my previously smaller view ever again. I am humbly grateful for every step that has led me to this deeper communion. There is no greater gift life can offer. In some ways it makes me wonder what I have done to deserve such blessing. But then, grace is never about deserving, only about love.

What's With All These Trees?

Author Anne Lamott once humorously described a malevolent presence that would use her teenage son Sam's body as a host. She named the entity "Phil." We could relate to her description, because in the past when Michael went through particularly rough patches with substance abuse, his personality would undergo a Jekyll & Hyde sort of change. So we took to calling him "Phil" when this alter ego surfaced. Our Phil was particularly oppositional and difficult. He was sullen, uncooperative and angry. And then just when we thought we'd never see our son again, Michael would show up out of the blue, usually after having cleaned up his act for a while. We used to say we never knew who was going to come through the door, Michael or Phil.

Michael is back lately. He's clean and sober and sweet, and I am reminded that it is always drugs and alcohol that turn him into that other ogre. Today he fed the dogs and took them out without a single suggestion from me. He thanked me for dinner. He even acquiesced to a game of Canfield, and beat me.

This most recent shift came right on the heels of my moaning about how weary I was of Michael's oppositional defiance and how eager I am for him to be free and on his own. It's as though he sensed my readiness to shoo him out of the nest and decided that maybe this little tree house wasn't so bad after all. I noticed the change when Michael went to see Jeff at the prison, or maybe just after that. We received such a joy-filled and enthusiastic letter from Jeff a day or so later, thanking Rob for sharing his family with him and going on and on about what a neat boy Michael is. Everyone always loves Michael. He's a likeable kid. Many times his teachers have remarked how they never see any of the sorts of behaviors we experience at home, but what young person isn't better behaved around adults other than his parents?

It was good for me to read Jeff's perspective on Michael for several reasons. One is that Jeff never knew Michael before his injury. The Michael he sees is the Michael he gets, and the picture isn't one of loss—of lost life, IQ points, cognitive functioning and speech fluency—but rather of incredible spark and vitality. This picture is true, of course. I think it's always good for any of us to see our all-too-familiar situations through someone else's eyes, particularly because we are often blind to our blessings due to their sheer repetitiveness. "Oh, my once dead son is still alive? Yeah, that was true yesterday. And the day before that. I have all of my daily needs met? Yeah, that has been true for the last, oh, I don't know, several decades." I sometimes forget what a miracle it is that Michael is here, that he is raising his eyebrows way up or getting his seventh helping of trail mix, eating all of the nuts first and saving the M&M's for last. I might miss the beauty of a sentence he slowly speaks such as, "Well, it didn't originate with me," given that when he first regained consciousness he couldn't articulate a single word, much less know what "originate" meant. I need to remember the good things, even if they are in front of me every day. Especially if they are in front of me.

I think we all have to guard against gratitude fatigue. Honestly, why am I so forgetful that life is astoundingly wonderful, as though my view of the forest of blessings is forever obscured by the abundant goodness of the trees? So not only was I was thankful for Jeff's newly acquired perspective on Michael, I appreciated his fresh joy and celebration of Michael's very life.

It was a good visit, Michael seeing Jeff. A death row inmate can offer advice in a way a mom just can't. The leverage is different. He has the right lingo and a communication style a teenage boy can understand. Jeff is intelligent, funny and articulate. And full of love.

So I can say again that "Every day that's a good day is a *good* day." And it is.

The Weave

God is continuing "the weave," as I am coming to call it. Here are a couple of the latest threads.

At a recent conference where a colleague of mine and I were lecturing and performing, I heard a presentation on the music of the white supremacy movement. This struck me as both unlikely and synchronistic, since I have only recently knowingly met a former white supremacist. I learned their music is available on Amazon and iTunes, and, if you research the movement, you should never use your real name or regular e-mail address. Their numbers have grown in huge proportion since President Obama's election. And by the way, if you are lecturing on the topic, your handouts can get confiscated at the border.

A second presentation I heard was on music in the state penitentiary in Angola, Louisiana, one of the most notorious penal institutions in the country. The lecture touched on the power of gospel music among lifetime inmates as a means of finding identity and niche.

What were the chances, I wondered, that I would listen to presentations on prison inmates and white supremacists at a music conference? You might think that by now I would respond with, "Well, seems highly likely, Christine, the way things have gone so far!" Given how many connections God has made and continues to forge, I probably should have arrived expecting a presentation on the power of music on brain injury recovery or something like that.

I wrote the woman who presented on the music of the Klan and other neo-Nazi groups and shared a story of hope. I told her of a former white supremacist on death row who now has a 19th century black slave woman as his baptismal saint, and who has raised over $100,000 for poor black children in Darfur. I told her he's prayed for my son every day since October 11, and that we've become friends. She wrote back and told me the topic is intensely personal for her because a young member of her family, who has had a very hard life and was "failed by the system," recently joined the Klan. She said she would like to interview Jeff if it were possible. We have pledged to pray for one another.

God offers us constant threads of life, a million small ways to connect with and encourage one another. I am grateful for every lead and for the learning and blessing offered along the way. God is good, all the time. All the time, God is good.

Tea Time
Michael has begun a new term at Chemeketa. He is still in the high school portion of their Early College/High School curriculum and will retake the same placement exam he took last summer at the end of this term. Those results will afford a chance to see where he is now in relation to where he was before his injury. He'll also retake the school district's neuro-psychological tests at that time. These results will compare with where he was in early January after his injury. So the summer will be a time of taking stock for future directions and plans.

Michael's current schedule is an impressive indication of how much he's healed. His occupational therapist recently suggested that he is now ready for a lecture format class. Michael originally chose two Physical Education classes for his schedule, but with his therapist's recommendation has now replaced one with Physical Science. This will be a big challenge for him. One of the areas hard hit by the injury was his ability to process aural information. The fact that she feels he's ready for this leap is encouraging.

His other classes include English and Weight Training, and he will continue an independent study for Math. He's ready for Algebra I now, but that course isn't offered this term, so he'll continue practicing on his own. He has also begun working on getting a job, which is no easy task in today's economy. He began his hunt at the Goodwill Job Opportunities office since one of their missions is to employ people with disabilities. He was directed to two other leads for employment and is following up on one of them today.

I don't know if Michael will be considered mentally challenged forever. I know he is now, and I am thankful for special considerations for folks with his needs and abilities. I also realize I am thinking less and less about his long-term reality. I don't consider whether or not his indications from his injury will become permanent as often as I once did. I think I am settling into "this is who Michael is," as in "this is who he is now and no other person exists since the future is simply an idea." Yet again I realize that it truly isn't my thoughts that get me into trouble but rather when I believe that they are true. Anything I think about Michael's future is only a thought, and sometimes those thoughts take the form of grand possibilities and other times they manifest as quiet discouragement. But they are all only thoughts, none truer than another. What is true is *now*, and now is beautiful.

As I practiced the presence of God this morning in prayer, I thought of tea leaves in water. I do very much like tea, particularly green tea with jasmine. I thought of the dry, bristly leaves and how they soften when wet, sharing their scent and flavor with the liquid. I felt that's how God's spirit works on me, taking what is dry but full of potential, and softening and spreading it to the world. It's a simple and perhaps basic analogy, but it describes my spiritual experiences in a tangible way. I often feel I'm steeping in the presence of God where it is warm and fragrant and delicious. This comforting presence is never meant for us alone. We are supposed to share. Just as I find it's nice to make a whole pot of tea rather than only a cup. That way there is enough to go around.

❧

Natalie and Michael were baptized years ago on Easter eve. It was during the time we lived in Moscow, Idaho, when I worked as Music Director at Pullman Presbyterian Church. Since I had been on a hiatus from faith when they were babies, they were baptized when they were six and three years old. Attendance was sparse at the Saturday evening service in the newly constructed sanctuary. The building was so new the baptismal font had yet to be installed, so someone had placed a crystal bowl filled with water on a small pedestal in the front of the chancel. As I think on it, it was likely a punch bowl. Churches always seem to have an excess of those.

Reconciling to the liturgy of the baptismal service required some creative thinking on both the pastor's and our parts. As a young adult I had left church and turned my back on the faith I learned there, so I was still struggling with making a personal statement of belief. I just couldn't wrap my brain around the traditional baptismal question, "Is Jesus Christ your Lord and Savior?" which is asked of the parents on the child's behalf. But I very much wanted this sacrament for my children. So the pastor graciously found an alternate order of worship for the baptismal service with questions that still met the criteria but which were phrased in a way that made sense to my fledgling understanding. I wanted to be honest, and wanted at least to think I knew the meaning of the question I was answering.

We talked with Natalie and Michael beforehand, explaining that we felt they were already God's and that their baptism was a way of activating that truth by claiming and affirming it publicly. At the time this ritual struck me as a means of enacting something communally that is already true individually and spiritually. I have always believed there is power in naming truth. I realize every denomination thinks of baptism differently, so I make no claim to be explaining any sort of absolute here. I'm merely expressing the ideas we shared with Michael and Natalie at the time. Because whatever we said, and whatever Michael heard, he came to the service that night with a great sense of expectancy.

I will never forget how he looked as he stood in front of that bowl of water, gazing into it with awed anticipation of the mysterious, holy, magical power it held. I can still see his face wide with wonder. When Pastor Dan dipped his hand in the water and dumped the full scoop of it on Michael's head three times, as it ran down his face and all over his blue button down shirt in streaks and blobs, he drank it in with the joy of a child playing in a downpour on a hot summer night in Kansas, except that he was as still as a saint.

Later in the service came the hymn. I don't think Dan could have known that this particular song was a special one from my youth in the days before I walked away from God, though by now he was familiar with my faith journey. He knew I had abandoned belief in favor of cynical intellectualism, and that I wore this mantle in an effort to obscure and escape irreconcilable differences within myself. And he knew God was currently pursuing me like the Hound of Heaven.[1] So he pulled out "For Those Tears I Died."[2] And I wept.

You said you'd come and share all my sorrows.
You said you'd be there for all my tomorrows.
I came so close to sending you away,
But just like you promised you came in to stay.
I just had to pray.

And Jesus said "Come to the water,
    stand by my side.
I know you are thirsty, you won't be denied.
I felt every tear drop when in
    darkness you cried,
And I long to remind you that
    for those tears I died."

Your goodness is so great, I don't understand,
But dear Lord, I know now that
    all this was planned.
I know you're here now and always will be.
Your love burst my chains, and in you I'm free.
But Jesus, why me?

Jesus, I give you my heart and my soul.
I know that without you I'd never be whole.
Savior, you opened all the right doors,
And I thank you and praise you
    from earth's humble shores.
Take me, I'm yours.

Reading over the words now I see why I loved
the song as a youth. It has that immediate, emotional
appeal that youngsters crave, and it also speaks to
being known in our sorrow. I remember quiet, angst-
filled nights crying into my pillow as an adolescent,
wishing someone would notice or understand. I look
back on those experiences now and understand them
as puppy-like pubescent urges, fraught with so much
immediate need and longing. But I think as adults

251

we simply morph our youthful needs into ever more complex and less recognizable incarnations. Instead of hoping to be noticed by the right girl or boy, we might seek professional acclaim or prestige. Rather than looking for a friend in the "cool" group, we might seek heart to heart, reciprocal understanding in a soul mate or close friend. We might still feel betrayed if the world doesn't understand us. And if we lack deep intimacy in relationships, we recognize that something essential is missing from our lives. Our desire to know and be known, to matter, to be free and claimed at the same time grows up with us, but it doesn't go away. I also see how the song now sounds to me like God reaching toward my son, saying, "Remember the best love you've ever known in your life? That is me, except much, much better." In the end, whether we are teenagers or octogenarians, the answer to our needs is the same.

I think as Michael stared into the water, motionless and ready, he beheld a truth, even if he didn't know what it was. Something very special was in that water, and he knew it. It was the love of God, crystal clear.

Everything Gained, Nothing Lost

I don't know how to love him,
what to do, how to move him....

I remember these words so well from *Jesus Christ Superstar.* I loved the show as a youth and thought it was one of the most powerful things I'd ever seen or heard. Now it strikes me as a timepiece, something that simultaneously conjures up the emotions it first aroused right alongside a full appreciation of its datedness. The song lyrics came to me the other night, probably because I was fresh from a Good Friday service, and they came as I thought about Michael.

I imagined myself saying the line to him: "Michael, I don't know how to love you. Sometimes our entire relationship seems to be reduced to a single issue: you want freedom to do whatever you please, which mostly means to do drugs, and I won't let you without imposing major consequences. How can I possibly express my love through that limited scope?" I thought about the rules I place on Michael, how much freedom and/or restriction he has. Virtually every restrictive rule has to do with using. For instance, lately he has to check in at home in person every two hours. Calling won't suffice, because too much can be disguised over the distance of a phone call. He's pretty much free to go and do as he pleases, but he has to check in. Mostly he chooses not to go anywhere at all.

I realize Michael has very few ideas on how to engage in social activities or interaction apart from using drugs or alcohol. That world has been his modus operandi for his entire adolescence. On top of that very limited realm of experience, he still suffers from a brain injury, now complicated by depression. Initiation remains elusive. There aren't many friends around who don't use. None, really. Well, maybe one, and that one has already separated from Michael out of self-preservation. It hurt that young man too much to watch Michael repeatedly hurt himself and others with his choices.

A response from the inner realm came to me as I thought about Michael. Don't resist. Don't force solutions. Just be. Keep reaching out. Keep your eyes open. And mostly just remember you aren't alone, and neither is he.

Rob calls it the ministry of presence, when all we are called to do is be with someone. So it occurs to me that maybe I do know how to love him. I don't know how to fix him or help him or control him, but I know how to love him. That I know very well, and one of the best ways I can do it is by witnessing, even if that witness is silent. Any time

I'm with Michael, I can know we are both with God. It's one of the simplest ways I know of praying for someone. Simply connect with the presence of God and then mentally bring the other person into the fold of that communion. Suddenly they are in the same peaceful and grace-filled space that you are. We are all spiritually porous, whether we know it or not. God permeates. The object of our prayer might not even know we are blessing them this way. Likely they won't. But love is being nurtured nonetheless.

Well I got all excited about this idea so I trotted right down to the family room where Michael was watching TV. I had heard it thumping and booming so I guessed whatever was on might not be my first choice, but I went anyway. I was centered and still, spiritually speaking, and was looking forward to being with Michael in that state. It didn't work out. I lasted maybe a minute and a half. He was watching a slasher movie and I really can't stomach those. The screaming and horror was a shock to my system, which was still in a contemplative place after the Good Friday service. Within moments I was reevaluating my sense of spiritual adventure and retreating up the stairs. I'd need to try again.

I did give it another go the next night, and this time he was watching *The Two Towers* from the *Lord of the Rings* trilogy. I like those movies, in spite of the violence. I read the entire series twice many years ago, so I enjoy seeing my old friends Frodo and Gandalph and all the others. We watched together, making some jokes. He asked me a question about something a friend of his had posted on Facebook. It was a good time.

And then today was Easter. As soon as I started singing the first hymn I began to weep. I fought it at first, thinking I couldn't stand there in church shaking with sobs, knowing if I gave in I might do just that. But then I simply let go and cried, for several verses. The enormity of life after death was overwhelming me. We really did lose Michael, and yet he is here. Every now and again this realization hits me and brings me to my knees in gratitude. This was one of those times.

In a stroke of God's synchronicity, I've been reading *90 Minutes of Heaven*. I went to the study the other day to find something by Thomas Merton but this book caught my eye instead. More than one person had recommended it to us, and apparently now was its time. It tells the story of Don Piper who died instantly in an auto accident when a semi-trailer truck crushed his car in a head on collision. He had no pulse and was pronounced dead at the scene, his mangled body covered with a tarp. Ninety minutes later another man was moved to pray for him, and the dead man regained his life. What struck me this weekend as I read it was what a hell this man's existence was upon his return to life. He miraculously came back from the dead only to be met with excruciating pain and suffering that went on and on. He spent over three months in the hospital, had 34 surgeries and was in a hospital bed at home with virtually no movement for 11 months. During this time he never slept but only ever passed out from pain. He was not at all grateful to be alive, and he was deeply depressed.

Oddly enough, it was reading about his trials more than his time in heaven that encouraged me. Michael is struggling right now, and his life is difficult. He is depressed. He is going through the motions okay, and actually just made stellar grades from his first term back at school. But often his spirit is heavy. And why wouldn't it be? His situation is tedious and the road of recovery is long. The gift of a miracle does not come with the promise of ease afterward. But it occurred to me I had been thinking it should. Doesn't blessing mean that we are *blessed*? If God saved Michael in such a dramatic way, shouldn't he be specially guarded and tended from now on? And wouldn't such blessing mean his life would be happy and good?

Well, no, it wouldn't. More likely, God's saving grace in Michael's life means Michael has a purpose here, and ultimately that purpose is probably not merely his own happiness but the joy that comes in giving himself away to others in love. His ultimate purpose may not be for him at all. I believe this is true for all of us and it surely has been true for Don Piper. To this day he lives with constant pain and is ready to go back to heaven whenever God will have him. But his life and story are an encouragement to countless others, many who need that good word in a desperate way.

So today I feel patient and grateful. Michael has been given another chance at life, but the chance doesn't mean his life will be easy or smooth. But it is *life*, and that is enough. For now when I can't think how to help him I'll simply be with him. I'll be patient. And I will remember that he is God's, as we all are. Rob shared these words of Henry Nouwen in his sermon this morning:

The resurrection is God's way of revealing to us that nothing that belongs to God will ever go to waste. What belongs to God will never get lost. The resurrection doesn't answer any of our common questions about life after death such as: "How will it be? How will it look?" But it does reveal to us that love is stronger than death.

Michael's Days

Michael has been around home a lot lately. We haven't received any visitations from his alter ego Phil for some time. We know our boy is clean, even without drug testing. We know because his naturally sweet spirit is shining through undiminished, which is always the case when Michael is sober. Alternately, when he's off the wagon he can't find or reveal that sweeter side of himself to save his life. He has always been a naturally tender and sensitive person (probably not the easiest attributes for an adolescent male to bear), so even now as he struggles with depression, he still smiles easily when something tickles his fancy or when one of us goads him a bit. While his face looks and moves differently than it did before his injury and while some of his expressions might more readily identify him as mentally challenged, there is a genuineness in his eyes when he smiles that was usually missing in the past. I'm not sure what accounts for the sincerity. Perhaps more of him is simply more visible, as if there are fewer layers damping his brilliance. In either case his gentle smile is handsome and winning.

I've been spending some time with him in front of the TV each evening. I'm not much of a TV watcher, probably taking in an hour or two per week at most. But Michael is in front of the TV a lot lately, so I try to meet him where he is. I look at television as a safe sort of drug for him right now, offering a bit of escape from the hours upon hours of alone time. Nothing is required of him when he watches TV, and I imagine he can temporarily forget about the parts of his brain or body that no longer work the way they used to. I've noticed that he laughs more at comedies when I'm there. I know I laugh out loud more when watching a funny movie with someone else, or even better, with a whole, lively group. Isn't it wonderful how laughter is contagious, feeding on the levity of those around us?

Michael is still on the job hunt. Sometimes he follows up on leads, sometimes he doesn't. He's going to school every day and keeping up with all of his work, though it holds no interest for him. But then, he has very little interest in anything right now, so his lack of academic enthusiasm isn't surprising. Like so many who suffer from depression, he is going through the motions of the days without experiencing any sense of their meaning, waiting for the time when some feeling of purpose returns. I think he's brave.

I was thinking about Michael while driving alone yesterday morning and I blurted out, "I love you so much, Michael." I realized what a saving grace love is, but not *my* love. A parent's love can never save their children or anyone else they care for. Love is a good thing, a right and incredible blessing for every child that is on the receiving end, but human love doesn't save anyone. No one ever reaches paradise or

serenity or happiness or fulfillment through the sheer, loving
determination of her own or anyone else's will, though many
of us have tried. These gifts only come in surrender to our
lack of control, which opens the door for divine love to flood
our broken, aching places. I have wished with all of my heart
that the love I feel for Michael could somehow manifest as
a particular positive aspect in his life, that it could magically
translate into hope or inspiration or courage for him. How
powerless we are in the end, even with the greatest power
in the world at our disposal. I suppose our love is powerful
in general but not in specifics. Love matters. It just doesn't
chart the course.

I do think love helps us chart our interior journey,
though. In the end our greatest power of influence is over
our own choices, both internal and external, which is apt
since the only person we will spend every day of our lives
with from beginning to end is ourselves. Choices made in
love have great strength. Choices made from fear are weak.
Thus we have both the power and responsibility to choose
what we want to manifest on the inside, what thoughts we
want to loop in our heads, what impulses we want to deliver
to the world, what kinds of words we want to share with
others, what ideas we want to feed. Only we can choose how
we respond to a situation, whether we assume the role of
victim or grateful student. God's grace helps us work with
the challenges life presents, so that instead of responding
with bitterness or self-pity we can unearth compassion, even
if we've been wounded along the way. Especially if we've
been wounded along the way.

Michael can now rattle off tongue twisters with impressive
speed, but still chooses silence nearly all day long because he
can't abide the sound of his speech. He has a perfect driving
record in his Mustang: no fender benders, no tickets, no
problems. His teachers like him. His memory is astounding,
which is particularly remarkable given that short-term
memory usually takes a very hard, long-term hit from brain

injuries such as his. He remembers appointments a couple of weeks out, never forgetting the day or time. He can navigate his way wherever he needs to go. We no longer hire someone to come stay here when we're out, partly because he hasn't relapsed again and even more because he has long been completely self-sufficient in personal care and safety. His Parkinson's-like jerkiness persists, and he resolutely refuses to see a counselor, again largely due to his self-consciousness over his speech but also due to a deep reticence to discuss internal issues. I know there is no hurrying a person's readiness to examine their tender, inner places with a magnifying glass, and I fully respect the boundary he's drawn. At the same time, I'm encouraged that he is considering seeing a brain injury psychologist now that he's learned depression occurs in nearly 100% of cases like his. When a person's old self is replaced with a new, partially diminished one, there is bound to be some upheaval and adjustment, including depression. All in all I see him manifesting the miracle of his very life every day in ever more wonderful ways. He's 130 days away from being 18.

I am learning to better respect each of his choices in spite of a nagging desire to alter many of them. That's an itch I just can't scratch, but I'm finding the longer I ignore the itch, the less attention it commands. Recently I read an entry in an Al-Anon book that went something like this: "I am not responsible for the alcoholic's drinking, sobriety, job, cleanliness, diet, or dental hygiene." It was strange, reading that, because as the mother of a minor I am responsible for nearly all of those things. But one day soon, one fine day about four months out, I will technically no longer be responsible for such details in Michael's life. I don't think I'm naive. I realize I can't throw a switch that suddenly moves him from semi-dependent teenager to fully independent adult. It is just strange to consider the impending balance shift, which I believe will be a very good thing. I've been working toward it for a long while. God grant me the serenity to accept the things I cannot change, the courage to change the things I can, and the wisdom to know the difference. And while you're at it, please help me not to confuse caring with control. And God, please bless Michael, now and in all his days to come. Amen.

Let my trust be in your mercy, not in myself.
Let my hope be in your love, not in health,
strength or ability or human resources. If I trust you,
everything else will become for me strength,
health and support. Everything will bring me to heaven.
If I do not trust you, everything will be my destruction.
—Thoughts In Solitude, Thomas Merton

Chapter 15
Not Looking Ahead

To Trust or Not to Trust

Merton's words about trust were a real gift to me. They incubated overnight and then birthed a little epiphany in me this morning. I saw how the entire balance of our lives rests in our response to life's events, in our ability to receive experiences with an attitude of "How might God use this in a transformative way?" rather than "Why me?" or "This isn't fair." Because God *will* transform us through our pain, if we're willing to follow love's lead. There is blessing offered in our brokenness. When life offers us a blow, we can either retreat like an animal to lick our wounds and die, or we can walk forward into the miraculous healing of God's light in ever greater fields of grace.

I often wonder why some receive the gift of faith and others don't. Why can some trust God in the midst of difficulties while others believe the difficulties to be the very reason to discount or abandon belief? And why do those who claim faith respond with trust at times and with blind doubt at others? What is the barrier that refuses God's saving love? Is it just pain? If so, what is so horrible about pain? What gives pain more leverage than love?

When life's challenges come our way, when our hearts are broken or we are at a loss as to how to go on or manage or climb our way out of a deep, dank pit of fear or pain, the first response needs to be surrender to God's love, because that love is what initiates the subtle but necessary internal shift. When we quit fighting, quit clawing up the slippery sides of the pit, quit trying to escape by the force of our own strength, merit, or mental effort, we make room for God to move in and take over. What comes then is peace, peace followed by great growth and beauty and health.

If we can let God in.

If we can remember we can't do it by ourselves.

If we can *trust*.

If we can't, as Merton said, those very things that could lead us to heaven instead lead us to hell. It isn't the experiences that define the course, but rather the humility of our response. The very same experiences, *exactly the same ones*, can usher us into paradise or destruction.

Michael's injury has already become one of the greatest blessings in my life, as has his struggle with addiction. I have been given opportunities for growth I never wanted, have been stretched far beyond my comfort level and this has blessed me immeasurably. Through the tragedy of October 11, God broke my heart open with grief and planted the seeds of sharing. Michael's journey has given me the opportunity to grow into a part of myself I hadn't yet found, and I'm grateful.

I can't say what blessings Michael's suicide attempt might offer him or others. That is for each person to discover on his or her own. We are all responsible for mining our own jewels from the pit. And oh how beautiful they are, these abundant jewels. There is no limit to their number, richness or beauty. When we are ushered or dropped or thrown into one of life's pits and are standing in the dark wondering which way to go, remember there are always two options: trusting or not trusting. One opens the door to heaven, the other to hell. If we can't yet trust, we can pray for the ability to trust. God respects and cheers on our desire. Trusting will come in equal measure to how much fear we can release. Like faith, it grows over time, so we can try trusting God in some small way first and see how that goes. I often want to ask those I know who haven't yet given God a try, "How is that working out for you?" If the answer is less than you'd like in terms of peace, joy, compassion, generosity, and happiness, why not try trusting the Love that will not let you go? It doesn't mean you won't have pain or loss, but it means you will find jewels in the pit of your despair. Seems to me the other option is merely wallowing in the muck. What have we got to lose?

O Love that wilt not let me go,
I rest my weary soul in thee,
I give thee back the life I owe,
That in thine ocean depths its flow
May richer, fuller be.

O light that followest all my way,
I yield my flickering torch to thee,
My heart restores its borrowed ray,
That in thy sunshine's blaze its day
May brighter, fairer be.

O Joy that seekest me through pain,
I cannot close my heart to thee,
I trace the rainbow through the rain,
And feel the promise is not vain,
That morn shall tearless be.

O Cross that liftest up my head,
I dare not ask to fly from thee,
I lay in dust life's glory dead,
And from the ground there blossoms red
Life that shall endless be.
– George Matheson (1882)

The Boy in the Portrait

Michael is past the halfway point of the magical first year of brain injury recovery, the year when many of the changes we will see are supposed to occur. He continues to be a miracle: a walking, talking testament to the enormity of life, a present witness to the sheer power of love.

The most remarkable differences we see now seem to happen quietly inside of his brain, such as cognitive gains that open up new levels of understanding and processing. His physical attributes have been constant for a while, not showing much noticeable change. Considering what is and isn't in flux led me to think on this new Michael, the one who gets up every day, eats cereal for breakfast and watches multiple episodes of *The Office* in the evening, the one who had a fender bender right after I bragged about his perfect driving record.

I realize I remember the old Michael less and less. Just as when a person we love dies and we expect the very force and depth of our attachment to produce a clear and lasting picture of them in our mind's eye, I thought I would always remember exactly what pre-October 11 Michael was like. But just as the visual memory of our loved ones can fade from our inner view over time, I find the specifics of Michael's pre-injury life are becoming increasingly difficult to remember. This is poignant. His old personality, mannerisms, expressions and sounds are becoming remote, like an echo that has bounced off one too many canyon walls to maintain the sharp definition of its initial strike. When I look at his senior portraits made to celebrate his GED and impending launch into college, it no longer seems like Michael who looks back at me. It is that other young man, the pre-injury Michael, the person who no longer exists. While I may recognize him, he has become a stranger to me, that one on the inside looking out through such an intimately familiar physical form.

It is interesting how much a person's thoughts and personality determine the look of his face. Michael's face is so different now, and while a bit of his muscular control has changed, it seems the greatest difference is how his insides have reshaped his outsides. Is this why, when couples remain married for a very long while, they sometimes begin to look like each other? Is it because the number of their shared experiences so dramatically outpaces the number of their separate ones that something in their physiques begins to reflect their shared commonality? I wonder.

That other person who inhabited Michael's body for 17 years, one month and 13 days no longer looks out at me from behind his eyes. I don't think we'll see him again. This realization brings fewer tears than it used to. I'm grieving the past less and living the present more. This is good. The unstoppable and miraculous force of life propels me forward just as it does Michael. Resisting would be as futile as trying to push a wave up a hill. Life is going the way it's going, and I'd be well advised to ride along rather than brace stubbornly against the current. I'm learning to love this new Michael. No, that isn't right. I'm certain I love Michael more now than I ever have. I guess I'm learning about who it is that I love. I'm getting to know him again for the first time. He is my boy, becoming a fine young man, and I love him.

Is it God or the Devil in the Details?

"Mike will never change. I can't imagine him ever being different." Casey, one of Michael's best friends, spoke these words during a time of intense frustration a year or so ago. He was having a hard time watching Michael repeatedly make self-destructive choices. This pain was particularly up close and personal since Casey was living with us at the time. Through many days and nights he was there for Michael, trying to be a good friend by discouraging him from going down the road to ruin. Michael's disregard for this care was also painful for Casey. He saw how entrenched Michael was in his lifestyle, how committed he was to it over all other relationships, even his relationship to Casey, who was like a brother to him.

I remember my response very clearly. "Casey, *never* is a long time." "Yeah, but I just can't see it. I just don't think he'll ever change." I told him we all have a hard time imagining the dramatic ways God might work in our lives, because we never see those truly transformational events coming. If we did, we'd probably run like rabbits! I know that I believe in solutions much more readily when I can imagine them, when I can see some genesis of their later manifestation and envision how they might unfold or develop, even if those scenarios are unlikely. But if I can't imagine the way at all it's very difficult for me to hope for it. Maybe this is a defense mechanism. My imagination has always been limited by my vision, and my vision is helplessly finite. "Now faith is the assurance of things hoped for, the conviction of things not seen," proclaims the book of Hebrews.[1] Like Casey, my problem is I'm often not too good at imagining the unseen, and since I don't know what to hope for, I have no conviction. Am I hoping for Heaven? Honestly, sometimes that seems a bit vague or too remote. My attraction to the idea of universal salvation aside, I've always experienced heaven as both an "already" and "not yet" reality. But if the kingdom of God is already among us here on earth, why are we behaving like resident aliens who are reluctant to take up full citizenship? Are we hoping for heaven now or later? Or just for a taste of the promise here or there?

I think God has taught me through this year to hope in what I can't even imagine, and maybe even more than that, I've learned it's better not to imagine at all but simply to hope in whatever God may provide. Now *that* I can hope for. Maybe that's what the author of Hebrews is getting at. Maybe such faith is the best way to move beyond the limited scope of my imagination, to hope in the big picture rather than the details. This seems so obvious to me as I write it since we can never see the impending details, though I hadn't considered this perspective before. I do trust God in the big picture, I know I do, and since the details are part of the big picture, I guess by default I trust God there, too. If I'm at a loss to trust in specifics, I have completely missed the truth that if I am trusting in the largest sense I must already be trusting in the minutia as well, because one is embodied in the other. Thank you, God!

It brings to mind the old phrase, "The years go by quickly, it's the days and nights that are slow." I think I need to pull back from the noise of the daily grind and look at the scope of the years more often. Just yesterday I was telling a student of mine who was in the midst of a small crisis how things almost always work out in the end. The only variable is how long we're going to spend stressed, angry or anxious. While we can't circumvent the initial, reptilian emotional responses to crises or offenses, we surely can decide how long we'll remain in their grip. Often our tenure there depends on how much drama we need in our days, a need which is determined by our self-image. As one friend put it, "I'm always thinking I'm either hot s*** or a piece of s***. I need to find the middle ground." If I'm supremely offended at someone's treatment of me, I'm probably thinking I'm hot stuff. If I am overly mortified by what I said or how I behaved, I'm probably thinking I'm worthless. Both of these perspectives are errors in judgment. I am who God says I am, no more, no less. God is in the details of me, too.

Michael's journey has taught me a great deal about this. God, help me to trust you in the days and nights, not only in the years. Please help me transfer some of my trust-in-general to trust-in-specifics. Help me to see how moments and eternity are ultimately one and the same, all parts of the same whole, which belongs to you.

~

Jeff and I have now developed a real friendship. We write every week, often several times a week. He is a prolific correspondent, not just with me, but with many across the globe. I have visited the prison three times, twice by myself and once with Michael, and we will continue the visits. Our written communications have ushered us past the mere idea of a relationship, beyond a sort of cardboard cut-out connection between the "death row inmate who was praying for a son" and the "mother who appreciated it" to a real friendship, one complete with tensions and interpersonal negotiations as well as deep affection. An example: Jeff had been lecturing me a bit about some behavior of mine with which he disagreed, choices which were related to basic differences between male and female perspectives, and I eventually wrote him that apparently he was stubborn and so was I, so I planned to continue doing my job and to let him do the same. He wrote back humorously that we could each have new names. His could be "Rocks Between Ears" and mine could be "Head Like Stone." He affectionately dubbed us "Rocky" and "Stoney." From there we moved past the friction into deeper rapport. Our friendship is real now, and I'm grateful.

Once when he got behind a bit on his writing he told me he had 70 letters in his inbox awaiting replies. Many of his friends are members of holy orders (monks, nuns and bishops in the Catholic church), others are doctors who work in Africa on behalf of those with AIDS, and others are folks like you and me who for one reason or another have come in contact with this man who has a gifted ability to "connect the dots for God." We have found we experience similar connections with the Divine. We both have mystics' hearts, so we are able to share conversation about experiences that to many would seem implausible or unlikely. We have grown to trust one another. He continues the appeals process that all death row inmates pursue, and there are some bright, hopeful spots on the horizon. We both pray, along with a great cloud of witnesses that literally spans the planet, that God's will may be accomplished in his life and that he will accept that will with trust and grace.

We have prayed together and shared our individual circles of prayer with one another. He has quite an extensive network of supplication and intercession and Michael has received literally hundreds of heartfelt prayers in response to letters Jeff sent out to various corners of the globe. I am reminded of the huge circle of prayer Natalie organized when Michael was in the hospital. Many (most?) of those gathered on behalf of a young man lying in a coma with a telling, raw, red circle around his neck had never met Michael. Jeff has prayed tirelessly for Michael's healing and wholeness since that day, and now stands poised to become a spiritual mentor and friend to him. Michael trusts him, too, as Jeff has opened his heart to Michael as well as to me. We're both praying that one day Michael will find it safe to do the same in return.

Jeff has become an integral part of Michael's (and our) story. He reminds me how God is found in the most unlikely places and always wildly exceeds our expectations. He is also a perfect manifestation of the way God honors the signals we send out to the universe and respectfully responds in kind, whatever our communication may be. I once heard it described this way: when we dwell in anger or judgment, we are giving a signal to the cosmos that we'd like to draw more of that experience to ourselves. This happens not as a matter of personal evaluation but through the principles of an impersonal energetic law of attraction. The vibrations we emit attract similar electromagnetic impulses, simply because it is their nature to respond, much as magnets attract other magnets of the proper match. Jeff now sends out love and grace to the long list of people for whom he prays, and he receives it in kind. I know I am in the middle of this current of grace and will remain in communion with him. God has gifted the two of us with this friendship forged through mystical hearts and a young man's desperate choice, and I think I can safely speak for both of us when I say we are grateful.

Friends and Family

We had a lovely evening at the beach yesterday. It was a spontaneous, early Mother's Day celebration, as miraculously all of us were available at the same time for the short trip. On the way we stopped at the Otis Cafe, a tiny diner just east of the Oregon coast that has been reviewed in the *New York Times* for it's culinary offerings and simple charm. They are particularly famous for their black molasses bread and German hash brown potatoes. The town of Otis was for sale a few years back. The entire municipality consists of the café, a post office, and a general store/gas station. A rich Californian was going to buy it, but I believe the deal fell through. The idea of buying a town struck me as fanciful fiction. Can a person really do that? I know major league teams have owners, but towns?

Natalie brought a Frisbee to the beach and we brought our Golden Retriever (Max was a good boy!). There was a lot of happy running and leaping. It was a perfect day, weather-wise. The Oregon coast isn't a swimming sort of beach; the water is around 45 degrees year round. Yesterday qualified as a balmy day, meaning the air temperature was in the upper 50's with sun and wind. We wore our fleece and sweatshirts and I sported a headband along with a hood to keep my ears warm. But the sun was out and it sure felt nice.

Rob snapped a picture of Michael and Natalie (Max elbowed his way in there, too). I was struck by the sincerity of Michael's smile and the way his arm wrapped around his sister. Both the expression and gesture were open and full. He was happy to be there, happy to be with her and with us. I was thankful for this irony. Before Michael's injury his family was nearly the most objectionable thing to him. His disdain for us was often palpable, and he made no secret of where we stood in terms of his loyalty: behind a long line of drug-using losers. He was fiercely loyal to his comrades, often to the detriment of his own safety or wellbeing. This loyalty never extended to his family. Most of the time we felt like we were there to be used when convenient and to be managed and handled when not. I know this sounds harsh, but it was true. Michael pretty much only engaged relationally with me when he wanted something. I realize in many regards this behavior is on task for a teenager, this separation from parents and identification with peers. Maybe I was impatient with it. Maybe he was particularly difficult.

Yesterday morning I sat down with Michael to review his recovery goals. He's still on track with most of the remaining objectives. Regarding "going to college," he continues to go to class at Chemeketa every day and to keep up on his work. His recent progress report boasted two As and two Bs. He's looking into what would be required to become an emergency responder such as a fireman or EMT.

I asked him about his goal to "hang out more with friends" and how he felt about his social life. He responded, "It's non-existent." This is true. There are no more phone calls, no more outings. Which has also meant no more using. The other day I recalled his response to me some weeks back when I suspected he was using (he was), and I told him we were going to do a UA (urinalysis). "Great, Mom. It's nice to know that after all of this time you still don't trust me." It was the using Michael trying on that old, ratty garment of shame and blame for size, but it didn't really fit him any more. Michael lost his cunning to his injury. He is almost without guile now, so when his speech-impeded mouth spouted that well-worn, deflecting response to being busted, it just didn't fit.

For years we begged in prayer that Michael would abandon his old using circle and set out unanchored in a new direction. We particularly prayed it during the two times he went through in-patient drug treatment. Every drug counselor tells addicts that they will need to start from scratch socially, that there is no way to stay clean if they drop back into their old circles, their familiar snake pits. Each time Michael was released from treatment he went right back around and down as fast as he could. These were his friends, he would argue, and he wasn't going to abandon his friends.

But now those friends have become the old misfit garment in his closet. He rarely checks his My Space account any more while watching TV, and often doesn't even bring his computer downstairs. He no longer asks me when he can have his cell phone back. It appears he has quit pursuing those relationships altogether. When he spoke yesterday about his non-existent social life, I said, "That world doesn't really fit anymore, does it?" "Nope," he said, "it doesn't." I wonder if he could hear the loud rejoicing in my head: "Hallelujah thank you God!" I doubt it. This loss is sharply painful for him. While it may feel like his new lease on life to me, I'm guessing he feels only abandonment and loneliness. His old world is gone and a new one has yet to appear. He is in a little cocoon of sorts, waiting for the next incarnation to reveal itself.

Rob and I reflected this morning that God seemed to know just how much of Michael needed to die that fated night back in October in order for his old way of being to become ultimately inaccessible. It occurs to me that if Michael had regained all of his functioning and old personality, he would also reclaim his manipulative cunning as well as his mask, the mask that always left his eyes shaded and guarded. God seems to know Michael shouldn't own those qualities in the end, that they truly are contrary to his nature.

As Michael put his arm around his sister yesterday and his other hand assumed the "thumbs up" position, his eyes were open and joyful. They weren't hiding or calculating. How is it that God is so smart? We had also prayed and prayed that Michael would value the family he lives with, that we would count at least as much as the next guy who cut the deal. Now we matter to him more than almost all others. We are his social circle, his safe place, and he now knows with assurance what he never was able to take in before: that we love him unconditionally. What's more, this love now matters to him. The friends who he thought were worthy of all of that loyalty are nowhere to be found. We won't remain in this singular position forever, and it wouldn't be right if we did. I fully trust and believe that there is a rich, relational world ahead for Michael, though I have no idea what form that manifestation will assume. But perhaps it will be one where his eyes can remain open and unguarded, where it will be safe to smile genuinely and hug his sister, and to love opening and freely, even his mom and step-dad.

While I was putting the last of my annual spring flowers in the ground this afternoon, Michael came outside and said, "Happy Mother's Day, Mom." He gave me a hug and smiled, and I said, "I love you, Michael." "I love you too." As he turned to go inside I said, "Michael? I *really* like being your mom."

Epilogue

It's been almost a year since Michael's suicide attempt. Anniversaries are significant occasions, and I confess I have felt some dread thinking about the approach of October 11. Then one day a few weeks ago it occurred to me that rather than expecting to relive trauma or loss, we could choose to remember that day with a celebration, because October 11 was not only the day Michael died, it was also the day he came to life. In fact, we could celebrate it every year as a second birthday. I told Michael that he is special, that most people don't get two birthdays.

Much has happened in the months since we ceased providing updates on Michael's progress. Most of the challenges we now face with him are regular teenage issues rather than brain injury or substance abuse ones, such as disputes over dishes left in front of the TV, or the volume of the movie sound system late in the evening, or doing chores, or saving some hot water for the rest of us.

The significant milestone of his 18th birthday came and went without trauma or incident. He is still on track with his brain injury recovery goals: He got a summer job working for the Boys and Girls Club, a non-profit organization in town, and this fall he started college courses at Chemeketa. He has moved to the next level of the Early College/High School program, taking high school classes in the morning and college ones in the afternoon. He remains under the umbrella of special education services.

Michael completed further therapies in ST and PT, improving coordination issues with his gait and balance as well as gaining greater control of facial expressions and the volume of his speaking voice. His speech therapist even taught him how to keep his eyebrows from reflexively going up all the time. He is still frustrated with his relatively slow and labored articulation, but I am reminded that he is just now one year into recovery, and we were told we would see significant changes for up to two, perhaps longer. So we're hopeful his speech will continue to improve. He worked with a brain injury counselor and most of his depression has lifted. We are so grateful his mood is noticeably brighter and more stable.

He continues to have occasional relapses, about once a quarter by my count. After a recent one I explained that while he may be correct in asserting that at 18 he should be able to make his own choices, such freedom is trumped by the house rule that if he wants to live here he has to be clean. I suggested he think about how much money he'd need to earn in order to have his own place, and that he might also consider how much time it would take him to earn it given that he is in school full time. After clearly articulating the ground rules, I paused and said, "So what do you think?" I braced for his answer, fully expecting him to say, "I'm moving out." To my surprise and relief he replied without deliberation, "I think I'm not gonna use." I think I almost cried. Whether he can manifest that reality remains to be seen, but I believe his intention is sincere.

A neighbor turned left in front of his Mustang without warning and totaled the car (no one was injured), so he's now driving a much less sexy but functional Ford Focus. And he has a new girlfriend, a cheerleader from one of the local high schools. He also has a new cell phone with a different number, so my phone no longer recognizes the number that sent those last, pre-injury text messages as his (he never did use that old phone again). Those messages now belong to a random number with no name. They no longer indicate "Michael," no longer name the person who wrote them or who he is now. They are floating in both my and my phone's memory, unattached and remote. But I still save them.

A new semester has begun at Willamette, teeming with a fresh crop of bright and talented students. Rob continues pastoring in Vancouver, and our daughter Natalie is getting married in December. Kat moved out this month to live on her own for the first time. Jeff continues the lengthy process of appeals, and he and I enjoy regular correspondence and visits. I shared my experience of encountering the burn patient Geoffrey in prayer with one of my missionary friends at the hospital in Maua, Kenya, who then shared it with the staff. They were grateful for the encouragement. Geoffrey continues to visit me from time to time in the still space.

Some friends have asked how Michael feels about his story becoming a book. Throughout the months of his recovery I repeatedly asked him if he would like to read the manuscript. I explained that I would feel much better if he reviewed it before I shared it any further, since it contains so many intimate details about his life. He always answered, "No, I don't want to read it, and whatever you want to say is okay." "But what if there is something there you'd rather I leave out?" "It's okay, Mom. Really, it's fine." I let it rest a while, but then one day down the line I asked again. I told him if he didn't want the project to go forward I would put it away without another thought, but that now was the time to speak up. He answered, "Yeah, okay, I'll read it." He sat down and spent most of an evening pouring over the pages. He did the same the next evening, and the next. He told me that reading his story was a bit like hearing childhood tales that he only vaguely recalls, or remembers only because repetition has etched them into his memory. He said he was glad to know some of the details and while the book was interesting, it held no emotional charge for him, because it felt like he was reading about events that happened to someone else.

He told me nothing made him uncomfortable, and that I should go ahead with plans to publish. Half of any proceeds will be his.

So life is mostly normal: incredibly joyful at times and quite challenging at others. We have made it past this particular tight spot and are back out into the easier, open flow. Life takes each of us through such narrows where we are tossed and tumbled by turbulence as the stream searches for the way through. I know there will likely be more tight spots in the future, but I am learning that I don't need to live as if they are here now. As Jeff said, life is a bit like working at the fire station. We know the bell is going to ring at some point, but there is no sense living all of our days in a state of emergency. When the bell rings, I'll spring into action, but until then I'm just going to enjoy hanging out at the station and playing cards with my friends.

God continues to teach me about the deep challenges and blessings of the spiritual path, and I am writing about much of what I learn. I hope to begin work on the next book project soon. I remain a grateful student of God's grace and love, and I am thankful we travel the path together.

With love and gratitude,
Christine

Michael, Natlaie and Max on the Oregon coast

Endnotes

Introduction
1 Words spoken to her sister, Corrie, before dying in the Ravensbrück concentration camp after being arrested for hiding Jews in WWII.

Chapter 1 – The Bend in the Road
1 Encyclopedia of Death and Dying, www.deathreference.com

Chapter 2 – Bleak
1 Acts 9:3-19
2 Acts 17:28
3 Psalm 37:4
4 Matt Redman
5 Philippians 4:13
6 II Corinthians 12:9
7 Tobias 5:21

Chapter 3 – Graduation
1 *Let All Things Now Living*, Katherine K. Davis © 1939
2 Matthew 18:3

Chapter 5 – Ordinary Miracles
1 Luke 17:21
2 Ephesians 3:17
3 Romans 8:9
4 Luke 1:46
5 Reinhold Niebur, known as the *Serenity Prayer* in AA and Al-Anon
6 Psalm 37
7 From *The Healing Light* by Agnes Sanford
8 Mark 4:24
9 St. Francis of Assisi on Luke 6:37
10 I John 1:5
11 John 1:5
12 Romans 8:38-39
13 Matthew 5:45
14 http://psychology.about.com/od/theoriesofpersonality/a/ hierarchyneeds.htm?p=1

Chapter 6 - Home
1 Words and music by Bill Carter, copyright © Presbybop Music, recording available at Presbybop.com, reprinted with permission.
2 Mark 5:1-13
3 Matthew 11:30
4 Colossians 1:17

Chapter 7 - The Long Steady Climb
1 Reprinted with permission
2 A Christian band
3 Psalm 28:7
4 From Bill Carter's CD by this name at presbybop.com
5 References in the Bible found in Isaiah, Proverbs, Psalms, Acts, and II Corinthians
6 I John 4:18
7 Mark 5:21-43
8 Matthew 6:34

Chapter 8 - Exploring the Territories
1 Matthew 18:20
2 Psalm 16:10
3 Psalm 16:7
4 From the Nicene Creed
5 John 14:18
6 John 14:16-17

Chapter 9 - Another Day in Earth School
1 Matthew 18:21-22
2 Romans 8:26
3 Luke 12:32
4 *Catholic Sentinel*, 2008, reprinted with permission.

Chapter 10 - Hope is a Waking Dream
1 Aristotle, *Lives of Eminent Philosophers*, Diogenes Laërtius
2 Matthew 15:11
3 From step 12 of the 12 steps of Alcoholics Anonymous (AA)
4 Mark 4:24 and Luke 6:38
5 Ecclesiastes 11:1
6 Luke 15:11-32
7 Bob Dylan

Chapter 11 - High Life, Low Life

1 *The Tender Land* by Aaron Copland and Horace Everett(c) 1954, 1956 by The Aaron Copland Fund for Music, Inc. Copyright renewed. Boosey & Hawkes, Inc., sole licensee. Reprinted by permission.

2 Proverbs 16:18

3 Matthew 16:18

4 Matthew 16:23

5 Flannery O'Connor on John 8:32

Chapter 12 - Finding North Again

1 Philippians 2:15

Chapter 13 - The Insatiable Beast

1 II Corinthians 12:7-10

2 Psalm 139:22

3 Mark 4:1-20

4 John 1:1

5 Matthew 25:14-30

6 From *The Selected Poetry of Jessica Powers*, published by ICS Publications, Washington, D.C. All copyrights, Carmelite Monastery, Pewaukee, WI. Used with permission.

7 Luke 17:21

8 II Corinthians 5:17

9 Matthew 25:39-40

10 *Let All Things Now Living* – Katherine K. Davis © 1939

11 John 6:1-14 and Matthew 15:32-38

12 Ephesians 3:20

13 I John 4:8

14 Psalm 23:4

15 Zechariah 13:9

Chapter 14 - Taking it as it Comes

1 A reference to Francis Thompson's 182 verse religious poem

2 *For Those Tears I Died*, Marsha J. Stevens, copyright © 1969 Bud John Songs (ASCAP) (adm. at EMICMGPublishing.com) All rights reserved. Used by permission.

Chapter 15 - Not Looking Ahead

1 Hebrews 11:1

༆

If you have been touched or encouraged by this story,
remember, as pastor Hunter said, "God had something to
do with it." As our blessings are never meant for us alone,
please pass this book along so that others might
experience the God hug.

To order copies, please visit:
brokenblessings.com
or contact Christine Elder at
Christine@brokenblessings.com.

༆